40 Critical Thinkers
in Community Development

Praise for this book

The ideas in this book reveal the great treasures of knowledge and wisdom that can enrich our lives. Indeed, inspiring thoughts are much needed in this time of fear and panic. The book is an essential companion for anyone involved in the citizen and professional project that is community development.

Professor Sue Kenny, Deakin University Australia

Good community development requires critical thinking, otherwise we will just prop up the existing neo-liberal order, with its economic and political injustices, its unsustainability, its patriarchy, its racism, its heteronormativity and its colonialism. This book provides a rich and varied collection of wisdom and critical scholarship, challenging taken-for-granted 'normality', which contributes to our understanding of living and working in community in these troubled times. It contains many 'gems' which will inspire and enhance the practice of community workers.

Professor Jim Ife, Western Sydney University

Ideas change the world! Here is an inspiring collection of good ideas to steer a kinder, fairer future out of the wreckage of neoliberalism.

Professor Margaret Ledwith, University of Cumbria

40 Critical Thinkers in Community Development

Peter Westoby, David Palmer, and Athena Lathouras

Practical
ACTION
PUBLISHING

Practical Action Publishing Ltd
27a, Albert Street, Rugby, Warwickshire, CV21 2SG, UK
www.practicalactionpublishing.com

A catalogue record for this book is available from the British Library.

A catalogue record for this book has been requested from the Library of Congress.

ISBN 978-1-78853-0-644 Paperback
ISBN 978-1-78853-1-221 Hardback
ISBN 978-1-78853-1-238 Epub
ISBN 978-1-78853-1-245 PDF

Citation: Westoby, P., Palmer, D., Lathouras, A., (2020) *40 Critical Thinkers in Community Development,* Rugby, UK: Practical Action Publishing <http://dx.doi.org/10.3362/9781788531245>.

Since 1974, Practical Action Publishing has published and disseminated books and information in support of international development work throughout the world. Practical Action Publishing is a trading name of Practical Action Publishing Ltd (Company Reg. No. 1159018), the wholly owned publishing company of Practical Action. Practical Action Publishing trades only in support of its parent charity objectives and any profits are covenanted back to Practical Action (Charity Reg. No. 247257, Group VAT Registration No. 880 9924 76).

Cover illustration by Sarah Govus
Cover design by RCO.design
Printed on demand

Contents

http://dx.doi.org/10.3362/9781788531245.000

Foreword

Good ideas have a magnetic attraction; they can clarify complexity, stimulate energy to keep going, and provide hope for better things to come. But also, good ideas can demand our moral and intellectual attention and challenge the comfort of our taken-for-granted day-to-day world. Good ideas give all of this and a lot more. When we attempt the complex task of living together peaceably and well, we need the companionship not only of our current colleagues but also of those companions who have gone before and who lent their best efforts and shared their best ideas to make our world a gentler and fairer place for all.

This little book is generous in its gifts, for it shares good ideas, not just of one person or their pathway but of many. My wish for this book is simple, that the gift of these good ideas nourish all of its readers on their many diverse life-journeys, as they contribute in both small and big ways to build that gentler and fairer world.

Anthony Kelly
Brisbane 2019

Acknowledgements

To the many people who have made this work possible.

To Anthony Kelly who seeded the idea of such a book some 20 years ago. It has grown, and now here it is.

Peter

To Lynda Shevellar and Ann Ingamells, as long-term comrades in community development teaching and activism.

To Gerard Dowling for the endless coffees with me as this book was crafted and soulmate Verne Harris who journeyed daily from afar.

To Community Praxis Co-op comrades that always make my world richer.

To the many students whom Tina and Peter have asked to write reflections on author-activists and critical thinkers, and who continue to inspire us.

Tina

To the colleagues and comrades who are members of three groups that help to ground and sustain my academic work: Community Praxis Co-operative; Community Development Queensland; and the Coalition of Community Boards.

Dave

To Jen Buchanan as my intellectual, road trip, and community work partner, whose analysis is so deeply sharp.

To Callum Palmer Buchanan for his clever and eloquent introductions to the beautiful and poetic wisdom that comes from the literary traditions.

To Matt Palmer Buchanan for teaching me about the magic of the arts, music, and film.

Us

To Tracy Adams for her boundless editing efforts.

To Clare Tawney at Practical Action Publishing, Schumacher Centre for trusting us.

Finally, our deep thanks to the many un-named people who have been so supportive and helpful in shaping the ideas in this book.

Author biographies

Peter Westoby works, teaches, and researches on the borderlands between community development and other disciplines and fields of practice, from phenomenology, dialogue, depth psychology, peace and conflict, and forced migration. He has worked accompanying youth, community, and organization for 30 years, from places as far afield as South Africa, Uganda, Vanuatu, PNG, Nepal, Philippines, Brazil, and Australia. He is an associate professor in Social Science – Community Development at the School of Public Health & Social Work at Queensland University of Technology (QUT); a visiting professor at the Centre for Development Support, University of the Free State, South Africa; and a director with Community Praxis Co-operative.

Dave Palmer lives in Perth, Western Australia. This means if he wants to visit Peter and Tina, he needs to drive about 4,500 kilometres by road or sit on a plane for over five hours. He currently teaches community development at Murdoch University. Much of his work takes him to remote parts of Central and Northern Australia supporting community-controlled projects carried out by Indigenous groups. Often this means he gets to see first-hand both the challenges facing communities, some of whom had their first contact with non-Indigenous people as recently as the 1970s, and a range of creative and culturally grounded projects that involve both the use of state-of-the-art digital technologies and the oldest traditions on the planet.

Athena Lathouras, known as 'Tina', has had 30 years practice experience in the areas of community development, disability support, and with peak bodies. She is a senior lecturer in the social work programme at the University of the Sunshine Coast; a member of Community Praxis Co-operative and volunteer liaison with Community Development Queensland. Tina engages in community work practice and research working to weave the links back and forth between these spaces so that one informs the other. Through this dialogue she seeks to promote better teaching, research, and practice in community issues.

Preface

Before we move too far into our discussion, we would like to make a point about where we sit geographically, socially, and culturally. All three of us share the heritage of colonizers/migrants and live in different parts of Australia, a country with a deep and traumatic history of Indigenous communities being robbed, usurped, marginalized, and made refugees in their own lands. This history includes the imposition of legal and policy regimes grounded in eugenics, the removal of families from one another, physical, spiritual, and emotional violence, and the extraction and theft of knowledge and cultural capital. This history has been felt differently across the continent of Australia, partly because the imposition of outsiders to these communities occurred at different times (e.g. 1788 in Sydney, 1984 in one part of Central Australia, right through to the present by governments, mining companies, and other interests). Presently Peter and Athena live on Gubbi Gubbi/Kabi Kabi country and Dave on Noongar country.

As well as acknowledging this history and the First Nations people who have maintained knowledge and culture in our home communities, we would like to make the point that we recognize one author in particular for her special place in shaping this book. Dr Mary Graham stands for us as one of the many Indigenous Australian critical thinkers that offers much to those working in community development. This is partly because Mary is a philosopher of 'high degree' in Indigenous knowledge and practice. Mary is a Kombumerri person through her father's heritage, and connected with Wakka Wakka through her mother. It is also because, like an emerging group of scholars, she brings together these elegant insights and deep conceptual frames with her training as an academic, government practitioner, and community worker.

So, as well as recognizing that we sit on the country and intellectual shoulders of the Indigenous elders and bosses (knowledge custodians) we specifically recognize Mary Graham for her work in this collection.

CHAPTER 1
Introduction
Towards a reflective community development practice: Integrating the gems and wisdoms of critical thinkers

By Peter Westoby, Dave Palmer,
and Athena Lathouras

The purpose of this book

In writing this book, in curating 40 critical thinkers in community development, our purpose is threefold. First, our aim is to *deepen, expand*, and *disrupt* the practice of people who think of themselves as community development (CD) practitioners. We explain what we mean by 'people who think of themselves as CD practitioners' below, but in terms of deepening, expanding, and disrupting we mean:

- **Deepen**: we aspire to practitioners reflecting on the roots of their practice, what informs it, what wisdom is either conscious or unconscious, and cultivating a sense of being on 'firm ground', perhaps 'standing on the feet of giants' (a phrase we will use).
- **Expand**: we introduce practitioners to thinkers who perhaps they have not heard of before and, therefore, new ideas can percolate into newer practices.
- **Disrupt**: we want practitioners to re-think taken-for-granted assumptions or habits about their practice.

We believe it is important to deepen, expand, and disrupt CD practice for two reasons related to the current context for CD. In the first instance, it is because of the drift from community development

http://dx.doi.org/10.3362/9781788531245.001

practice to forms of service delivery that are prevalent, especially in work funded by the state or external donors. Are we straying into 'top down' practice where the service workers largely set the agenda, obtain the resources, and pre-determine the outputs associated with the work, forgetting the 'bottom-up' or citizen-led nature of CD practice? And in the second instance, deepening, expanding, and especially disrupting practice is important because of the dominant political ideology of our times, neoliberalism. With such an emphasis on individualism and *personal* transformation that comes with individual achievement we can forget about the root causes or the social sources of oppression, those that perpetuate poverty, exclusion, and disadvantage. We can forget that working for the pursuit of social justice is about *social* transformation – changing the life chances of large numbers of people and empowering whole communities.

Second, our aim is to offer a wide range of community development wisdoms that will help reflective practitioners build what is sometimes understood to be a 'practice framework'. We have opted not to say much about this here, but point readers to the book *Participatory Development Practice: Using Traditional and Contemporary Frameworks* (Kelly & Westoby, 2018) to support the process. With that book outlining a process for framework development, this *40 Critical Thinkers* book provides much wisdom that practitioners can draw into their framework.

Third, we hope to offer a 'new' way of thinking about how practitioners cultivate wise practice. To do this, we have offered wisdom from the 40 critical thinkers, but also suggest particular ways of using these gems pedagogically. Our pedagogical approach to learning is that community development practitioners learn best 'on the job' and then reflect on what they are doing – deepening, expanding, or disrupting their practice. They can do that alone simply through thinking, or reading, or in groups, or via supervision or mentoring. We discuss some of these options below.

With these purposes, we have therefore curated 40 authors whom we have called critical thinkers. Originally, we talked of 40 'author-activists', and then we almost settled for 40 'crucial thinkers', but instead we have opted for 40 'critical thinkers'. As Hannah **Arendt** has said, we want people to think, and see thinking, as a key practice, and an element of activism anyway – hence 'thinkers'. As 'critical' thinkers, we hold to a perspective that things are not okay as they are. Change is needed, radical change in society – social transformation, emancipation even – and more critical thinking and practice is needed to achieve that. However, we are not using the idea of 'critical' within the critical sociological tradition alone, but in the broader sense of critical reflection processes to understand how values, beliefs, and assumptions shape and influence world views, and therefore CD practice. Such thinking helps practitioners to see or notice, and challenges everyday practice when it falls short of our social justice or ecological commitments.

Here we are also noting that thinking and doing are interconnected. Pedagogically, we also suggest that 'the doing' often comes first and sometimes we get to do some thinking before the doing. Often times community development practitioners are thrust into action without the time and resources to first carry out much planning and thought. Indeed, if we were to be honest, we would have to confess that this is what has happened most of the time. This can actually be good, as reading, thinking and coming across new ideas can be all the more illuminating when we have had some experience to help us make sense of the 'frameworks' that others offer.

People who think of themselves as CD practitioners – both a citizen and professional project

As three authors we think it is best to think of community development as both a citizen and professional project that has been going on for centuries. This is a broad enough way of thinking to be inclusive of volunteers, citizens, workers, those with the occupation of community development, and so forth. We propose this broader way, underpinned by the principle of diversity, where we are not wanting to narrow CD down to just a professional or academic project. If you, the reader, think of yourself as a community development practitioner, this book is for you.

You might be involved in your own neighbourhoods – helping out in a school, or with your church, or mosque, or in your community garden. You might be doing some service-oriented community work through the RSL, the Rotary Club, or the local neighbourhood centre. You might be gathering neighbours for annual barbecues, or a group of friends for a monthly reading club. Alternatively, you might be involved in more edgy community development practice, such as First Nation solidarity groups, or reconciliation initiatives; maybe you are involved in refugee support or policy advocacy groups. You might be working within a community-based organization (CBO), or non-government organization (NGO), which involves engaging with people, setting up groups, initiating projects or community programmes, reporting to managers, negotiating for funding, and related activities. For people doing this as paid work, maybe you have qualifications in community development – you may have even read the occasional article from the *Community Development Journal* or attended a workshop or conference. This book is written for all of you.

When people as citizens get together and solve problems or work on their aspirations as groups, when they cooperate together, they are doing community development as a citizen project. This kind of citizen or people's action has been going on for more or less all of history and in this sense, 'our' community development practice has deep roots, resting on the co-operative capabilities of people through time immemorial. However, as a professional project, that is, with professional and often paid community development practitioners, it has been around since the 1900s. Indicators of this kind of professional project are the development of architecture supporting the work such as associations (see for example, the International Association of Community Development (IACD) established in 1953) and journals such as the *Community Development Journal* (Oxford University Press), *Community Development:* Journal of the U.S.A. Community Development Society (Taylor & Francis) and the many books available about the field.

From a community development definition to understanding the key movements

In understanding community development as both a citizen and professional community development project, we do, however, unlike the IACD, avoid proposing a definition of community development. For example, the IACD defines CD as a 'practice-based profession and an academic discipline …' (see Banks & Westoby, 2019: 6).

From our perspective, there are hundreds of definitions – many contestable, representing diverse values, models, and traditions – so instead we prefer to suggest thinking about community development as representing some *key movements*. The three key movements are simple. The first movement is 'I' to 'we'. The work is always a movement from people being alone, struggling, and thinking that whatever their problem is, it is their fault. For example, 'I'm lonely because I am incapable of making friends', or 'I'm poor and unemployed because I'm stupid and useless.' That's often how people feel when suffering alone. But when people can come together with others having the same experience, they can support one another and also transform that idea that 'it's my fault' because in fact all social problems, unemployment and isolation for example, are not individual problems, they are public and shared social problems.

Then there is a second movement. Enfolded within the 'I' to 'we' is the recognition that the problem 'I' am experiencing is not my fault but it is a social problem and it needs to be tackled socially. Hence the movement from 'private' to 'public'.

A crucial and third movement is from working 'for' others, or delivering a service 'to' others, to working 'with' or 'amongst', eschewing the traditional service delivery paradigm of experts or professionals doing stuff 'for' people. More is said about this below.

Meaning of community

But it's not only about movements. Community is crucial, and a key premise for readers who think of themselves as community development practitioners is that whatever task you might be doing, you are doing it *with others*. What you are doing can be understood as community development work because it involves *groups of people* (small or largish) and the work is weaving a web of relationships that ultimately creates what might be thought of as community. Community then, is not just understood as synonymous with neighbourhood or place. Community is instead something that emerges, as a felt experience, or a social phenomenon, when people *create* it together: when they are in *relationship* with one another, drawn together by a *shared concern* (reading, refugee advocacy, reconciliation, wanting to garden, and so forth) and make commitments to act together. It might occur in neighbourhoods, villages, towns, places; but community is not synonymous with those words.

From definition to traditions

Along with avoiding a definition, we root our understanding of community development within the notion of 'traditions'. For example, there are, among others, the community building, community education, community action, community planning and community-of-intention traditions.

The community-building tradition represents the work of bringing people back together, reconnecting socially when many have become socially isolated and there is a pandemic of loneliness. Then there is the tradition of community education, where communities say, 'let's get together and learn about the issues we are facing'. Whether it be climate change or transport challenges: 'let's educate ourselves'. Then there is the third tradition of community action, where citizens decide that they do not like what is happening in their neighbourhood or wider society. Perhaps somebody else has made decisions about what is going to happen (or not happen e.g. government inaction on climate change), and these decisions are not liked. Then citizens organize and campaign, and challenge: 'let's not stand for this; let's send a message'. Then there is a fourth tradition of community planning, where people think about the public infrastructure in their communities and ask themselves 'how do we partner with local authorities'? Here citizens say to them, 'you are meant to be planning about our neighbourhood, so we want to participate and be a part of that planning.' Lastly, there is a tradition which is called the community-of-intention tradition, where people come together and create their own communities, such as eco-villages, co-housing and housing co-operatives. They ask themselves 'with our shared values can we live together and share common resources?'

A reflective question would be, what other traditions of community development are being practised all around the world? Our work is rich in diversity and tradition and goes beyond any simplistic definition.

Poverties and power in community work

However, the work is not only about movements, community, and traditions; it is also about working with people who can be understood as poor or marginalized. Historically, community development practice has been about a method of social change that is used by the poor to bring change to their lives. They do it through joint action; for example, by pooling small amounts of money to buy in bulk, or to grow their savings, or insure one another against the fragile nature of life; or they co-operate through learning together in non-formal education, or through advocating for a common cause. The point is that they gain power through co-operating. In many ways the community element in community development practice is about this ability for people to co-operate (Sennett, 2012). There is a huge historical legacy of this kind of work – of small savings and loans groups growing into mutual societies; of reading groups providing the seeds that germinate into community libraries; of small groups meeting to advocate for themselves morphing into wide scale social movements.

However, in recent years, as community development practice has also become professionalized, the work is not only about a method of social change used by the poor to change their lives; it is also a professional practice concerned with paid professionals accompanying or supporting the poor in processes of change. There is a sense that while the poor have done things really well themselves, they could do with some help. And governments have put aside money to help, so a cohort of professionals is needed to guide how those funds should be spent.

Of course, whenever professionals step in to help and enact the social policy imperatives of government or the agendas of the donor/funder, the risk is that the professionals 'take over' or exercise their so-called expertise and end up 'servicing the poor'. In a sense then, without a lot of care or a strong developmental (bottom-up) framework, the professionals can undo the need for the poor, or for their energy to be directed to co-operate together. Then change can easily become a process of the poor co-operating with what the professionals decide to do. The poor become adept in the language of the professionals, their logics, and their industry. The work then becomes even more complex than it already is. Who is taking action, whose ideas get priority in working out what needs to be done, what vision of life is being argued for? Such questions become central ethical and practical concerns.

The ideas in this book represent an attempt to find a middle ground. It's not about either the poor or the professional; instead it's about a particular kind of relationship between them. From our perspective, poverty – or what is more accurately thought of as poverties – are often manifest in a form of stuckness (Max-Neef, 1991). There is a lack of animating or connecting energy in the poor to move forward, or if they do attempt to move forward, they find the energy of someone else, or some organization, working against them. For example, someone is stuck economically when they cannot get out of debt or find enough capital to start a livelihood. Or they are stuck socially feeling isolated or cut off; or they have mental ill health and no one wants to be their friend. Maybe they are stuck culturally in that they don't fit in with the mainstream culture and its norms of behaviour, so they feel excluded, hidden, stuck on the margins. Or they are stuck politically, seemingly unable to influence decision-making – it's done behind the closed doors of the powerful, or there's no seat at the table and resources are always allocated elsewhere. The point is that the stuckness means the poor usually remain poor.

Our understanding of community development practice offers a perspective on ways forward. It is a perspective in which a community development practitioner can get close to the experience of a person, or a group, and truly understand the kinds of poverties described above. In getting close they can engage in conversations that might tap into energies and in turn animate collective action. A community development practitioner comes alongside into the situation and becomes receptive to what might emerge. They might hear of an idea spoken timidly by someone, and instead of 'letting it go' they affirm that it is a good idea. A conversation is triggered and energy is generated.

But at times the community development practitioner also might need to 'inject' some new energy, particularly if people have been downtrodden many times. For example, most people who get stuck in their poverty have also developed a powerful story of who they are. Prize-winning economist, and author of *Small is Beautiful*, **E. F. Schumacher** (1974), argues that poverty is to be convinced of your own ignorance. Note that he is not saying to be poor is to be ignorant; in fact, the poor are usually experts on understanding what produces their own poverty, and their survival strategies often require incredible skills and tenacity. No, **Schumacher** is saying that poverty is to 'be convinced' of your own ignorance. That is, it is to have acquired a story about yourself. Like any story however, it is not going to be accurate; it will probably only tell a percentage of the truth. As the Nigerian writer Chimamanda Ngozi **Adichie** (2009) might say, a wise community development practitioner aims to create a space in which there might be receptivity to a 'new story', or a way of rescuing a story[1] that someone has forgotten; for example, that they have incredible skills and tenacity to survive. So, the community development practitioner, rather than servicing the poor, or 'taking over' – developing an innovative project *for* the poor – instead works *with* the poor, in trying to create receptivity to a new story. A new story is sure to contribute to animating energies, which in turn help people to get unstuck.

Our practice methodology and ethos

What should be clear by now is that we are advocating for a methodology and ethos that is primarily *a relationship practice*. Returning to the earlier mentioned third movement, and at risk of repeating ourselves, a well-practised community development practitioner would try to avoid doing things 'to people', and instead works 'with people'. At the heart of practice then, is the ability to build relationships and come alongside people: what Mary Watkins calls 'social accompaniment' (Watkins, 2019). One of our key messages around ethos, which will be unearthed several times in reading the critical thinkers in this book, is, as First Nation leader Aunty Lilla Watson from Australia says: 'If you have come to help me you are wasting your time. But if you have come because your liberation is bound up with mine, then let us work together'.

From our perspective, community development practice has a very clear approach, a clear practice. Practitioners build relationships with individuals. If employed as a community development worker they will go and meet many people, they will listen to their stories, they'll hear the key ideas that people are grappling with, the issues: unemployment, access to health, transport issues, loneliness, and so forth.

When they hear different people with similar stories they'll then invite them to come together. They will literally say: 'I've been hearing stories from other people who are really lonely. I've heard your story, and I've heard her story. I've met this guy who is also lonely. How about we get together, the four of us and talk about this issue?' When they get together the practitioner will say, 'We have shared concerns about these issues, what do you think about us doing something about it together ... and heh, there are a lot of other people in this neighbourhood who are lonely, and let's invite them as well'. Then *we* might start an activity, which might evolve into a project or even a programme.

The practice is clear – and by practice we mean 'doing something with a clear intention'. Our practice is to build relationships, to listen, to then bring community members together, and they create the solution. That is our intent, so supporting people to 'create their solution'. This is the practice. The practitioner never creates the solution. Some community development practitioners might try and create the solution and we would call this 'unwise practice'. This whole book aims to build practice wisdom, pushing against unwise work.

It is unwise practice because, for example, what happens when the practitioner leaves? Nothing is going to be sustained because people have got used to the practitioner creating solutions. Another key idea of community development is for practitioners to support people to find their own confidence, their own skills, connect them to resources so that they can sustain what they are doing.

As such, ownership is a crucial wisdom of community development – that people feel like they created a project or they started that process with others. We say 'with others' purposefully, because one of the big challenges is when someone connects with a practitioner and has a really strong agenda, or desire to do something in the community and wants your support. They say, 'I've got this idea, this is what I want to do'.

A wise and more developmental response to this might be something like, 'Well you can go it alone and try and make that project or why don't you hold that idea a bit lighter ...'. We actually say, 'Hold that idea a bit lighter', and, 'See if you can find two, three, four or ... five other people that together can shape an idea that is a group idea'. Then the idea has got legs, it has got the potential to sustain itself.

Working with energy

Another key wisdom that we would like to communicate in this introduction is that not many people are motivated to bring change just because they think something is a good idea. Many of us can name a lot of things that need to be done in our communities. But the only way most people are going to stay involved in something is if they really feel heart connection to it, a passion with it. One of our most loved mantras is Margaret Wheatley and Deborah Frieze's 'start anywhere, go everywhere' (2011: 91). Their point is, start where the people have energy and if this is nurtured and people's confidence and capacity grows, then they can 'go everywhere', that is, tackle other issues/concerns.

Learning about practice

As stated earlier, one of the purposes for this book is re-orienting thinking about how community development practitioners learn 'the practice'. Most people, caught in the Cartesian mind-body and theory-practice dualities still deep down believe, 'theory first, practice second', or 'ideas first, doing second' (that is, mind first, body second). Hence the emphasis on going to university to learn community development. While we acknowledge the usefulness of university education, this book suggests that most of us learn 'on the job' through doing, and reflection. That is, we 'practice' – sometimes in a muddled way – that is, our doing and intention is not so clear, yet with reflection (in reading, journaling, discussing with others) 'we' get clearer. In a sense, practice is discovered rather than learned. We hope that this book is a resource for discovery.

The quality of the practitioner and practice

Much of this discovery is linked to understanding ourselves. As such, community development practice has as much to do with our own internal worlds and our own stories, as it does with how to engage with the external world. The quality of the work is, as Otto Scharmer (2009) puts it, as much about the quality of the 'source' – that is, the practitioner – as it is about the practice. Community development practice is not something that can be applied by a computer program. It requires a *human response*. And a human response is by its very nature, fragile, tinged with personal limitations and vulnerabilities, shaped by norms, deeply affected by values and morality, and ultimately characterized by imperfection. From this perspective, community development practice moves from being a technical activity whereby a worker plays a relatively neutral role as 'applicator of technique', to being an embodied process that is as much about the ongoing development of the practitioner as it is about the development of the practice. Community development practice cannot be understood as purely scientific from this perspective. Indeed, the 'art' of practice becomes central (Kaplan, 2002), and the worker becomes a wholehearted participant (along with all the other participants) in the act of *co-creating* the work. Paulo **Freire** (1998: 108) captures this beautifully when he suggests that:

> It is fundamental for us to know that without certain qualities or virtues, such as a generous loving heart, respect for others, tolerance, humility, a joyful disposition, love of life, openness to what is new, a disposition to welcome change, perseverance in the struggle, a refusal of determinism, a spirit of hope, and openness to justice, progressive pedagogical practice is not possible. It is something that the merely scientific, technical mind cannot accomplish.

Therefore, in order to engage with community development practice, practitioners need to be able to see and hold onto their own truths – stories, passions, motivations, capacities, strengths, limitations, and weaknesses – *and to connect these with the stories of those with whom we work and live, to the nature of the work, and to the world in which we work.* From every perspective, the view of the work is personal and interconnected. The beginning and end points of community development practice are personal, as are its context and means. In this very personal sense, each and every one of us who is involved in the work needs to grow with it. It is work that is not done for and to others, it is mutual, co-creative work, it is our work, done for all our sakes. Because we are 'in it', there 'among others', and we need to proceed with ourselves as we proceed with others.

Our connections to the wisdom of others

Our own personal stories are not, however, *purely personal* – they are cultural, historical, communal, political, and spiritual. Partly because of this, *40 Critical Thinkers in Community Development* is a crucial resource for those wishing to reflect on, and further cultivate and curate their own practice, drawing on our synthesis of key wisdoms. It would be an almost impossible task for workers to read the full *opuses* of 40 thinkers.

However, these wisdoms cannot just be cherry-picked. One of the key tasks of each practitioner is to reflect on their own practice, engage with these wisdoms, and integrate into their own practice – build what we call a 'practice framework' – and ensure congruence between 'words' and 'actions'. To help with this we have offered a couple of simple pointers to practitioners, which is, some tools for self-reflection and then some guidance on how to engage the wisdom of the 40 critical thinkers. In turn, as authors, we make transparent some of the rationales for choosing the 40 that are included – recognizing that all acts of inclusion are also excluding.

Curating a practice

Curating an intentional community development practice is an exciting period of evolution for a practitioner, which is even further enriched when attempted with other comrades or colleagues. When community development practitioners learn 'in the field' or 'on the job', when they listen to the stories of well-known and published author-practitioners, when they access professional supervision for reflection, when they hear different views and values, sometimes supportive, sometimes challenging and even divisive, then their sense of practice expands. As a collegial process to cultivate a practice, there is need for a robust spirit of give and take in which there needs to be both a confidence in having a practice, that is 'I know what I am doing, with a clear intention'. Yet, there is also the need for humility, to accept we know very little and always need to be on the edge of learning something afresh or anew. Practitioners need to play their part in providing an environment that is safe, challenging, respectful, and, of course, participatory – no different from any good piece of developmental work. Some ways we have learned for curating and cultivating a practice include:

- Drawing a 'river' or 'tree' of life, as a way of reflecting on key influences (people/moments) that have shaped the practice – and sharing these with others;

- Reflecting on a story of practice, or ideally, asking a colleague to ask questions so that the development worker can really 'see' what they do (not necessarily the same as what they say they do);
- Reading a biography of a person who has inspired us; and
- Watching the work of others through the use of YouTube or Vimeo short documentaries.

Yet, reflection on our own practice – even with colleagues – can be limiting. That's where this book can further contribute, for there is the profound wisdom of those colleagues long-gone, or in their eldership years.

Ways to use this resource

We have imagined various options, including:

- A daily or weekly reading of one of the thinkers, chosen randomly (recognition of a name, or resonance with one of the gems) and then used to reflect on practice;
- Much as above, but less randomly – simply a working through the book – which we have collated alphabetically;
- Study groups that might form and reflect on a number of the critical thinkers – perhaps a group might find some of our reflections have sparked an interest in doing more research, reading, and reflection on a number of the critical thinkers;
- Working or project teams, grappling with a moment or stage in a community development project, needing some new input or ideas to help 'shake-up' taken-for-granted thinking;
- Stimulation for preparing for working with an external supervision session – again, to reflect on practice (at the same time, someone supervising could also suggest a practitioner go and read one of the critical thinkers);
- A resource for teachers of community development – recognizing that a community development course/unit, would probably engage deeply with a couple of authors (for example, Peter uses **Buber** and **Freire** extensively in teaching). This book offers students a sense of the broad array of possibilities as they expand their horizon;
- A whole course on author-activists or critical thinkers could be developed by community development teachers, with this as a text (with student assessments being in-depth study of a few).

How we chose the 40 critical thinkers

We worked over two phases. During phase one, in which we aimed to have drafted the first 20 of the 40 critical thinkers, we more or less allowed each of the three of us to work on a number of critical thinkers that excited us. This included familiar critical thinkers who we wanted to return to and go deeper with, and also new ones that we had aspired to read for a while. The book writing process gave an opportunity to do both.

We did have some basic requirements – that the critical thinker had a longevity of influence – they weren't 'flash in the pans' – that is, they did represent a depth of thinking that had survived the span of time. We were certainly aware of the risk of this – to exclude some new, fresh cutting-edge thinking, yet we opted to stay with depth and longevity.

In saying this, we made one exception, that of Greta **Thunberg**, aware that she represents the voice of young people, whose voices cannot yet 'survive the span of time' (that is, their work is not yet enshrined in books and subject to substantive commentary and critique), and yet are desperate for more time to live on a thriving planet. Furthermore, perhaps – and we say perhaps, yet with an adult passion of solidarity with her – much of the thinking of the other 39 critical thinkers means little if the planet becomes uninhabitable. All struggles for justice are now enfolded within the struggle for justice for future generations and current generations of non-humans.

We also preferred that the critical thinker could offer something for community development 'practice' – a gem, a meme, something memorable for a practitioner. We were also keen to make choices based on having some personal connection with the critical thinker, enabling each of us to write in a way that linked the author to our own practice, or what has influenced our practice. This aspiration attuned to our desire that we not write what can be found in Wikipedia, but that readers would get excited enough to want to learn, to go read the critical thinker for themselves. Each chapter has a list of the critical thinker's key works to help.

During phase two we worked on a further 20 critical thinkers based on the three of us getting together face-to-face to conduct a gap analysis – particularly in terms of gender and other identity markers (such as theoretical frameworks or types of social issues), and geography. The book includes 19 critical thinkers who are female and 21 male, and we use this simplistic binary framework of gender somewhat tentatively, also aware of the fluidity of sexuality and gender.

Geographically, despite all our attempts, the weight of scales leaned towards North America and Europe, yet we also worked hard for some kind of equity. Hence, there is relatively strong representation from Africa, South and Central America, and South and South-East Asia; and we have included a couple of thinkers from Oceania (Australia and the Pacific). The North American/European emphasis (20 of the 40) is mostly an indicator of those who write in English, or whose work is accessible to us in translation.

In Conclusion

'We are standing on the shoulders of giants' is very apt. Our 40 critical thinkers have been wonderful to research or revisit, and we have benefitted greatly from their wisdom. We were excited to write this book and wished it had been around when we were starting out in community development. We do hope you find it helpful to your community development and social change efforts.

Endnotes

1. We are indebted to the work of David Denborough at the Dulwich Centre for this idea of 'rescuing stories'.

References

Adichie, C. N. (2009) 'The Danger of a Single Story', *TED Talk*. [website] <www.ted.com/talks/chimamanda_adichie_the_danger_of_a_single_story?language=en> [Accessed 26 Sept 2019].

Banks, S. & Westoby, P. (eds.). (2019). *Ethics, Equity and Community Development*, Policy Press, Bristol.

Freire, P. (1998) *Pedagogy of Freedom: Ethics, Democracy and Civic Courage*, Rowman and Littlefield Pub., MD.

Kaplan, A. (2002) *Development Practitioners and Social Process: Artists of the Invisible*, Pluto Press, London.

Kelly, A. and Westoby, P. (2018) *Participatory Development Practice: Using Traditional and Contemporary Frameworks*, Practical Action Press, Rugby, UK.

Max-Neef, M. (1991) *Human Scale Development: Conceptions, Application and Further Reflections*, The Apex Press, London & New York.

Scharmer, C.O. (2009) *Theory U: Leading from the Future as it Emerges*, Berrett-Koehler, San Francisco, CA.

Schumacher, E. F. (1974) *Small is Beautiful: Economics as if People Mattered*, Abacus, London.

Sennett, R. (2008) *The Craftsman*, Allen Lane, New York.

Sennett, R. (2012) *Together: The Rituals, Pleasures and Politics of Cooperation*, Allan Lane/Penguin Books, London.

Watkins, P. (2019) *Mutual Accompaniment and the Creation of the Commons*, Duke University Press, Durham, NC.

Westoby, P., and Ingamells, A. (2011) 'Teaching community development personal practice frameworks', *Social Work Education* 31(3): 383–396.

Wheatley, M. & Frieze, D. (2011) *Walk Out, Walk On: A Learning Journey into Communities Daring to Live the Future Now*, Berrett-Koehler, San Francisco, CA.

CHAPTER 2

Jane Addams: *Practise mutual accompaniment*

By Athena Lathouras

Jane Addams 1860–1935

Rudolf Cronau, 1919

I first heard about Jane Addams when I was starting my community development practice in neighbourhood centres. Neighbourhood Centres, or 'Houses' as they are known today, are somewhat akin to a contemporary expression of the global Settlement House movement, which started with settlements founded in the United Kingdom, United States and other countries in the late 19th century. The key idea behind the settlements was that people concerned about social issues are only effective in making improvements if they have direct experience of existing problems by living among people in need and 'settling' into their neighbourhoods (International Federation of Settlements and Neighbourhood Centres (IFS), 2019). This view, of immersing oneself in a place and building relationships with the local people to truly understand them and the context is still seen as a crucial principle for community development today (Kelly & Westoby, 2018: 98).

Jane Addams was born in 1860, to a world of increasing industrialization and urbanization, innovations in communication and transportation, and growing imperialism as well as class, race, and ethnic tensions (Fischer, Nackenoff & Chimielewski, 2009). She was a prolific author of scholarly and popular writing, and many biographers have written about her humane social vision and life's work for just social change. Addams's civic contributions can be seen in her role as co-founder and head of the social settlement, Hull House; her role as a leader of social reform; and as a public intellectual (Knight, 2005: 411). The first American woman to be awarded the Nobel Peace Prize in 1931, she was a major leader in movements to promote peace, child welfare, women's suffrage, improved housing, education, juvenile justice, labour relations, and civil liberties (Carnes, 2012).

http://dx.doi.org/10.3362/9781788531245.002

Hull House and Addams's social philosophy

Inspired by the pioneering Toynbee Hall in London, Addams founded Hull House – the first settlement house in the United States – in 1889 with her trusted friend Ellen Starr. Addams's (1910) book, still in print, *Twenty Years at Hull House,* chronicles her struggles to improve the lives of poor immigrants in Chicago. The settlement residents comprised young college graduates who had trained as lawyers, teachers, economists, and physicians (Opdycke, 2012: 2), who chose to live locally and learn about their immigrant neighbours' lives and suffering. They saw that people were far from their home countries, and that they faced industrial and urban abuses such as unfair wages, lack of representation, child labour, lack of safety standards, unregulated hours, and also the failures of neighbourhood infrastructure (Watkins, 2019).

The settlement members' experimentation and responsiveness to community issues led to the continual enlargement of the Hull House settlement, eventually expanding to fill an entire city block filled with social and educational clubs and programmes. Through their work, the social problems they could *not* solve were also revealed. These experiences were the impetus for Addams's social policy reform advocacy at municipal, state, and national levels (Opdycke, 2012: 2–3).

Addams not only lived in the original Hull House settlement but also theorized about it and its place in the world, seeing activism in terms of social philosophy (Hamington, 2009: 5–45). Hamington (2009: 19) argues that Addams should be seen as the founder of the philosophy of critical feminist pragmatism. This branch of philosophy – pragmatism – does not get stuck in abstract debate or arguments for argument's sake, but rather suggests an extended dialogue between thinking and acting (Opdycke, 2012: 48). It stresses the relationship of theory to praxis and the continuity of experience as the starting point for reflection (Hamington, 2009: 42), resonating with 'the doing' of practice that is referred to in our introduction to this book.

Addams's practice was integrated with, and guided by, a critical-emancipatory analysis about class, race, and gender that challenged the existing structures of power (Hamington, 2009: 45). Her social philosophy centred on widespread progress over individual progress. She argued that:

> the best speculative philosophy sets forth the solidarity of the human race; that the highest moralists have taught that without the advance and improvement of the whole, no man [sic]

can hope for any lasting improvement in his [sic] own moral or material individual condition; and that the subjective necessity for Social Settlements is therefore identical with that necessity, which urges us on toward social and individual salvation (Addams, 1910: 61).

Democracy and social ethics through social ties

Addams's primary commitment was to a theory and practice of democracy (Fischer et al., 2009: 2). Knight (2005: 5), quoting Addams, defines democracy as, 'a rule of living and a test of faith in the essential dignity and equality of all men [sic]'. Addams knew that her upper-middle-class privilege had created ignorance of the conditions of those around her and their cultures (Watkins, 2019). Thus, she insisted that social reform must not take place solely at an institutional level, but also at the level of personal relationships through renewed social ties. She argued that democracy is attained and sustained by developing a profound sense of connection with one's fellow human beings and that a critical test of democracy lies in how people treat each other every day (Opdycke, 2012: 57).

In her book, *Democracy and Social Ethics* (1902), she highlights the importance of broadening sympathies, so people understand how the world looks to other people. Referring to factory workers and immigrants from the Hull House Settlement, she said that if people close such people out of their minds and hearts, 'we not only tremendously circumscribe our range of life but limit the scope of our ethics' (cited in Opdycke, 2012: 57). To Addams, the need for mutual understanding was one of the crucial elements of a democratic society; and one not easily achieved given the obstacles of the society's class, race and wealth divides at that time (Opdycke, 2012: 57–58). This deep sense of connection with fellow human beings as a vehicle for democracy was at the heart of the social settlement movement.

Mutual accompaniment

Watkins (2019) takes these ideas further and writes about the social settlement movement as a vehicle to create social democracy through *mutual accompaniment*, which is the gem of wisdom I've chosen for community development. Long before the emergence of the welfare state and the birth of competing and fracturing social services in a capitalist economy, settlement members practised psychosocial accompaniment in neighbourhoods, addressing individual and community wellbeing in a holistic manner. They settled into neighbourhoods not to 'help' others, or to gentrify the neighbourhoods, but to join in solidarity with their new neighbours, to share in all facets of life around them, and to work to create cross-class and cross-ethnic relationships that were reciprocal and mutual (Watkins, 2019). This notion of not setting out just to 'help' those in need harks back to community development as a relationship practice of solidarity, discussed in our introduction and in the chapter on **Esteva**. Aunty Lilla Watson's apt quote bears repeating here – 'If you have come to help me you are wasting your time. But if your liberation is tied up with mine, then let us work together.'[1]

This theme of mutual accompaniment is perhaps the greatest challenge for contemporary community developers today. Watkins (2019) writes about its erosion in a capitalist service economy. The model of voluntary residents partnering with neighbours in settlement house neighbourhoods has transformed into a growing cadre of paid professional staff, working for those 'in need of services' (Watkins, 2019: 58). People's welfare has literally become the business of others within the flourishing non-profit sector.

Watkins (2019) explains this has come about because of the emergence of the welfare state in the 1930s and 1940s and has resulted in a depoliticizing of citizens prepared to address structural injustice. As informal relationships of care and mutual aid are being displaced by these formal systems, Watkins argues there is a stigmatization of those caught in poverty, and as clients of human services people are subjected to the burgeoning clinical discourse of psychopathology (Watkins, 2019: 59).

This is far removed from the Hull House model of settlement in its first decades, which was an engine of social justice activism (Knight, 2012). It is also a far cry from Addams's view of social democracy and the notion of social accompaniment. Watkins (2019) argues that the displacement of hospitality from people's homes and hearts into formalized systems of care has separated us from our humanity and our humaneness. She makes a compelling argument for practices of mutual accompaniment being at the heart of their retrieval.

Conclusion

Writing not long after the closure of Hull House 123 years after it opened (due to welfare state funding cuts), Knight (2012) asks if the Settlement House legacy is something that should be brought back.

Addams stressed that one of the gifts of living in the settlement house was the feeling and reality of being in and part of a community. These mutual social ties were the impetus for citizens to cooperate for social justice. Jane Addams created and led an open-minded and flexible organization comprised of people willing to experiment. They had a great impact on thousands of people's lives and on social policy reform at all levels of government at the time. Residential settlement houses may have had their day, but using Jane Addams's words, Knight (2012) says, we could all benefit from finding new ways to come together 'on the common road'.

Endnotes

1. Words originally used by Lilla Watson, Aboriginal elder, activist, and educator from Queensland, Australia, in the 1970s and 1980s, and thence by other Aboriginal activists in Australia.

References

Addams, J. (1902) *Democracy and Social Ethics*, Macmillan, New York.

Addams, J. (1910) *Twenty Years at Hull House; illustrated and unabridged*, Feather Trail Press, United States, Reprinted 2009.

Carnes, M. (2012) 'Editor's preface', in S. Opdycke (ed.), *Jane Addams and her Vision for America*, pp.ix–x, Pearson Education, New Jersey.

Fischer, M., Nackenoff, C. and Chimielewski, W. (eds.) (2009) 'Introduction', in *Jane Addams and the Practice of Democracy*, pp.1–18, University of Illinois Press, Urbana and Chicago, IL.

Hamington, M. (2009) *The Social Philosophy of Jane Addams*, University of Illinois Press, Urbana, Chicago and Springfield, IL.

International Federation of Settlements and Neighbourhood Centres (IFS) (2019), *'About IFS, History'* [website] <https://ifsnetwork.org/history> [Accessed 28 September 2019].

Kelly, A. and Westoby, P. (2018) 'Table 4.2: The seven steps of mezzo method', in A. Kelly and P. Westoby (eds.), *Participatory Development Practice: Using Traditional and Contemporary Frameworks*, p. 98, Practical Action Publishing, Warwickshire, UK.

Knight, L. (2005) *Citizen: Jane Addams and the Struggle for Democracy*, The University of Chicago Press, Chicago, IL.

Knight, L. (2012) 'As Chicago's Hull House Closes Its Doors, Time to Revive the Settlement Model?', *The Nation* [website] (posted 25 January 2012) <www.thenation.com/article/chicagos-hull-house-closes-its-doors-time-revive-settlement-model/> [Accessed 15 October 2019]

Opdycke, S. (2012) *Jane Addams and her Vision her Vision for America,* Pearson Education, New Jersey.
Watkins, M. (2019) 'Creating social democracy through mutual accompaniment: The social settlement movement', in M. Watkins (ed.), *Mutual Accompaniment and the Creation of the Commons,* pp. 24–61, Yale University Press, New Haven, CT.

CHAPTER 3
Chimamanda Ngozi Adichie: *The danger of a single story*

By Dave Palmer

Wani Olatunde

Chimamanda Ngozi Adichie 1977—

Who is Chimamanda Ngozi Adichie?

Chimamanda Ngozi Adichie, born in the city of Enugu, Nigeria, is a novelist, and writer of short stories and nonfiction. Much of her work explores the relationships between men and women, parents and their children, Africa and the United States, and the multiplicity and complexity of identities and stories.

Adichie was raised in the university town of Nsukka in Nigeria with both her parents working at the University of Nigeria. During the Nigerian civil war, both pairs of her grandparents were killed and her parents lost all their material possessions. Initially studying medicine in Nigeria, she moved to the USA at nineteen where she changed to studying communications and politics. After arriving in the USA she had what she describes as her first experience of being identified by the colour of her skin. Suddenly her race became something that she had to understand and negotiate. As well as writing about the experiences associated with being a young African coming to America, she has become acknowledged for her public lectures on feminism, race, and the importance of seeking multiple stories about people, places, and communities.

The danger of a single story

Adichie is particularly recognized for her TED talk called 'The Danger of a Single Story', delivered in July 2009. In this public lecture, she talks about her concern that too often non-Anglo cultural experience

http://dx.doi.org/10.3362/9781788531245.003

is represented one dimensionally and points to the power of seeking out multidimensional accounts of identity, experience, and 'community' life.

Adichie starts her lecture with a tale drawn from her own life. As a young girl and the daughter of two Nigerian intellectuals she was encouraged to read often, and given the dearth of opportunities for Nigerians to write novels, to read established American and British authors. This meant that she grew up reading primarily about the experiences of characters who were from Anglo backgrounds, speaking English and often from middle-class families. Not surprisingly, as she began to write at an early age her stories replicated those she had read, with all their British sensibilities, subject matter, and discursive styles. She writes:

> My characters also drank a lot of ginger beer because the characters in the British books I read drank ginger beer. Never mind that I had no idea what ginger beer was. And for many years afterwards, I would have a desperate desire to taste ginger beer. But that is another story.[1]

When she began to read books written by African authors, she discovered that her stories did not have to contain accounts of growing up in Britain or the USA. Suddenly she could write about things she recognized, themes that were relevant to her with characters that looked like her and did things that she had done. This process she said, saved her from 'having a single story about what books are'.[2]

Throughout the lecture, she uses personal stories to illustrate the dangers of relying upon one-dimensional narratives. For example, she begins the second part of her lecture by discussing her ideas about a young 'houseboy' or domestic worker called Fide, who would work each day in her middle-class family home. Her mother had told her that Fide's family was 'very poor' and would scold Adichie when she did not finish her dinner with 'Finish your food! Don't you know? People like Fide's family have nothing'. This she says created in her a sense of pity and distance from Fide. However, when later she visited Fide's village and met his family, Adichie's ideas were turned on their head after Fide's mother showed them a basket that Fide's brother had made. Adichie said, 'It had not occurred to me that anybody in his family could actually make something. All I had heard about them was how poor they were, so that it had become impossible for me to see them as anything else but poor. Their poverty was my single story of them'.[3]

In another personal account, she speaks of what happened to her after leaving Nigeria to study in the USA. She recounts that her American roommate was shocked that she was such a capable English speaker and surprised that she did not listen to what her mate called 'tribal music'. 'She was very disappointed when I produced my tape of Mariah Carey'. Her friend had already imagined Adichie's story, that she was poor, 'backward', and someone whose life had been a combination of sorrowful and 'traditional'. This had clearly not been a story that Adichie had imagined. Rather it was a preconceived default position about 'Africa' and 'Africans', one grounded in patronizing ideas of underdevelopment and deficiency. She says of this: 'My roommate had a single story of Africa: a single story of catastrophe. In this single story, there was no possibility of Africans being similar to her in any way, no possibility of feelings more complex than pity, no possibility of a connection as human equals'.

Behind Adichie's stories in this lecture are accounts of the limits of one dimensional and taken-for-granted ideas about others. As she puts it, these stories 'flatten' the experience of both those who are being talked about and those who rely upon such stale and unoriginal accounts of others. She points out that the trouble with such accounts is not so much that they are untrue. Indeed, there may well be some elements of 'truth' in the experience. The major danger of relying on these kinds of simple stereotypes and tropes is 'that they are incomplete. They make one story become the only story'. The other important consequence of trading in single stories is that it takes the depth and quality away from the lives of humans, often reducing them to inert objects that are acted upon and enjoy no agency, no strength, no originality. As Adichie puts it, reproducing single stories 'robs people of dignity'.

Adichie's contribution offers much to those interested in community development. One of the strengths of this public lecture is that Adichie speaks plainly and clearly, covering in a few short minutes similar observations made by many great writers and political figures such as Edward Said in *Orientalism* (1978), Chandra Talpande Mohanty *in Under Western Eyes* (1984), and Gayatri Chakravorty Spivak in *Can the Subaltern Speak?* (1988). In this way she offers us something that is user-friendly and accessible to many, including those who have limited written literacy.

Another gift from this work to community practitioners is the clear reminder that we can all too easily fall for the simple and one-dimensional stories about the people with whom we work, particularly given the centrality of problematizing narratives in shaping policy and funding priorities. Often this puts us in a position where, in order to attract the attention of governments or others who could support the work, we need to frame the complex lives of people through the prism of social problems, needs, and issues. As those involved in the call to adopt an 'assets-based approach to community' have pointed out, this skews the work from its inception and importantly often results in community being 'type-cast' and 'orientalised' as deficient, indigent, and pitiable. These tropes of community in crisis also result in our being in a position where we constantly feel the need to defend people living in the communities where we work.

The solution proposed by Adichie is to build a programme of storytelling by those inside the communities with whom we work. The weapon against a single story is the telling of multiple stories by those within. Part of the practice of community workers then can be to encourage people to tell stories and plenty of them. Implicit in this project is that we in community development: 1) resist the urge to retell the conventional story of people's 'disadvantage'; 2) do not become the only story-teller on behalf of the community and in the name of representing their interests; 3) look up, out, and past the first stories, seeking multiple stories from the community; and 4) seek to encourage multiple versions of stories of community life.

Endnotes

1. Chimamanda Ngozi Adichie (2009) 'The danger of a single story' (annotated video scripts) [website] <https://ngl.cengage.com/21centuryreading/resources/sites/default/files/B3_TG_AT7_0.pdf> [accessed 23 September 2019].
2. Ibid
3. ibid

References and key works

Adichie, Chimamanda Ngozi (2009) 'The Danger of a Single Story', Ted Talk, *Ted Global* [website] <www.ted.com/talks/chimamanda_adichie_the_danger_of_a_single_story?language=en> [Accessed 23 September 2019].

Adichie, Chimamanda Ngozi (2016) 'The Danger of a Single Story', Annotated Video Transcripts, *Cengage Learning* [website], <https://ngl.cengage.com/21centuryreading/resources/sites/default/files/B3_TG_AT7_0.pdf> [Accessed 23 September 2019].

Mohanty, Chandra Talpade. (1984) 'Under Western eyes: Feminist scholarship and colonial discourses', *Boundary 2*. 12(3)–13(1): 333–358.

Said, Edward (1978) *Orientalism*, Penguin, London.

Spivak, Gayatri Chakravorty (1988) 'Can the subaltern speak?' in Cary Nelson and Lawrence Grossberg (eds.), *Marxism and the Interpretation of Culture*, pp. 44–111 Macmillan, London.

CHAPTER 4
Hannah Arendt: *Time to think*

By Dave Palmer

Hannah Arendt 1906–1975

Introduction

One of the great challenges confronting those trained in the art and science of community development is that we work daily with organizations and those operating under heavily regulated and compliance-driven regimes. Often this means that we are under enormous pressure to manage and be managed, carrying out work against the backdrop of outcomes-driven planning systems that pretend we can predetermine what is to be done in advance. Increasingly, risk management culture infects the work, with its obsession with technical rationality and great faith in planning as a means of limiting failure and hazards, and for resolving problems.

A consequence of this mentality of governance or style of working is that practitioners are discouraged from exercising judgement and are encouraged to rely upon procedures, plans, and highly regulated behaviour. For example, those preparing practitioners to work with communities (particularly those identified as problems or 'at risk') are expected to educate people in how to follow codes of professional ethics, build blueprints for action, set out 'best practice' models, and follow guidelines and frameworks. This codification of practice is usually carefully monitored by independent evaluators and line managers, who make assessments about the efficacy and success of the work based on predetermined measures that predominately test outcomes set by funding regimes and pay scant attention to the processes people use and the judgements workers make.

My intuitive mistrust of this style of working, with its heavy reliance on the values and assessments of experts and policy boffins who have little 'skin in the game' and almost no experience 'on

http://dx.doi.org/10.3362/9781788531245.004

the ground' led me to read the work of Hannah Arendt, the Jewish, German-raised intellectual with a deep scepticism of what she and others call 'technical rationality'.

Who was Hannah Arendt?

Hannah Arendt (1906–1975), was a political philosopher born in Hanover, Germany, in 1906, to secular Jewish parents. She began study at the University of Berlin and famously worked with philosopher Martin Heidegger, who acted both as her mentor and briefly her lover.

In 1933, she moved to Paris to escape the power and likely persecution of Nazis, who had just come to power. In 1936, she met her soon-to-be husband Heinrich Blücher, a German political refugee. She was briefly interned by the French during the German occupation of France, before moving to the US to write about the horrors of totalitarianism.

This work was to prove remarkable in its timely description of the distinction between old tyrannies and new forms of oppressive regimes. Arendt observed that older systems of domination had used terror as the means to an end, that of attaining and maintaining power. In contrast, contemporary totalitarian regimes were less strategic or rational in their adoption of terror. Rather, terror became the end itself.

On human judgment

Perhaps the most important facet of Arendt's enquiry is her outline of the importance of human judgment. She concluded that academics and others from the middle class are often invested in systems of power. She was also highly critical of the distance between the lived experiences of communities and political philosophers, with their abstract ideas, presuppositions, and universalizing principals. She argued that the greatest threat to human freedom came from the act of abstraction from action. Following the work of phenomenologists such as Martin Heidegger, Arendt insisted on a return to the study of 'the things themselves'. In particular, for her, the keys to understanding are in exercising judgement and thinking.

To help explain this, Arendt made a distinction between labour, work, and action, claiming it is only in action that humans can become free. Following Augustine, she saw human action as that which involves taking initiative, using judgment to respond to context. For her, the capacity of humans to take initiative gives them the unique ability to create something new and different from whatever happened before. The exertion of thought to shape such action distinguishes free human endeavours from other conduct that is driven by habit, regulation, imposition, and automation.

The 'banality of evil'

As a sobering case in point, Arendt's study of the trial of Adolf Eichmann stands as a powerful example of the consequences of failing to think. After hearing of Eichmann's capture and his planned trial in Jerusalem, Arendt contacted the editors of the internationally respected journal *The New Yorker* to have them support a trip to witness the trial – where she would test her ideas about totalitarianism and write about the work of the man seen as the architect of Hitler's Final Solution.

To help understand what she had seen of Eichmann she coined the term 'the banality of evil' to describe the potential for evil in ordinary and everyday acts. Challenging the taken-for-granted idea that evil is radical, out of the ordinary, and the act of the mad, she concluded that the actions of Eichmann and many Nazis were 'terribly and terrifyingly normal' (Arendt 1963). Rather than being motivated by extreme hatred of Jews, Eichmann was a bland individual. He acted without thought, technically following orders and the plans and instructions of those in authority, free from contemplation of what this would do to those subjected to his action. He was efficient, capable, and distant, all the hallmarks of a supposed 'good government official'.

Using Eichmann as a case in point Arendt concluded that rather than acts of terror being carried out by evil monsters, horrific deeds can emerge out of thoughtlessness, and from the tendency of people to obey orders and conform to popular opinion. As far as she could see, Eichmann was not mad, nor was his willing involvement with the programme of genocide a product of a failure or absence of the faculties of sound thinking and judgement. For Arendt, Eichmann's work was not driven by the presence of hatred but rather the absence or failure to imagine Jews as anything more than the subject of the machinery of Nazi government.

Arendt concluded that Eichmann's great failing was his inability to exercise independent thought, of having failed to have an internal conversation with himself about the consequences of his deeds. This connection between evil and failure to think and exercise judgement is an important observation and gift to those working with communities.

On thinking and community development

To be sure, all involved in work with communities must negotiate the sometimes-conflicting demands of community aspirations, funding bodies, the regimes that govern our organizations, and the constant impact of shifting policy makers. Some of our colleagues might argue that success comes most to those who artfully balance these demands so that tensions are kept to a minimum and the bosses are kept satisfied. Others who would take the moral and political high ground might suggest that the answer is in resistance, push back, and social protest.

If Hannah Arendt were still with us and was invited to give counsel to community workers, she might instead suggest that our greatest achievements will come when we apply our best thinking to the many complex and shifting challenges that confront our work and those with whom we work.

In her first volume of *Life of the Mind* (1971) Arendt makes the important distinction between knowing or understanding (*Verstand*) and thinking or reasoning (*Vernunft*). *Verstand* involves the quest for truth or knowledge. *Vernunft* involves the human quest to move beyond knowing, the act of constantly and persistently asking questions, and imagining how something might be other than what first appears. For Arendt, technically we can settle on *verstand* or that which can be known. In contrast, *Vernunft* is constant and continuous; a quest to move beyond understanding.

This, she claimed was a central element in politics. Drawing on features of the *Polis* in ancient Athens, Arendt posited that the constant process of thinking or reasoning in public is what allows humans to exercise freedom. Making public, through debate, discourse, and dialogue, the seeds of our thought is the way we can collectively maintain freedom. Maintaining institutions and practices that set us constantly and communally on the quest to imagine how things might be different is how we can be free from technical rationality and other forms of imposed government.

Perhaps, Arendt might say that this is intrinsic to the practice of community development – engaging the mind with others through relentless questioning. As she said, 'to think with an enlarged mentality means that one trains one's imagination to go visiting'. 'Going visiting' with others in this way might be another way of describing a most powerful practice of those who seek freedom for others in community.

References and Key Works

Arendt, H. (1951) *The Origins of Totalitarianism*, Harcourt, New York.

Arendt, H. (1958) *The Human Condition*, University of Chicago Press, Chicago.

Arendt, H. (1962) *On Revolution*, Penguin, New York.

Arendt, H. (1963) *Eichmann in Jerusalem: A Report on the Banality of Evil*, Faber & Faber, London.

Arendt, H. (1968) *Men in Dark Times*, Harcourt, New York.

Arendt, H. (1971) *The Life of the Mind*, Harcourt, New York.

CHAPTER 5

James Baldwin: *We have to go the way our blood beats*

Allan Warren

By Peter Westoby

James Baldwin 1924–1987

James Baldwin, a celebrated African American world-renowned author, analyst, and gay rights voice, left his home country of the USA in 1948, simply to 'go anywhere' (Baldwin, 2017: 88). A self-confessed maverick – in the sense that, 'I depended on neither the white world nor the black world … I would've been broken otherwise' (Baldwin, 2014: 51), he found himself in Paris which 'released [him] from social terror' (Baldwin, 2017: 88). Here, finally he found that he was no longer paranoid about his own mind and no longer felt as if he were constantly living with real danger – the social terror of violence from police and white folk. Being in Europe saved him and what is significant for this reflection is that leaving the USA 'gave [him] another touchstone – myself' (Baldwin, 2014: 51). In a sense *he got inside his own skin*. Since then, a well-known essayist, novelist, witness to the world, he has felt compelled to 'speak out against institutionalized and individual tyranny wherever he found it' (Baldwin, 2014: 81).

Linking to the idea of being inside his own skin, I have opted for the gem of wisdom to be a slightly adapted version of a well-known Baldwin quote, 'you have to go the way your blood beats'. And the metaphor of blood simply refers to life-force, identity, honesty, and courage. To go the way your blood beats is to be alive to your own life-force, your own identity, and to be courageous and honest in this.

http://dx.doi.org/10.3362/9781788531245.005

This wisdom can be summed up as the implicate method of community development practice (see Kelly & Westoby, 2018), whereby a community development practitioner is both in their own skin (confident to be oneself, not focused on pleasing others), and inviting people and community leaders to also be in their own skin. This is to imply that there's no universal right way of doing anything, no right response, nor should anyone act necessarily from some external pressure (to conform, to please others and so on). Live life your own way, albeit there are clearly ethical conversations and, perhaps imperatives to keep in mind.

There was a particular context for Baldwin's wise words, that is, his experience as a black man – and he shares how, '...I was not born to be what someone said I was. I was not born to be defined by someone else, but by myself, and myself only' (Baldwin, 2014: 92). To find the way our heart beats is to not be defined by anyone else, albeit recognizing that we are not just individuals (as per limp liberal ideology), but rather socialized beings.

In an address at an international community development conference I used this Baldwin quote, but slightly tweaked it to, '*we* have to go the way *our* blood beats', replacing 'I' and 'your' with 'we' and 'our' to signify the collective dimension of community practice. Each *group* in a community has to find its way. Each group has to be in their own skin so to speak. Each group has to go the way their blood beats. Each group has to work not to be defined by others.

To be in one's own skin, to be going where the heart beats is to also be connected to our own passion and, as Baldwin suggests, to bring social change 'you don't need numbers, you need passion'. But he does add that, 'the tragedy is that most people who say they care about it do not care' (Baldwin, 2017: 95).

However, in pressing for this kind of passionate authentic way of being in our own skin – not defined by others – Baldwin did not shy away from the tough issues of his day. Returning from his sojourn in Paris, now famous as a novelist and essayist, he had plenty to say about race relations and at other times about sexuality, in a somewhat fierce and yet nuanced way. In many ways his work was a precursor to what we now think of as intersectional thinking.

Sitting in a cinema in 2017 watching the acclaimed movie *I am not Your Negro*, a story narrated by Baldwin about his experience of, and reflection on, the 1960s deaths of three friends and comrades – Martin Luther King, Malcolm X, and Medgar Evers – I was transfixed by his humble yet potent words. I'd finally encountered the opus of Baldwin.

Race relations and white hearts: Time for White folks to do the work

Grappling with the enduring horror of race relations within the USA, Baldwin asks some hard questions that are still pertinent. For example, 'How [do we] communicate to the vast, heartless, unthinking ... white majority. ... They really don't think I'm human' (Baldwin, 2017: 39). In this, Baldwin, sees 'white as a metaphor for power' (ibid: 107), echoing Ghassan Hage's examination of *White Nation: Fantasies of White Supremacy in a Multicultural Society* (Hage, 1998) in contemporary Australia – and my use of White with a capital 'W' is an indicator that non-white people join the power system of White oppression. In a sense he was ahead of the game, as critical race studies have finally opened a place of studying 'whiteness'.

Foreseeing what Chela Sandoval's *Methodology of the Oppressed* (2000) argues, Baldwin understands that oppressed people have the advantage of 'double consciousness' – they see themselves, *and* how others see them. For example, he names how black people have an advantage – 'you [white folk] never had to look at me. I had to look at you' (Baldwin, 2017: 103). He suggests that basically, it's time for White folk, or those with power, to stop looking at others, and to instead turn the gaze on themselves.

Baldwin goes to the heart of the dehumanising system of what **bell hooks** called the 'imperialist white supremacist capitalist patriarchy'. Within this analysis he sees how, 'black people are trying to survive a very brutal system in which they are trying to stay alive' (ibid: 49), while white people experience emotional poverty, a mode characterized by constricted white imagination. As per **Fanon**'s reflection, colonization and racism destroy both the oppressor and oppressed in somewhat different ways.

Again, shining the light on white people, he suggests that 'the root of white man's hatred is terror ... an entity which lives only in his mind' (ibid: 60). The lack of imagination is a limited construction of the black man and Baldwin expands on this, arguing, 'If I'm not a nigger [sic] here and you invented him, you, the white people invented him, then *you've* got to find out why' (ibid: 109). He rightly insists that it's time for white people to start doing the work of change. Adding to this he invites white people to ask, 'In white hearts, why is it necessary to have a "nigger" [sic] in the first place?' (ibid: 108). Why this need to have someone to hate or/and to oppress?

Sexuality and straight infantilism

Baldwin talks of the 'forceful encounter' with himself as a 14-year-old young man, knowing he loved a boy. In his 1984 interview with Richard Goldstein he shared how, '[sexuality] was like everything else in my life, a problem which I would have to resolve myself … it never occurred to me to join a club' (Baldwin, 2014: 60). Not being a group-oriented person, instead a maverick, he found his way to understanding sexuality through writing. Writing was his public action, with a kind of 'responsibility because [he] would have to be a kind of witness' (Baldwin, 2014: 61).

He elevated the issue of homosexuality into the public realm as a writer, taking great risk in publishing the acclaimed novel *Giovanni's Room* (the risk was that his readership, the black community, would reject the book). While working out his own sexuality through writing, and 'alone', he did however have a social analysis of the issue. For example, in that same 1984 interview he suggests, 'the discovery of one's sexual preference doesn't have to be a trauma. It's a trauma because it's such a traumatised society' (ibid: 63). In a sense, the pain of feeling life as an 'other' is because people do the 'othering'. Here's the heart of the trauma – to be [not]seen and unloved, rejected. Much like Baldwin's analysis of race relations, with his asking white people, 'why do you need a "nigger"?', he asks the same of straight people, arguing:

> I know from my own experience that the macho men – truck drivers, cops, football players – these people are far more complex than they want to realise. That's why I call them infantile. They have needs which, for them, are literally inexpressible. They don't dare look into the mirror. And that is why they need faggots [sic] (Baldwin, 2014: 650).

Huge statements, forcing the powerful – White and straight – to ask why they need 'niggers' and 'faggots'?

In conclusion

Despite his deep and profound analysis, Baldwin proposes that 'I'm an optimist … I'm forced to believe that we can survive' (Baldwin, 2017: 108). Survival comes through that authenticity talked of early in this reflection and then everyone shining the light on themselves. Race relations, gender, and sexuality require a profound authenticity, a coming to terms with our own complexity, and an openness to learning, never thinking we know the world of an 'other'. Baldwin, with poignant final words, suggests 'you can't be taught anything if you think you know everything already; that something else – greed, materialism, and consuming – is more important to your life' (Baldwin, 2014: 117). I say poignant because this addiction to greed, materialism, and consuming in a hyper-consumer capitalist society certainly undoes all that's important for community development – self-reflection, learning, profound honesty, finding the blood that beats in our own hearts.

References

Baldwin, J. (1954) *Go Tell It on the Mountain,* Penguin Books, London.

Baldwin, J. (1983) *Notes of a Native Son,* Beacon Press, Boston, MA.

Baldwin, J. (2014) *James Baldwin: The Last Interview and Other Conversations,* Melville House, London.

Baldwin, J. (2017) *I Am Not Your Negro,* Penguin Books, London.

Hage, G. (1998) *White Nation: Fantasies of White Supremacy in a Multicultural Society,* Pluto Press, London.

Kelly, A. and Westoby, P. (2018) *Participatory Development Practice: Using Traditional and Contemporary Frameworks.* Practical Action Publishing, Rugby.

Sandoval, C. (2000) *Methodology of the Oppressed,* University of Minnesota Press, Minneapolis, MN and London.

CHAPTER 6
Homi Bhabha: *The value of colonial ambivalence*

By Dave Palmer

Homi Bhabha 1949—

Coming across Homi Bhabha

Like many with a history of working with young people, I was drawn to research because of a keenness to better understand what I was doing. One of my first pieces of work involved carrying out ethnographic research with non-Aboriginal Australians who, as youth workers, spent time with Aboriginal young people and their families. I was particularly interested in how these relationships took shape and how power and influence was negotiated between young people and youth workers. Having been introduced to the critical sociological traditions I began framing my discussions with youth workers by assuming that they had to start their relationships with Aboriginal young people from a position of 'structural advantage'. In other words, I began by asking youth workers to talk about how they dealt with the fact that they had power over young people.

Very quickly it became apparent that the 'lenses' I was using to think about this work did not help me understand the people whom I had invited to be involved in my research. Rather than Aboriginal young people being 'disadvantaged' in their interactions with youth workers, they were often able to exercise considerable influence. For example, in response to my question about how he had 'power over' his charges one youth worker said:

> I can tell you right now that Nyungar (Aboriginal people from the South West of Australia) kids aren't #@*% powerless. Some of them are real little operators that run rings around youth workers. I tell you what, in the last five years I've been shown a thing or two (cited in Palmer, 1995: 28).

http://dx.doi.org/10.3362/9781788531245.006

Confronted with people working directly in community contexts where their experiences did not easily match simple ideas about power, I was forced to seek out different conceptual lenses to help understand relationships between those living in postcolonial Australia. This is how I came to meet the work of writers such as Homi Bhabha, writers who themselves had been raised having to contend with the ideas, explanations, and analysis of members of the colonist classes.

Who is Homi Bhabha?

Homi Bhabha is an Indian (Parsi) literary studies intellectual and key figure in the postcolonial studies tradition. He is most known for his attempts to enunciate the complex forms of identity and new cultural forms that have emerged under late colonial discourse and intercultural relations. Although born in Bombay, Bhabha studied and has subsequently worked in some of the most hallowed of Western institutions, including Oxford, Princeton, and University College London. In his work, such as the book *The Location of Culture*, Bhabha lays open the complexity of colonial experience and the array of responses from people who sit inside 'communities' that have been imposed upon by outsiders.

Colonial discourse and colonizing practices

Often regarded as the catalyst for, or beginning of, postcolonial literature, Edward Said's *Orientalism* moved analysis to the West and how it constitutes 'the other' (Gandhi, 1998: 64). Importantly for Said (1978), the practice of producing discourses on the Other has several features. Firstly, the process of producing public and 'official' representations of the Other allows the West to make sense of itself as the powerful, the articulate, and the civilized. In contrast, the 'Orient' is almost always constituted as the defeated, the distant, the weak, the needy, the strange, and importantly those for whom intervention and help is essential. According to Said, the formal study, research, and policy work that emerges from Orientalism has long been used as a tool for intervention, often seeing the intelligence gatherers as part of the armour of military and imperialist projects. Secondly, Said makes the sobering observation that Orientalism almost always involves public talk (often described as research) about the Other in their absence.

Ambivalence and stories about the Other

Since *Orientalism*, theorists have revisited Said's analysis and argued that stories about the colonial Other are often more ambivalent, complex, and available to the colonized. Foremost has been the work of Homi Bhabha who reminds us that discourses on the Other are never as fixed and settled as we imagine. On the one hand, the Indigenous Other is often despised as a barbaric alien who looms as a dangerous threat. On the other hand, the Indigenous Other is sometimes the subject of much desire, serving as a source of inspiration because of its ancient wisdom and its ability to hold up the inadequacies of the West (Bhabha, 1986).

This ambivalence stems from a deep-seated contradiction at the heart of the colonial enterprise. On the one hand, colonial discourse sets out to delineate the Other as 'radically different' (Bhabha, 1994). At the same time the colonizer must maintain sufficient identity and contact with its Indigenous counterparts in order to maintain control over them.

According to Bhabha this has the effect of challenging and disrupting the discourse of the colonizers and producing possibilities for the subversion and transformation of colonial life. This means that built into Orientalist discourse is the seeds of its own subversion.

So, we can say at the very least, the 'West's' construction of the 'Orient' is not a unified or unidirectional one (Gandhi, 1998: 17). Nor are stories about the 'Orient' always and only available to the West and used against the colonized. In other words, Orientalist discourse is available to and used by its antagonists in the colonized world (Bhabha, 1985).

Ambivalence in community work

How might this play out for those involved in community work? As Benedict Anderson (1983) reminds us, the act of colonizing and modern nation-making is intricately tied up with the act of making community. We might paraphrase this and observe that the will to govern 'community' comes out of old practices tied to the will to colonize the minds, lands, and lives of local and Indigenous peoples. Not surprisingly, the subjects of community work are often local people who have a long experience of being treated as the Other; long managed by outsiders who do not share their languages, interests, and values. To help with this let us turn to an example from Australia and how this gets played out with Indigenous groups.

On the one hand, the history of policy interventions by governments, universities, and non-government groups into the lives of Indigenous Australians has been devastating. Legislative and policy incursions into Indigenous communities have been premised upon many and varied racist tropes, sometimes couched in old eugenics, sometimes in more liberal rhetorical arguments. One thing remains, the lives of Indigenous Australians unequally bear the scars of generations who are poor, have little equity in the marketplace, struggle with health, and are dying much younger. This is something that modern governments must address (or at least be seen to address). On the other hand, Aboriginal people are central to the solutions and critical as practitioners, policy architects, and leaders in the work that has too often failed in in the past because of the inability, lack of knowledge, and inexperience of outsiders. At the same time, the fact that 'Indigenous communities' exist as a problem group becomes a problem in and of itself in that it contradicts governmental aspirations for a society politically administered according to principles of fairness and equality.

This can and does create possibilities for challenging the way we deal with the needs and aspirations of Aboriginal groups. For example, Mickler suggests that Indigenous leaders regularly and routinely use Aboriginal victimhood and pauperism as a political tool to call attention to government inaction (1996: 283). In the last 40 years Aboriginal groups have successfully argued for increased expenditure, intervention, and the necessity of Aboriginal involvement in the solutions. In this way the two-century-long failure of successive governments to improve the circumstances of Aboriginal communities has forced many to turn to 'engagement' with community as a modern mantra for policy solutions. In other words, one effect of two hundred years of 'troubling talk' about Aboriginal communities is that many organizations, largely staffed by non-Aboriginal community workers, are forced to turn to Aboriginal groups and representatives for counsel and strategies.

In conclusion

Community workers often stand in contradictory and ambiguous positions, particularly in their relationship to the communities they support. Their and other people's talk about these communities constantly drags them in a multitude of directions so that they are never entirely sure of their course and never successful in their objectives.

Bhabha might say this is extremely menacing and disruptive to the authority and certainty of their work.

However, this may not be all bad news for those involved in community development. Indeed, Bhabha argues that the absence of closure produced by ambivalence in colonial discourse 'allows for native intervention' and often produces conditions that turn discourse on its head (Bhabha, 1985). In other words, discourse around 'the community', unsettling as it is, can challenge community workers and those who attempt to direct their work to reassess their ideas and practice. In addition, it may force resources to be directed towards initiatives aimed at improving the circumstances of the communities that they are charged to support. It might also open space for them to respond creatively, adopt novel approaches and imaginatively build new and innovative ways that involve community.

References and key works

Anderson, B. (1983) *Imagined Communities: Reflections on the Origin and Spread of Nationalism*, Verso, London.

Bhabha, H. (1985) 'Signs taken for wonders: Questions of ambivalence and authority under a tree outside Delhi, May 1815' *Critical Inquiry* 12, Autumn: 144–165.

Bhabha, H. (1986) 'The other question: Difference, discrimination and the discourse of colonialism', in Barker, F., Hulme, P. and Iversen, M. (eds), *Literature, Politics and Theory*, pp. 148–173, Methuen, London.

Bhabha, H. (1994) *The Location of Culture*. London, Routledge.

Gandhi, L. (1998) *Postcolonial Theory: A Critical Introduction*, Allen and Unwin, St Leonards, Sydney, Australia.

Mickler, S. (1998) *The Myth of Privilege: Aboriginal Status, Media Visions, Public Ideas*, Fremantle Arts Centre, South Fremantle, West Australia.

Palmer, D. (1995) 'Getting shown a thing or two: The adoption of Nyungar cultural forms by youth workers', *Youth Studies Australia*, January 1995: 22–28.

Said, E. (1978) *Orientalism: Western Conceptions of the Orient*, Penguin, London.

CHAPTER 7

Ela Bhatt: *Start with women; may our action be one of nurturance*

By Athena Lathouras

Mohan Juneja

Ela Bhatt 1933—

I consider myself lucky to have heard Ela Bhatt give the *Les Halliwell Memorial Address*[1] in 2009. This took place at the joint International Association for Community Development / Community Development Queensland conference in Brisbane, Australia and I loved listening to her deep wisdom. Her philosophy for women's empowerment comes from a belief in building collective strength and becoming self-reliant – the path of *Swaraj*, or self-rule (Bhatt, 2017). Fifty years ago, she set out to work with poor women, to help them organize and to stop their economic exploitation, founding the Self-Employed Women's Association (SEWA) in India.

Bhatt's key belief is that where there is poverty, there is injustice. To her, poverty is a form of violence perpetuated with the consent of society (Bhatt, 2012). This kind of injustice sanctions the exploitation of individuals, communities, and the environment. Where there is poverty, she argues, there is discrimination, fear, intimidation, and enormous vulnerability. Whereas, with economic freedom, dignity and self-respect ensue.

Women, work, and peace

When accepting the Niwano Peace Prize in 2010, Bhatt claimed her activist philosophy can be said in three words – *women, work,* and *peace.*

Within the context of traditional values and practices informed by patriarchy, class, caste, and religious divisions, Bhatt asserts that women's liberation can be transformative – for individual women and for

http://dx.doi.org/10.3362/9781788531245.007

their communities. She focuses on women as leaders – those who are building a 'gentler economy' (Bhatt 2009), asserting that women are key to building a community as they are the forger of bonds – they are both creators and preservers of family and community. Women may be materially poor and vulnerable, yet they possess enormous strengths – they are survivors.

Bhatt (2010) emphasized that productive work is a key thread that weaves society together. When people have work they have an incentive to maintain a stable society, to think of the future, and to plan for the future. In these sets of circumstances life is no longer about just survival, but about investing in a better future. Work builds peace because work gives people roots, it builds communities and gives meaning and dignity to one's life. Work forges an individual's identity and provides livelihoods that produce goods and services, and thus builds a society. Hence, much of her work is focused on women's work.

Peace, she claims, is under threat (Bhatt, 2010). We live in a world with widening divides – between nations, between peoples, and between governments and their own people. Where there is an unfair distribution of resources, there is unrest. Peace and poverty cannot co-exist, hence the inextricable link between peace and work. When people cannot enjoy the fruits of their labours fairly, this is the basis of an unjust society. Livelihood invokes life values and life vision. But when erased, she claims, a livelihood – a memory, a competence, a community, and culture – are destroyed. Such a belief system explains Bhatt's decades-long commitment to creating opportunities for women to work as a form of livelihood.

SEWA – building peace through poverty eradication

SEWA, an acronym that means 'to serve', spans the labour movement, the cooperative movement, and the women's movement. SEWA's approach is to organize around work – to see poor women as workers and producers rather than just as income-deprived or vulnerable people. Women get the strength to organize when they tap into their collective strength through women's to women's organizing. Equipped to deal with challenges in life, women then move out of poverty.

With a critical analysis of economic and social structural issues, SEWA seeks to address real barriers that the poor encounter (Bhatt, n.d.). Barriers in entry to labour exist, and product markets are closely connected to social structures. For example, gender, caste, class, and social needs such as health, child care, education, and housing are all linked to economic capabilities. Bhatt argues that since the economic and social structures are so interrelated, the solutions too have to be integrated. There is no one formula for poverty reduction, rather it must be an approach that addresses the various economic and social factors that perpetuate poverty, simultaneously.

With such an analysis and a clear vision, since the 1970s SEWA has been facilitating women's self-employment and economic security and has now nearly two million members (Chen, Bonner & Carré, 2015). SEWA is also seen as a social movement as its organizing principles have been generative. Its current work with women also takes place in Afghanistan, Pakistan, Nepal, Sri Lanka, and Bhutan.

Many examples of the projects women undertake to achieve economic freedom and to live with dignity and self-respect are documented through Tedx Talks (see, for example, Nanavaty, 2015) and SEWA's website (www.sewa.org). Women form their own co-operatives, now numbering over 100, and they provide decentralized and affordable services for and by poor women. When they come together, women innovate and take on new risks; they take out small loans and build businesses. SEWA has established its own bank, savings and credit groups, health care and child care services, social security, insurance schemes, and legal services.

A social economy of nurturance

Now in her elder years and after a lifetime of working against the violence of poverty, exploitation, and injustice, Bhatt pleads for a social economy of nurturance. Exploitation, she argues, is a learned behaviour, whereas nurturance comes naturally to human beings (Bhatt, 2017). In today's world, though, we are encouraged to be exploitative rather than nurturing and this results in a threefold crisis – rising poverty despite abundance; the rise of intolerance, hatred, and violence; and environmental catastrophe. She asserts that this has to be corrected, not by our 'leaders', but by us, 'the common people', as a local-global movement. We need to rebuild a new social economy of nurturance and reject the current anti-social economy of exploitation and destruction. In our work, and in our commitments to action, we need to use our human and social capital to reclaim our access to natural and physical capital.

I conclude this reflection on Ela Bhatt's significant life's work with what I have chosen as the 'gem' of her wisdom – the hope that our action be the kind that builds the social economy of nurturance. She challenges activists, development practitioners, and social change agents to carefully and critically reflect on the impact of all action. According to the *Bhagavad Gita,* the way to liberation is *karma* – generally understood as fate or destiny. However, Bhatt (2012) explains that in Sanskrit, *karma* means action. Her challenge is for us to consider the impact of our action, on life today, but also on future lives. For all of us she claims, our good deeds have an impact on the lives of others across the globe. And because all our action is inextricably linked we are bound by mutual responsibility. It follows then that a social economy of nurturance is one that is deeply reflective of its impacts, on ourselves and on the world. She poses three key questions and asks community development practitioners to carefully consider these as a guide for their work and practice:

What impact will my action have on me?

What impact will my action have on the people around me and on the global community? And lastly, what impact will my action have on Mother Nature?

Endnotes

1. Les Halliwell was the first head of the newly established School of Social Work at the University of Queensland, Australia in 1956. He is remembered for his strong commitment to a people-first approach and influencing the practice of a unique model of community development in Queensland. See: CD Queensland - www.cdqld.org for Ela Bhatt's speech.

References and key works

Bhatt, E. R. (n.d) *Approaches to Poverty Removal [website]* <www.sewa. org/Archives_Poverty_Removal.asp> [Accessed 7 December 2018].

Bhatt, E. (2009) *Les Halliwell Address – Where Women are Leaders: Building a Gentler Economy* [website] <www.cdqld.org/ uploads/7/0/8/6/70862165/bhatt.pdf> [Accessed 7 December 2018].

Bhatt, E. (2010) *Acceptance Message on Receiving the Niwano Peace Prize, 13 May 2010, Tokyo* [website] <www.sewa.org/Archives.asp> [Accessed 6 December 2018].

Bhatt, E. (2012) *Speech to Graduating Students Georgetown University, 19 May 2012* [website] <www.sewa.org/Archives.asp> [Accessed 5th December 2018].

Bhatt, E. (2017) *Gandhi is with Us: Building an Economy of Nurturance, Speech to Azim Premji University, Bangalor, 26 October 2017* [website] <www.sewa.org/Archives.asp> [Accessed 6 December 2018].

Chen, M., Bonner, C. and Carré, F. (2015) *Organizing Informal Workers: Benefits, Challenges and Successes,* UNDP Human Development Report Office, New York.

Community Development Queensland (2018) [website] <www.cdqld. org> [Accessed 7 December 2018].

Nanavaty, R. (2015) 'SEWA – Interplay of Women, Work and Peace' TEDx Talks [online] <www.youtube.com/watch?v=nRom5d9p5S4> [Accessed 6 December 2018].

SEWA – Self Employed Women's Association, *'SEWA Services'* [website] <www.sewa.org/Sewa_Services.asp> [Accessed 12 April 2019].

CHAPTER 8
Augusto Boal:
Rehearsing the possible

By Dave Palmer

Augusto Boal 1931–2009

Introduction

In many of the projects I follow, much of the success of the work can be attributable to the central role that singing, music, art, and performance plays. In some measure this is due to the strength of the arts in the histories and traditions of these communities. In part, it is because expressions of art and performance are so important, interesting, and fun to many of us. However, as Goffman (1956) reminds us, the practice of performing is literally a way of life, a way of bringing ourselves and our community to life, and in turn the way we come to life in our community.

To separate the practice of looking after the health of communities from singing, dancing, and performing is an abstraction that often does not help to explain life for communities (see sections on **Bird Rose**, **Freire**, and **Sennett**). This happens in a number of important ways. Not only does people's understanding of community come into being through performance of different roles, activities, and practices, but daily and yearly interactions with each other in communities are performative events; many of the metaphors used to describe community work are taken from the arts and theatre. For example, we invite communities to 'give voice' to their stories. We 'sing up' solutions. We take on different roles. We often take on collective action as part of social movements. We ask people to find 'harmony' with one another.

Another important observation for First Nation and other poor communities throughout the world is that, consistently throughout the history of colonial encounter, performance has been central to attempts by groups to give expression to their political aspirations.

http://dx.doi.org/10.3362/9781788531245.008

Music, dance and performance in particular have regularly been used in campaigns to reclaim land tenure lost to colonial conquest, human rights violations through discriminatory laws, and governmental acquisition of community land title.

Not surprisingly then, it was only a matter of time before I came across the work of Augusto Boal and his project to encourage communities to reframe the stories that confront them through theatre and performance.

Who was Augusto Boal?

Augusto Boal was born in Brazil in 1931 and studied theatre in the USA where he was strongly influenced by experimental theatre forms shaped by Brecht, Stanislavski, and the Black Experimental Theatre tradition. He met Paulo **Freire** and was moved by his ideas about the need to support the interests of the 'oppressed'. During the 1950s and 1960s, Boal started to develop a philosophy that led to a practice he called *Theatre of the Oppressed*. In this he initially sought to invite audiences to participate more fully in the experience of theatre by discussing the work at the end of its performance. After some experimentation he concluded that this was too restrictive on the audience as they merely took on the role of relatively passive viewers to the story and action performed by others. In his mind this risked maintaining the 'oppression' of poor audiences by confining them to consumers of other people's stories. This led him to mature the process so that members of the audience could take more control of the story, reconfiguring and reimagining its performance. What emerged was a form of theatre where the audience would be invited to stop a performance at any time and suggest different actions, stories, and narrative for the actors. In this way, the Theatre of the Oppressed model provided a chance for community members to come up with their own solutions to their problems examined in the theatre piece.

Rehearsing new futures and reconfiguring community into dialogue

As has been suggested by other critical thinkers in this collection (e.g. **Bird Rose**, **Sennett**, **Freire**), critical to the maintenance of community, economy, language, stories, and culture are what the West often calls arts and creative production. Partly this has been recognized in what is called 'community cultural development'. The intention behind this style of work is to use various art and creative forms to help draw out people's taken-for-granted or tacit knowledge, imagine how things can be different, and help them take action for a better future.

Sometimes this work attempts to shift the routines, perspectives, and responses of individuals so that practitioners can help people see things from a different perspective, suggest connections and transform the lives of people living in communities. As my 'gem of a wisdom', often the work seeks to help enliven the imagination of community and provide opportunities for people to 'rehearse' what might be possible. In other words, this approach can help individuals and groups to inhabit the character of the person or community they could become (Boal, 2007: 13).

Boal is a central contributor to this kind of work. We can see that he was influenced by the work of **Freire** and **Buber**, and following these two he understood oppression as 'a relationship in which there is only monologue, not dialogue' (Boal, 1995).

In his experiments with theatre he tested out the assumption that dialogue is the means through which all humans can build a healthy and respectful dynamic, and that oppression occurs when a dialogue becomes a monologue. For him theatre was a beautiful and powerful tool for helping people reconfigure monologue into dialogue. He said, 'while some people make theatre, we all are theatre' (1979: 30).

This idea of theatre provides a place in which audiences are offered the opportunities to directly participate in theatre, through taking that which is presented and reformulating it. This, according to Boal (1998: 180) is because we all possess an ability to reinvent our future, and he suggested that, 'Today, in the present, as we think on our past, we have a duty to invent the future. This duty will be the task of these centres, units, or nuclei: to invent the future, rather than await it' (Boal 1998: 180).

Theatre of the Oppressed

The style of performance that has been adopted from Boal's social theatre methodology is called 'Theatre of the Oppressed'. 'Theatre of the Oppressed' offers a methodology that encourages an exploration of people's possible trajectories. It is designed to enable participants to imagine alternative actions in order to transcend social challenges, problems, and obstacles (Boal calls this oppression) that block healthy outcomes (Boal, 1995: 13).

One expression of this kind of methodology has been called 'forum theatre'. Here a script is built around a key set of social problems or difficulties that affect the community or group that created it. The actors and non-actors perform it once through while the audience observes. The play does not have a resolution. The actors then perform the play again from the beginning and the audience, reframed as 'spect-actors', are given the chance to stop the performance, often a short scene in which a character is being oppressed, violence is occurring, or a problem is being poorly dealt with. The audience then steps up on stage and performs different actions or interventions in an attempt to change the outcome of the play. Forum theatre has two important aims: 1) to help the 'spect-actor' transform into the 'protagonist of the dramatic action and rehearse alternatives for his [sic] situation' or behaviour; and 2) through this rehearsal to take into real life the actions that have emerged in the forum space (Boal, 1995: 40).

This style of performance attempts to do several things. It is designed to undo the traditional divide between actor and audience, by bringing audience members into the performance. It also aims to reconfigure dramatic action and encourage communities to build their repertoire for dealing with social problems. The idea is that people are able to identify the points of controversy or difficulty and reimagine the fate of the characters. In this way, forum theatre invites the audience to identify points of conflict and struggle in their own lives and show the 'performers' what they see as the best solutions to these challenges.

The process begins when a group workshops a particular theme, using local and colloquial language and cultural forms to lead to a short play. The play is then performed to an audience, perhaps from the same or similar community or one that is trying to deal with similar problems. Unlike traditional plays, a forum performance does not have a fixed or positive outcome or resolution. Rather, it is written in such a way as to encourage the audience to adjust the script and come up with outcomes they consider useful for their lives.

Where they are confident, the audience or 'spect-actors' are encouraged to join the play by adding themselves as new characters or replacing older characters. They are then asked to interact with the actors to find a solution or look for alternative ways of responding. As the play is performed twice, once as scripted and the next impromptu, forum theatre requires impressive skills from the actors who must realistically respond to what is offered. This theatrical process requires a neutral person to be at the centre of proceedings, coaxing out the audience or spectators, managing the logistics, timing, and positioning of the intervention as an outsider. This person is often called the facilitator, although Boal used the term 'joker', after the neutral joker card in a deck of playing cards.

In conclusion

One way I describe community development as distinct from other ways of working is as an approach that seeks to encourage members of communities who have been acted upon to find ways to become agents themselves. Much of our experience of culture today has us sitting in the back seat and watching where others are taking us; instead, community development practitioners can facilitate and assist communities to take up the steering wheel themselves and start to drive their lives in a direction that serves their interests.

Boal was not satisfied with a world in which communities were merely acted-upon. His contribution to practice invites us to use our bodies and our imaginations, and through theatre become active participants in a process that includes identifying personal and structural challenges, building alliances, as well as beginning to generate solutions in conjunction with others. Boal's inspired forum theatre approach is now a tried and tested set of methods that through participation in performance, sees the audience become 'empowered' to begin the process of publicly imagining changes, using their bodies to rehearse these changes, and reflect together on the solutions that come out of this performance to generate social changes and different ways of moving into the future.

Through fun, sometimes humorous and often familiar performance of stories, members of a community can create scenarios, images, and narratives to think about how to respond powerfully by: 1) showing what they would do if they had influence; 2) speculating about what they would propose if others listened to them; 3) imagining what they would need to achieve this; and 4) coming up with a range of responses and solutions to the everyday challenges they face.

References and key works

Boal, A. (1979) *The Theatre of the Oppressed*, Pluto Press, London and Urizen Books, New York.

Boal, A. (1992) *Games for Actors and Non-actors*, Routledge, New York.

Boal, A. (1995) *The Rainbow of Desire: The Boal Method of Theatre and Therapy*, Routledge London & New York.

Boal, A. (1998) *Legislative Theatre: Using Performance to Make Politics*, Routledge, London, UK.

Boal, A. (2007) 'Poetics of the oppressed', in P. Kuppers and G. Robertson (eds.) *The Community Performance Reader*, pp. 13–23. Routledge, London.

Goffman, E. (1956) *The Presentation of Self in Everyday Life*, Penguin, Harmondsworth, UK.

CHAPTER 9

Behrouz Boochani: *Bearing witness in the face of cruelty*

By Dave Palmer

Hoda Afshar

Behrouz Boochani 1983—

On Thursday night, the 14th of November, I bought Behrouz Boochani's (2018a) book *No Friend But the Mountains*. It was late and I'd been out so didn't get started reading that evening. Like the rest of the world I had no idea that he was in the air and on his way to speak at the WORD Christchurch Writers Festival. I awoke to the news that he had arrived in New Zealand, escaping six hellish years of imprisonment in various Australian 'overseas' detention centres including those on Christmas Island, Manus Island, and in Port Moresby.

Peter had described Behrouz Boochani as the 'Anne Frank of our time', saying his work 'offered us an intimate and first-hand account of the horrors of off-shore detention, the cruelty of our government and the extent to which officials will go to cover up brutality.'

Over the next week, Behrouz's first week of 'savouring life as a free man' in many, many years, I carefully read his work and listened to others speak of the beauty of his poetics, and the deeply disturbing and intimate accounts of life under my own government's cruel regimes, euphemistically called the 'Pacific Solution'.

As I read, I was reminded of how the US soldiers felt as they first saw the bodies of Jews imprisoned and murdered at Buchenwald concentration camp in April 1945. Under the instruction of General Dwight D. Eisenhower, soldiers carefully photographed the bodies of those who endured the Holocaust, the design of the German-built concentration camps planned with the specific intent of mass extermination, and the cruel treatment by German guards and public officials. Eisenhower specifically wanted his front-line soldiers to bear

http://dx.doi.org/10.3362/9781788531245.009

witness to the horrors that had been distant and made invisible to the eye of the rest of the world.

Who is Behrouz Boochani?

Behrouz Boochani is a journalist who was born in Ilan, Iran, in 1983 to a Kurdish family. In 2013 Behrouz went into hiding in Iran when the Islamic Revolutionary Guard Corps raided the offices of one of the newspapers for which he was writing. Three months later and fearing for his life Behrouz fled Iran and headed for Southeast Asia.

After a previous failed attempt to make a sea crossing to Australia from Indonesia, Behrouz set off on a boat with 60 other asylum seekers. The Royal Australian Navy intercepted the boat and all on board were taken to Christmas Island to be detained. As part of what the Australian government called Operation Sovereign Borders (previously called the Pacific Solution) he was later transferred to the Manus Island Detention Centre.

While detained on Manus Island, Behrouz published a range of articles and poems in media outlets, smuggling out stories about the lives of refugees held by the Australian government via text messages sent from a hidden phone. He also used his phone to create and narrate an award-winning documentary called *Chauka, Please Tell Us the Time*.

Life in exiled community and the Kyriarchal system

In *No Friend but the Mountains*, Behrouz describes with sickening intimacy the process of subjecting people to deep despair, overcrowding, heat, hopelessness, boredom, and cruelty. Drawing on the work of Elisabeth Schussler Fiorenza, he labels the political system operating at Manus as 'kyriarchal'. This concept combines the Greek word *kyrios*, meaning 'master', with '*archein*', meaning to 'rule'. Here different forms and layers of oppression, power, and cruelty intersect so that people begin to act as both oppressor and the oppressed. Behrouz carefully and cleverly details how this works on Manus with those detained sometimes exercising cruelty upon one another, those 'guarding' being controlled and manipulated by their masters, and all suffering from ethical dissonance as a result of forced compliant behaviour (prisoners and guards alike).

He describes how this is not accidental but purposeful – with prisoners isolated from one another, from their futures, from any hope of knowing what is ahead of them – and designed to turn people against each other in the vicious daily struggle for survival (Boochani, 2018a: 126). This is done by those who seek an organized strategy to warn potential and future refugees of what they can expect if they dare attempt a sea crossing to Australia.

This not only impacts those who are imprisoned. It also produces a level of human suffering for those who guard and protect this system. Indirect and often unrecognized, this has a massive impact on the minds and lives of those who establish and govern the prison.

The most damaging element here is the creation and licensing of contempt. Indeed, this contempt is the very fabric of relationships between prisoners and guards, between policy makers and the idea of 'illegal immigrants', between political leaders and their constituencies. Prison guards are forced to exercise and accentuate a mixture of feelings of abhorrence, envy, and barbarism towards prisoners, and repress their guilt, grief, and sense of decency towards others. As Behrouz (2018a: 141) puts it, those working at Manus are forced to take on an 'approach to work [that] is based on being a bastard. You need to be a total bastard to work in a place where you detest everyone'.

On the power of words and creativity

Like so many beautiful and evocative poets, Behrouz points us to the power of words in conjuring up the minutiae of daily life, moving the reader so they can see something of the cruelty endured. An example demonstrates:

> Here, in the neighbourhood of the people who stare for twenty-four hours solely at walls and metal, the presence of animals is a virtue; That flock of birds gliding at night under the dramatic moon creates a magical and striking scene in our minds; So too the orchestra of frogs that have no home except a lagoon that clings to the ocean; Shunning the ocean as they grow old, the eldest crabs sink into the damp mud under the fences and after a while drift into a deep sleep; Slithering under the fences curious snakes sometimes enter the prison like strangers and usually lose their lives for their innocent trespass; When the unique fish-eating eagle with a white neck dives into the ocean bed it catches a big fish; Colourful parrots love to hold their family gathering on the tallest coconut trees. Here animals are the finest elements in the mind of a lonely prisoner who has no interests but the sky, the ocean and the jungle, all beyond the fences (Boochani, 2016b).

In his foreword to the book, Richard Flanagan points out how Behrouz uses words as weapons when all other power seems impossible (Behrouz, 2018a: vii-ix). Central here is the powerful use of devices such as flashbacks, flashforward, antonyms, oxymorons, paradox, juxtaposition, movement between prose and poetry, and rich description. This produces writing that speaks to our historical, philosophical, and visceral sensibilities. It literally touches us.

As well as using this to influence Australian politics and bear witness to the circumstances on Manus, Behrouz's writing keeps himself going. Indeed, he claims this as a central element in overcoming the devastating effects of being detained indefinitely:

> The only people who can overcome and survive all the suffering inflicted by the prison are those who exercise creativity. That is, those who can trace the outlines of hope using the melodic humming and visions from beyond the prison fences and the beehives we live in (Boochani, 2018a: 128).

Behrouz and understanding community

No Friend but the Mountains offers us a sobering reminder of what happens to communities that are detained indefinitely. Like the Jewish psychologist Viktor Frankl in his book *Man's Search for Meaning*, Boochani offers an honest exploration of the psychological destruction that gets created inside detention that is fuelled by bigotry.

There are several characters Behrouz describes to show what happens to members of a community in custody. *Maysam the Whore* is a clown, a farceur who sets up and performs ridiculous, rebellious, and comic soirees. Often this is done to spite the onlooking guards who stand by with silent contempt. *The Cow* is a master of queues, sitting for hours to take control over meals, toilets, telephone access, cigarettes, and paracetamol. For Behrouz *the Cow* is the ideal Manus inmate who has resigned himself to live to eat, sleep, and not question. The *Prime Minister* is a dignified and honourable man that is initially respected by all for his mild and mannered respect of others. *Maysam* is his opposite and cruel public tormenter. As a consequence of this element of the new culture of the Manus community, the *Prime Minister* is publicly shamed and dishonoured. Not long after he agrees to accept what the officials want and returns to his home country to face what awaits him.

Behrouz's work also provides remarkable insights into what happens to the community of oppressors. The kyriarchal system exaggerates difference and necessitates the debasing of other humans. For example, Boochani describes with detail the way nurses on Manus use the threat of malaria to instil fear and manage prisoners, knowing full well that this is a lie. He makes the point that when they take up the work and enter the prison they become 'motherfuckers ... with their ridiculous clothes, their spotty faces and their particular kind of arrogance' (Boochani, 2018a: 305). In this way Behrouz points to the deep psychological damage, repressed guilt, ethical dissonance, and shutting down of the capacity to love, to be kind, to receive hospitality, and to be warm to one another. As he so powerfully suggests, a consequence of the 'Pacific Solution' is the creation of a generation of Australians who are cruel, trained to repress their capacity to care for those who are close. A consequence of Behrouz's gift to us is the reminder for those who work with community of the power of bearing witness to these kinds of acts of 'motherfuckery'.

References

Boochani, Behrouz (2016a) 'The day my friend Hamid Kehazaei died', *The Guardian*, 28 November 2016.

Boochani, Behrouz (2016b) Untitled (poem), *Cordite Poetry Review* [website] <https://web.archive.org/web/20180913030202/http://cordite.org.au/poetry/explode/untitled-16/> (posted 1 November 2016) [Accessed 23 December 2019].

Boochani, B. (2018a) *No Friend But the Mountains: Writing from Manus Prison*, Picador, Australia.

Boochani, Behrouz and Tofighian, Omid (2018b) 'The last days in Manus Prison', *Meanjin Quarterly,* Summer 2018 [website] <https://meanjin.com.au/essays/the-last-days-in-manus-prison/> [Accessed 23 December 2019].

Flanagan, R. (2018) 'Forward', in B. Boochani, *No Friend But the Mountains: Writing from Manus Prison.* p. vii–x, Picador, Australia.

Manne, Robert (2018) '*No Friend But The Mountains* review: Behrouz Boochani's poetic and vital memoir', *Sydney Morning Herald,* 10 August 2018 [website] <https://web.archive.org/web/20181030122031/https://www.smh.com.au/entertainment/books/no-friend-but-the-mountains-review-behrouz-boochanis-poetic-and-vital-memoir-20180801-h13fuu.html> [Accessed 23 December 2019].

Tofighian, Omid (2018) 'Translator's tale: A window to the mountains' in B. Boochani, Behrouz. *No Friend But the Mountains: Writing from Manus Prison.* p. xi–xxxiv, Picador, Australia.

Viktor E. Frankl (1964) *Man's Search for Meaning: An Introduction to Logotherapy*, Hodder and Stoughton, London, UK.

CHAPTER 10

Martin Buber: *Practice as an encounter*

By Peter Westoby

The David B. Keidan Collection

Martin Buber 1878–1965

To encounter Martin Buber's work is to be drawn into a 'life of dialogue', his key contribution to the world. I use 'encounter' particularly as this depicts what Buber calls an I-Thou relation, which is to be contrasted with an I-It relation. I-Thou depicts a living encounter, moving beyond, 'I see', 'I feel', 'I sense', and so forth (all 'I-It' ways of being in the world) – notice the 'I's – to a relational way of being in the world characterized by being fully present to the other, to be inside the 'in-between space' of I and the other. This *in-between space*, as a place of encounter, *is the Thou*. For Buber, this two-fold attitude of being in the world through either I-It or I-Thou, are both necessary, but he also discerned that the former was becoming so predominant in the world that people were losing their capacity to be human, which is in essence an 'I-Thou' relational inter-human way of being in the world.

I also use 'encounter' alluding to Maurice Friedman's seminal biography of Buber, *Encounter on the Narrow Ridge* (1991). Buber referred to the 'narrow ridge' as that edgy space in which people encounter the world as 'lived concrete', that is, 'as it is' – a living phenomenological disclosure. The abyss on either side of the narrow ridge involves avoiding the real present encounter with life through various forms of 'abstraction-psychologism, historicism, technicism, philosophizing, magic, gnosis, or the false either/or of individualism versus collectivism, freedom versus discipline, action versus grace' (Friedman, 1991: 44). Again, this narrow ridge of the encounter is the 'in-between' space of dialogue/relationship, one in which there is no certainty about anything other than the 'confidence in the genuineness of a meeting that yields the knowing of mutual contact' (Freidman, 1991: 246).

http://dx.doi.org/10.3362/9781788531245.010

This reflection on Buber's work, perhaps read early in this book, invites an encounter, as Thou, with the text (the whole book). Such an encounter is to transcend the habit of defensive debate, instead insisting on being open wholeheartedly to something new, fresh, a genuine dialogue between reader-author-text. If a reader is not up for a real meeting or encounter perhaps it's best to put the book down. For this reason, 'practice as encounter' is the chosen 'gem of a wisdom'. How does a community development practitioner engage in their work open to encounter?

I-Thou and development work

Some years ago, I was teaching some community development students from Vietnam. They were telling me how they felt 'tortured' by a feeling that their four years of work on a large Australian-government-funded project in northern Vietnam had failed. Independent evaluations had shown how the local indigenous people had hardly gained anything from the multi-million dollar initiative. In talking with the students about their sense of failure we started to reflect on how the project workers had engaged with the villagers.

After some discussion, one of the Vietnamese students had an 'aha!' moment and shared it with the class. She realized that, 'what we did wrong is that we didn't really approach these villagers as people equal to us; we didn't go and sit with them around their village fires, hear their stories and understand their world. We didn't create the project together'. I asked her what they did do. She thought about the question for some time and then reflected back to us how the project workers would turn up in four-wheel drives, facilitate meetings, talk about the importance of participation, empowerment, and natural resource management, then draw up a list of activities and actions for local people, and leave.

I then introduced Buber's contrast between I-It and I-Thou to reflect on the workers' unintentional but disastrous process and the story's sad outcome. The student realized that the project workers as subjects (that is, as active agents making decisions, using their creativity, resources, relationship, and intelligence) related to the villagers only as objects – in a sense the villagers became people to whom a project could be done *to* or *for* rather than *with* or *amongst*. There was no sense of the villagers as equal participants in a process of inter-subjective dialogue and co-creation. This is an example of Buber's I-It, with workers 'using' people for their own purposes.

The student's 'aha!' moment also incorporated a renewed vision of what a different kind of relationship could bring to the work. She recognized an inter-subjective and co-creative kind of relationship – what Buber called the I-Thou relationship in which a space for relationship building, for storytelling, for deep listening, and for building a shared commitment to change could be activated. A real encounter! As I went around the class reflecting on this student's analysis, others started to realize that many of their failed attempts at community development work came down to this failure to truly be with people in this mutual way – as an authentic encounter.

For many people such I-Thou kinds of relationship are not easy to imagine in contemporary society. The analysis within the above reflection could be challenged by arguing that it is unreasonable to expect such project workers to take the time to build such relationships with the villagers. It could be argued that there are simply too many villagers or that the project schedule itself would not allow for it. In the same vein, some people could argue that contemporary life is too fast, relationships are too many and there are too many needs. However, the irony is that while for many there is a sense of 'too fast, too many', there is also a sense that relationships are lacking in deep connection, solidarity, and meaning. Many people are so overloaded with diverse kinds of relationships that they have lost their capacity to discern a moment of true, genuine encounter with the other (characterized by I-Thou qualities); or if such an encounter is discerned, people move on so fast that they fail to cherish or celebrate it, and then build on it. The opportunity for a more meaningful sociality, which is a foundation for community development, is missed.

A Life of dialogue

Martin Buber was a German Jewish man born in Vienna in 1878 – a man of encyclopaedic knowledge who was fluent in nine languages. When he was three years old his parents separated and he was sent to live with his grandparents in a region that lies between Poland and Ukraine. From his earliest years, he was fascinated by relationships, particularly the nature of dialogue and the struggle humans have to make respectful connection with one another. A philosopher, poet, novelist, dramatist, anthropologist, sociologist, and philosopher, he was nominated for numerous prizes, including by Herman Hesse for the Nobel Prize of Literature. Buber died in 1965, and to this day is more or less the starting place for anyone of any discipline or field of practice curious about dialogue.

Community as dialogue versus collectivity

Of significance to community practitioners, Buber (1947) articulates an understanding of 'community' that has challenged me throughout my 'life of dialogue'. For him, community is contrasted with collectivity. Collectivity is group-think, something ever present in today's echo-chambers of social media and expanding gated communities. Instead, community is the space 'in-between' collectivity and individuality. For Buber:

> collectivity is based on an organised atrophy of personal existence … it is a flight from community's testing and consecration of the personal, a flight from the vital dialogue, demanding the staking of the self, which is at the heart of the world (Buber, 1947: 37).

In contrast, community happens through genuine dialogue. Community is a 'dynamic facing of the other, a flowing from *I* to *Thou*' (Buber 1947: 37). In this, Buber offers some fundamental wisdom for community development practitioners wanting to see community unfold through such vital dialogue. For example, as Kramer explains, 'Real community, in Buber's view, originates and continually renews itself as a group of people participating in and around a dialogical centre' (Kramer, 2003: 81). People come together with a common yearning, but their challenge is to renew this dialogical centre, sustained also by awareness of that *Thou* (a relational way of being), which is also 'the very plasma of community', which in turn is 'the spirit of relational trust permeating each *I-Thou* relationship in the group' (Kramer, 2003: 96).

The social versus political principle

Finally, while a philosopher-poet, Buber's life was filled with politics, as he found himself alive during both world wars and the establishment of the Jewish Zionist state. For example, in dialogue with the likes of Carl Jung and Mahatma Gandhi, he advocated for a spiritual resistance to Nazism. Never afraid to step backwards in his views, Buber is also one of the few Jewish leaders who argued strongly for Arab–Jewish solidarity and suffered profoundly for that view.

Arising from a deep and profound depression about Nazism and the militaristic pathway of the Jewish state, he was a strong advocate for a 'federalistic communal socialism'. Aligned with the community economies tradition (see **Schumacher** in this book), in *Paths to*

Utopia (1988) Buber suggested that social restructuring was a necessity, flourishing with cooperatives and village communes (Freidman, 1991: 299) – a vision clearly linked to the success of the kibbutz. His life-long commitment to adult education was also linked to his dream of the 'social principle', understood as people creating a federal community socialism 'from below' as opposed to a socialism of power being constructed by the lifeless 'political principle'.

As a lover of the social principle, dialogue, community and relational ways of being Buber is a real gem for community development practitioners.

References

Buber, M. (1947/2002) *Between Man and Man*, 2nd edn, Routledge Classics, London and New York.

Buber, M. (1958) *I and Thou*, Charles Scribener's Sons, New York.

Buber, M. (1988) *Paths to Utopia*, Macmillan, New York.

Kramer, K. P. (2003) *Martin Buber's I and Thou: Practicing Living Dialogue*, Paulist Press, NJ.

Freidman, M. (1991) *Encounter on the Narrow Ridge: A Life of Martin Buber*, Paragon House, USA.

CHAPTER 11

Judi Chamberlin: *Nothing About Us, Without Us*

By Athena Lathouras

Judi Chamberlin 1944–2010

Tom Olin

My connection to Judi Chamberlin's activism stems from my two decades of practice with the Uniting Church as a disability support worker in the 1980s and 1990s. This was a period of incredible social change in Australian social policy where people with disabilities finally started winning the fight for their human rights. I was part of the deinstitutionalization movement and assisted people, many of whom were moving into their own homes from institutions for the first time in their lives. No longer hidden from society, they started to live ordinary lives like most of us deem to be our inherent right.

The catalyst for Judi Chamberlin's life's work occurred in 1966 in the United States. At the age of 21 she was in severe emotional distress after a miscarriage and was committed to a psychiatric hospital. Once institutionalized as a mental health patient she discovered it was nearly impossible to regain her freedom. She was stripped of her human rights and told she would never be allowed to live outside the institution (Chamberlin, 1978: 22–62). After she regained her liberty, she went on to research people's experiences of the mental health system. Over years she collected thousands of narratives about people's experiences of loss of personhood and sense of injustice because of the power psychiatrists have to remove a person's liberty for treatment (Chamberlin, 2007).

These experiences fuelled a burning anger and desire for just change. Following in the footsteps of the civil rights, women's and gay liberation movements, Chamberlin and others drew courage and inspiration and founded what became the psychiatric user, survivor and ex-patient movement. Her 1978 book, *On Our Own: Patient Controlled Alternatives to the Mental Health System*, is a scathing critique of mainstream psychiatric practice. The book has become a seminal

http://dx.doi.org/10.3362/9781788531245.011

text and is still used by the movement today. It is a bold vision for self-help, mutual support, and non-coercive, peer-run alternatives.

Power and the mental health system

Provocatively, she claimed that the mental health system is all about power, not illness or treatment (Chamberlin, 1978: 3). Unlike physical illnesses, which affect parts of a person's body, mental illnesses affect that abstraction known as 'the mind'. Once it has been decided that a person has a sick mind, enormous social consequences ensue. Often determined judicially, a finding of mental illness frequently results in loss of liberty. Chamberlin claims that for people who have been put into a hospital involuntarily, it feels like a prison and is ultimately harmful (1978: 211–214).

Chamberlin (2007) is highly critical of the use of psychiatric coercion in the context of the mental health system. She recognizes the state's legitimate right to take away one's liberty, that is, when a person has broken the law. In this context laws are written, codified, and if a person is accused of breaking the law there are legal safeguards and entitlements – to a defence, a trial, a right of appeal. It must be proven in this context that a person has committed a crime before they lose their liberty. Whereas, in the mental health system, when people are labelled as having a mental illness, they lose their liberty without breaking the law. Moreover, the standards of determining if one is a danger to oneself or others varies according to jurisdiction and is a very elastic standard (Chamberlin, 2007).

Combating mentalism through alternative practices

Chamberlin foregrounds the term 'mentalism' (1978: 196) and defines it as the unreasonable fear of mental patients. Thus, she is describing the oppression of mental health service users in the same way as 'racism', 'sexism', and 'ageism' describes the oppression of other groups. More perniciously, she argues, mentalism infects its victims with the belief in their own inferiority (Chamberlin, 1978: 173). This kind of internalized oppression, she states, harbours the kinds of beliefs that must be deliberately rooted out through consciousness-raising processes.

The main thrust of Chamberlin's book is to describe psychiatric-system-survivor-controlled alternatives to mainstream services to combat mentalism. Since the 1970s, people from across the world have been forming their own organizations - co-operative and democratic structures that are support systems for people experiencing mental and emotional distress. These alternative services fundamentally alter the unequal power relationships that are at the heart of the mental health system. They provide services to people without the demoralizing consequences of the authoritarian, hierarchical structures of traditional mental health services (Chamberlin, 1978: 7).

Nothing About Us, Without Us

Chamberlin takes an ethical stance known as the 'dignity of risk' (2007). This means, people should not be treated like children who are incapable of making decisions. Rather, they should be given the opportunity to make decisions, to possibly make mistakes, and to have the opportunity to learn and grow from the process. She asserts that people with psychiatric disabilities have human rights and the legal capacity to make decisions about their own lives. That decision making should be appropriately supported if people need it and want it. For Chamberlin, this is a moral challenge, one that sees a shift from paternalism to self-determination and creates human dignity (Chamberlin, 1998). She posits that the most apt slogan for their worldwide movement is, *'Nothing About Us, Without Us'* (2007). This is the gem of wisdom I have chosen for community development.

Chamberlin's central thesis is that because of ongoing circumstances of disempowerment, the psychiatric-survivor movement takes a fundamental stance that no-one can speak *for* them. They insist they must speak for themselves, and that this is their right. Other people may claim to speak for people, or represent the views of people affected, but that is not a substitute for the authentic voice of people who themselves are affected by mental ill health. Freedom and self-determination are basic human rights that must not be eroded or ended because of a medical diagnosis (Chamberlin, 2007). Oftentimes, she argues, the best form of support comes from self-help and peer-led programmes operated and controlled by people who have experienced psychiatry. Known as peers, these people are experts by experience, have lived through and thrived (not just survived) in the experience of recovery from mental health challenges (Fong et al, 2018).

It would be apt for community developers, who arguably connect with a broad range of citizens in local communities, to read the *Manifesto for Compassionate Change*. Developed by The ReAwaken community, this manifesto reflects the collective work of international leaders in the fields of mental health, addiction and trauma.

Decades after Chamberlin commenced her activism for radical change in the mental health system, the ReAwaken community argue that the current medical model of mental health support is still not working and requires a paradigm shift. They argue that healing happens through connected relationships and in community. Their call to action expresses the critical need for connection, compassion, and meaningful responses to promote the health and welfare of the populace. People's pain does not occur in a vacuum, they say, instead it is often caused by greater societal problems such as poverty, violence, environmental destruction, and broken institutions (ReAwaken, 2019).

Chamberlin's Legacy

Today the psychiatric user, survivor, and ex-patient movement founded by Chamberlin and others has evolved. Epstein (2013) states that the movement today is a broad church of groups across the political spectrum and is claiming space as people with a range of expertise – their own lived experience of the mental health system and of alternatives to psychiatry. Bradley (2014) posits that Chamberlin's seminal text is foundational to the current Mad Pride movement. This movement today is about a community of people with shared experiences of mental ill health questioning the effects of mental illness labels, combating stigma and increasing their sense of empowerment by purposefully reclaiming what has been a pejorative term, 'mad' (Bradley, 2014). The body of knowledge referred to as 'survivor research' has grown significantly in recent years, challenging the basis of mainstream mental health knowledge through scholarly literature, and is known as 'mad studies' (Faulkner, 2017). This emerging field is being shaped and constituted between the academy and the Mad Pride Movement with co-designed research and co-produced new knowledge.

Conclusion

Alarmingly, today, we are seeing a staggering increase in statistics of people affected by mental ill health globally. Depression is predicted to the leading cause of disease burden across the world by 2030 (Black Dog Institute, 2019). And in Australia, one in five Australians aged 16–85 experience a mental illness in any year, with almost half (45%) experiencing mental illness in their lifetime (Black Dog Institute, 2019).

It seems that Judi Chamberlin and the consumers of peer-led mental health support have always known that the need for community care – creating a sense of belonging and connection to others – is crucial. I'd suggest that community development practitioners need to keep working to bring people together and to build meaningful connections, and whilst doing so, remember the words of Judi Chamberlin – *Nothing About Us, Without Us* – to lead from behind so that communities themselves can determine what is important to them and their wellbeing.

References and Key Works

Black Dog Institute (2019), 'Research updates and insights' [website] <www.blackdoginstitute.org.au/research/evidence-and-policy/updates-and-insights> [Accessed 6 September 2019].

Bradley, M. (2014) 'Viewpoint: The Mad Pride movement', *Mental Health Today*, November/December 2014: 22.

Chamberlin, J. (1978) *On Our Own: Patient-Controlled Alternatives to the Mental Health System*, Hawthorn Books, Inc. Publishers, New York.

Chamberlin, J. (1998) 'Citizenship rights and psychiatric disability', *Psychiatric Rehabilitation Journal* 21(4): 405–408.

Chamberlin, J. (2007) 'Whose voice? Whose choice? Whose power?' Speech to the World Psychiatric Association, Dresden, Germany, 6–8 June 2007, [website] <http://ki-art-multimedia.de/dresden/judi.htm> [Accessed 5 September 2019].

Epstein, M. (2013) *The Consumer Movement in Australia: A memoir of an Old Campaigner*. Our Consumer Place, Melbourne, Australia.

Faulkner, A. (2017) 'Survivor research and Mad Studies: The role and value of experiential knowledge in mental health research', *Disability & Society* 32(4): 500–520.

Fong, T., Meagher, J., Stratford, A., Jackson, F., & Jayakody, E. (2018) *Peer Work in Australia: A New Future for Mental Health*, Flourish Australia, Sydney, Australia.

ReAwaken (2019) 'Manifesto for compassionate change' [website] <www.reawakenaustralia.com.au/the-manifesto> [Accessed 7 September 2019].

CHAPTER 12

Angela Davis: *Unlock the gates of poverties and prisons*

By Dave Palmer

Columbia GSAPP

Angela Davis 1944—

I live in a place where one in every 12 of the state's Indigenous adult males are presently in prison. Across Australia more than one in every seven Indigenous people have been to prison at some point in their lives. Proportionately, Australian Indigenous people are gaoled at a higher rate than anywhere else in the world (Halsey, 2015). According to one estimate, Indigenous people are five times more likely to complete a prison sentence than finish a university degree. This means my country invests in prison as the future for Indigenous communities massively more than it invests in education for Indigenous communities. My prime minister has recently said 'Aren't Australians great?' I suspect that Angela Davis, prison abolitionist and civil rights activist, has things to say about this!

Who is Angela Davis?

Angela Davis was born into an African American family in Birmingham, Alabama. Alabama was famously segregated in the 1950s and unsafe for those African American families who did not know and keep their place (Davis, 1988). Her family experienced firsthand the racist violence handed out by the Ku Klux Klan, living in an area that was to become known as 'Dynamite Hill' because of the frequency of white terrorist-led house bombings.

Davis is an activist, academic, writer, and community organizer. She has worked in universities, been sacked by universities, campaigned for new ways of responding to crime and violence, argued against prisons, and has herself been imprisoned for over a year during the

http://dx.doi.org/10.3362/9781788531245.012

active struggles for civil rights. She has been a member of the US Communist Party, the Black Independence Movement (often known as the Black Panther Party), the movement against the Vietnam War and the breakaway Committees of Correspondence for Democracy and Socialism. She has written over ten books about the intersection of class, gender, and race as well as about prisons and the importance of change led by 'the people'.

Most famously, in 1970, Davis was arrested and imprisoned for purchasing firearms and later giving these to men who used them in an armed attack in a courtroom in Marin County, California in which four people were killed. Although not directly involved she was prosecuted for three capital offences, including conspiracy to murder, on the basis of the argument that she had earlier supplied the firearms to those who committed the offence. She subsequently spent a year in prison until a nationally supported campaign was successful in having her acquitted.

Since this time Davis has worked in a range of US university positions, writing about and organizing against the cruel consequences of unbridled capitalism, particularly massive levels of social inequality for African American communities, women, working people, and those incarcerated in American gaols. For example, African Americans are incarcerated in prisons at 5.1 times the imprisonment rate of whites (Nellis, 2015). Twice she has stood as an independent candidate for the US presidency.

Change is a lifelong commitment and comes from individuals forming communities of struggle

An important gift of wisdom from Davis comes from her observation that in making individual figures the central element in the history of political struggle we fail to see the important influence of coalitions or 'communities of struggle'. In response to a question about the role of political movements, Davis reminds us that the great and courageous modern figure of political struggle, Nelson Mandela, always insisted that his accomplishments were part of a long and collective history of African struggle against colonialism. She said, 'it is essential to resist the depiction of history as the work of heroic individuals in order for people today to recognize their potential agency as a part of an ever-expanding community of struggle' (Barat, 2014).

In her mind, indeed in Davis's experience, change and political movements are at their most powerful when they emerge 'from communities' that are themselves subjects of struggle. She explains her view: 'I think change comes from below ... it sounds like I am praising

Obama (former US president) ... which I am not ... but what I did appreciate about him was that he always indicated that he could not make these changes alone.' (Davis, 2018).

For Davis, the act of participating in change is not to be taken lightly or entered into for short periods of time. Furthermore, 'revolution' is not a thing that young people do before 'settling down' to adult life. As she put it, being involved in political struggle 'was no fashionable club with newly minted jargon, or new kind of social life – made thrilling by risk and confrontation'. In her mind, 'revolution is a serious thing' (Davis, 1988: 162).

Prisons as microcosms of community

Another important element in Davis's work is the connection between prisons and community. For Davis, a mark of the ill-health of capitalism, modern forms of government, and the lives of communities across the globe, is the sheer number of people who are incarcerated. She argued that two consequences of capitalism relate to prison. The first is that most of those who end up in prison are the poor, those who are locked out of the spoils of a market economy, and those who threaten the interests of the ruling classes. The second is that increasingly prisons are places where private enterprise make lots of money, building, managing and running what she called the 'prison-industrial complex'.

In a 1972 speech she gave just five days after her release from prison, Davis made the observation that we can learn a great deal about a society by looking at the way it manages its prisons:

> Look towards its dungeons and there you will see in concentrated and microcosmic form the sickness of the entire system. And today in the United States of American in 1972 there is something that is particularly revealing about the analogy between the prison and the larger society of which it is a reflection (Davis, 1972a).

In a description that echoes **Behrouz Boochani's** account of Manus Island, Davis draws on the work of political prisoner George Jackson to remind us that, not surprisingly, the most marginal of all communities are those who endure prison. Before he died in Soledad Prison, Jackson described life in incarceration:

> This place destroys the logical processes of the mind. A man's thoughts become completely disorganized. The noise, madness streaming from every throat, frustrated sounds from the bars,

metallic sounds from the walls, the steel trays, the iron beds bolted to the wall, the hollow sounds from a cast iron sink, a toilet, the smells, the human waste thrown at us, unwashed bodies, the rotten food (cited in Davis 1972a).

More recently she has observed that indicative of the failure of modern politics is that increasingly the task of managing prisons, for which many claim is the goal of 'protecting the community', has been given to private and for-profit interests (Barat, 2014). Strongly critiquing this feature of social life across the globe she sees the increasing profitability of holding prisoners captive as one of the most depraved and vile symptoms of allowing global capitalism loose on the world. She claims the current system is more like a new form of slavery than about justice and protection of the community.

According to Davis, this has occurred because prisons are political weapons that function to contain both those within and those communities without. They target people who threaten the status quo, those who act in ways that challenge the 'masters who control the keys to freedom' (Davis, 1972). She named as example of these groups people who run Standard Oils, General Motors, all the giant corporations and their government protectors. She maintained that prisons act as self-perpetuating systems of terror that contain communities both without and outside their own walls.

Angela Davis and community

Perhaps Angela Davis's greatest contribution to thinking about community work comes from her observation that life in many communities has people 'locked' into deeply regulated, diminished, and trapped existences. From her own experience and from work with political prisoners she concluded that for many millions around the globe, many people of colour, and working class women and men, the conditions with which they are confronted bear 'striking similarity to the condition of the prisoner'. We live in a world where leaders constantly claim that we are free, that we live in communities that are egalitarian, that we treat each other with care and kindness and that harmonious community is what we can expect. However, says Davis, this freedom is in stark contrast to how most of us live, unable to exert political agency, access the most basic of human rights, enjoy healthy life, and live free of fear, anxiety, and trauma. This she says is because of the small numbers of those who hold the keys to systems, laws, and economies that keep people 'locked up with the ugliness of racism and poverty and war and all the attendant mental frustrations and manipulations.' (Davis,1972a). In other words, the situation confronting many communities is much like the situation of prisoners except that we all too often forget or become blind to this. This, says Davis, we must never forget, 'for if we do, we will lose our desire for freedom and our will to struggle for liberation' (Davis 1972a).

For Davis, most are not able to enjoy freedom from the worst elements of a capitalist system that casts people aside, sentences them to a life of pain, isolation and poverty. She concludes that our leaders hold the key to unlock the gates of this freedom. She observes, however, that there is little motivation for these people to act. The solution she proposes is for 'the people' to take hold of the keys that lock people behind bars, lock them into life trajectories of poverty, and lock them out of access to civic participation. The solution she proposes is in part the closure of our prisons and the movement towards communities that are organized in a human-centric way rather than a crime-centric way, where people-oriented communities take care of the material and spiritual needs of those who are free to live with full bellies, in meaningful work, and able to build character rather than be judged on their skin colour, gender, social background, and sexuality.

In reflecting on her own experience of prison and freedom she provides wisdom for those who seek to unlock the lives for people in community. Here she shares:

> My freedom was achieved as an outcome of a massive, massive people's struggle. Young people and older people, black, brown, Asian, Native American and white people, students and workers. The people seized the keys which opened the gates to freedom. And we have just begun. The momentum of this movement must be sustained and must be increased. Let us try to seize more keys and open more gates and bring out more sisters and brothers so that they can join the ranks of our struggle (Davis, 1972b).

References

Barat, F. (2014) 'A Q&A with Angela Davis on Black Power, Feminism and the Prison-Industrial Complex' *The Nation,* September 2014 Issue [website] <www.thenation.com/article/qa-angela-davis-black-power-feminism-and-prison-industrial-complex/> (posted 27 August 2014) [Accessed 10 December 2019].

Davis, A. (1972a) 'The Gates of Freedom', Edited version of the speech given by Angela Davis gave on 9 June 1972 at the Embassy Auditorium, Los Angeles California. On website of The Almeida Theatre and Figures of Speech [website], <www.speech.almeida.co.uk/new-page> [Accessed 10 December 2019].

Davis, A. (1972b) Pearl Mackie reads Angela Davis' speech 'The Gates of Freedom' [video recording on website], On website of The Almeida Theatre and Figures of Speech, <www.speech.almeida.co.uk/speech/the-gates-to-freedom> [Accessed 10 December 2019].

Davis, A. (1988) *Angela Davis: An Autobiography*. Random House, New York.

Davis, A. (2018) 'Angela Davis on Feminism, Communism and Being a Black Panther During the Civil Rights Movement', Interview on Channel 4 News, [video recording on YouTube website], <www.youtube.com/watch?v=x3q_qV5mHg0> [Accessed 10 December 2019].

Halsey, M (2015) 'State of imprisonment: South Australia's prisoner numbers soar, with just 10% of budget for rehab' *The Conversation* [website] <https://theconversation.com/state-of-imprisonment-south-australias-prisoner-numbers-soar-with-just-10-of-budget-for-rehab-38906> (posted 14 April 2015) [Accessed 10 December 2019].

Nellis, A. (2015) *The Colour of Justice: Racial and Ethnic Disparity in State Prisons*, The Sentencing Project, Washington, DC.

CHAPTER 13

Jacques Derrida: *Deconstruction, a community development 'yet-to-come' and 'the hauntology of justice'*

Arturo Espinoza

By Peter Westoby

Jacques Derrida 1930–2004

> That [community development] died yesterday... and [community development] should still wander toward the meaning of its death – or that it has always lived knowing itself to be dying ...

This is the kind of thing Derrida *might say*. He used these words, but about philosophy (replace 'community development' with philosophy), early in his career writing an essay on Emmanuel Levinas in a journal of his time called *Critique*. Like such a provocation to philosophy, Derrida's deconstruction invites critical reflection and a possible re-constituting of community development in the light of what he calls the 'hauntology of justice'.

I met Derrida in 1998, an encounter in Johannesburg, where he was fully immersed in the debates around the South African National Truth and Reconciliation Commission. In a sense, his work has haunted me ever since, someone I come back to regularly, inviting me to deconstruct any community development tropes that have become empty mantras.

The word 'deconstruction', as used by Derrida, is a play on Heidegger's *destruktion* – which in German and French is not so much about destroying, but about a critical re-constituting. For Derrida the deconstructive task is not so much destroying but about opening up text, programmes, and institution – not with the purpose of anarchy,

http://dx.doi.org/10.3362/9781788531245.013

but with a view to *more just* programmes and institutions (Smith, 2005: 11).

Derrida's deconstructive episteme is also a profound affirmation about a future yet-to-come. In pronouncing the death of community development, he *would be* inviting a community development that is 'yet-to-come'. As he said in his final interview, 'deconstruction is always on the side of the yes, on the side of an affirmation of life' (Derrida, 2007: 51).

Why the need for a 'community development yet-to-come'? Community development has engaged with many key historical issues, from marginalization and poverty, feminism and patriarchy, colonization and the concerns of First Nations peoples – just to name a few. But a community development 'yet-to-come' is also needed to address new issues, those coming towards us, such as: How is community development responding to the globalization of right-wing populism and its accompanying patriarchal politics? In what ways does community development have a robust response to human-induced climate change and species extinction? What does community development look like under the public-policy responses to COVID-19 and other such pandemics? What does community development say to the concurrent neoliberal assault on the university and democracy? There is certainly, *as is always the case for any fields of practice*, an urgent need to renew community development. I suggest Derrida's philosophy could play a role, albeit recognizing that community development scholars and practitioners rarely engage directly with philosophy – and rightly so, because most practitioners are grappling with real everyday concerns, and also because scholars in the field are mostly influenced by the social and political sciences.

Deconstruction is Derrida's main contribution to the world, which I will briefly explain below, yet for this short reflection I will focus on his contribution of a 'hauntology of justice'. First, however, a quick sketch of key aspects of his life.

A sketch of Derrida's life

Sketching Derrida's biography, there are a couple of angles I want to draw on. The first is an unusual recognition by an intellectual that biography counts. He was one of the few intellectuals who left behind many fragments of autobiography or memoir. Importantly, he himself argued that, 'you must put philosopher's biographies back in the picture and the commitments, particularly the political commitments ...' (cited in Peeters, 2013: 1). So, this brief biographical sketch counts. It is not just background fluff. Read Derrida asking what his commitments were.

The second angle, and perhaps the most significant, is that he often was, and felt himself to be, an outsider. Shaped as both an Algerian-born Jew – but living most of his life in France – and also an outsider to the academy who was never quite accepted by the gatekeepers of orthodoxy, he lived with a profound sense of exclusion. This embodied experience of often feeling like the outsider was crucial in his theorizing of what he called alterity, or 'the other' – which led to another key principle of his: 'vigilance for the other', which played out in a proposed ethic of hospitality towards the other. The 'other' is an important element of his deconstructive episteme and how his philosophical sensibility played out in many disciplines and fields of practice – from law to architecture. Deconstruction as a vigilance to the other, and deconstruction as being open to the disruption of the other.

One of the upshots of this experience of exclusion was a commitment against communitarianism – and I am conscious, as a community development scholar, that he was very ambivalent about the idea of 'community', living with the spectral haunting of the *dangers of community*. He explicitly shared how 'I don't much like the word community. I am not sure I even like the thing' (Derrida's lectures, in Caputo, 1997: 107). Community as unity or uniformity smelled of danger for Derrida, which makes sense in the context of his biographical experiences of anti-Semitism. Alternatively, he talked of 'community as hospitality' always arguing for an opening of the social, never allowing it to be closed (as it often does in the name of community) (ibid: 109ff).

Of importance for this reflection, 1989 represented a key turning point in Derrida's career, signalled with a lecture he gave in Greenwich Village, New York at the Cardoza Law School – a well-known school of radical legal theory, most graduates of which become defenders of the poor against the rich (Caputo, 2018: 191). This lecture represented a turn towards more practical things – ethics, justice, politics – which occupied him for the last 20 years of his life.

You could more or less say that he was now taking his radical deconstructionist episteme into the practical and political realm of public life. From here on he published work on issues as wide as the law and justice, memory work, refugees and hospitality, the death penalty, our relationship with animals, and so much more.

Deconstructive episteme

Deconstruction could be described as an episteme (a way of thinking and understanding 'text') oriented around re-thinking language, ethics, and politics, *focused on reforming programmes or institutions*. One institution he often had his eye on was the university (because he loved it dearly), always reaching for a reformation of the university and particularly the way philosophy was understood and taught within it. Derrida yearned for a university-yet-to-come, a key institution in what he talked about as the 'democracy-yet-to-come' (Derrida, 2005: 41; Smith, 2005: 84) – one more fully alive to justice than ever before.

In the same way that Derrida loved philosophy and the university, I suggest that Derrida *would* (for he never talked of community development) love community development to be constantly reforming in a way that is more fully alive to justice. Importantly from a Derridean perspective, there is no 'essence' of community development. There are simply diverse theories and practices, held in a dialectic tension that produces a particular praxis, hence an openness to constant reform. No-one needs to fight for a truth of community development. Reform implies a constant engagement with the contradictions, tensions, and fissures within community development – allowing for a plurality of possibilities.

However, if this is true, meaning community development can constantly be deconstructed (as it should be), what of justice? Can this too be deconstructed? This leads to the main wisdom presented in this reflection.

A hauntology of justice

Derrida argues that everything is open to deconstruction *except justice*. In fact, he argued that deconstruction is justice (Caputo, 2018: 201). Many sceptics of Derrida's philosophy thought deconstruction was a form of anarchy – anything goes (with that removal of truth), yet later in his life Derrida clarified his thinking and writing, making the case that deconstruction is justice. In this case he argued that all 'things' are deconstructable – for example, the law, ethics, professional practices – *but that justice is not a thing*. Justice instead is 'an appeal', an imperative – 'it is like a ghost' (ibid, 203). In this sense, the law is a thing as a historical construction, as is a community development programme. These 'things' can always be deconstructed, which is a good proposition and is the basis for constant reform. And here is the crux of it: for Derrida, we reform the law and community development, and all things in the light of the call, imperative, or summons to justice – this undeconstructable haunting presence. Together, the deconstructability of community development and the undeconstructability of justice go hand in hand to make up deconstruction (Caputo, ibid, 205). The imperative of justice puts pressure on community development to be in constant reform.

References

Caputo, J. (1997) *Deconstruction in a Nutshell: A Conversation with Jacques Derrida,* Fordham University Press, New York.

Caputo, J. (2018) *Hermeneutics: Facts and Interpretation in the Age of Information,* Pelican Books, UK.

Derrida, J. (2001) *Cosmopolitanism and Forgiveness,* Routledge, London and New York.

Derrida, J. (2005) *Rogues,* Stanford University Press, USA

Derrida, J. (2007) *Learning to Live Finally: The Last Interview,* Melville House Publishing, NJ.

Peeters, B. (2013) *Derrida: A Biography,* Polity Press, Cambridge, UK.

Smith, J. (2005) *Jacques Derrida: Live Theory,* Continuum, London and New York.

CHAPTER 14

Gustavo Esteva: *The work of deprofessionalizing ourselves*

By Peter Westoby

Gustavo Esteva 1936—

Some years ago I was in Mexico City and planning a visit to meet Gustavo Esteva in the southern state, Oaxaca. He lived and worked there, both at the *Universidad de la Tierra* (University of the Earth), which he founded, and in solidarity with the Zapatista. In one exchange I thought he'd invited me for some 'drinking time', but realized he meant 'thinking time' (I'd not heard him quite right). An advocate of what he calls a 'Thinkery', Esteva suggests we cannot really think alone, and even more intriguingly:

> It's how to talk about ideas that you do not have. You cannot really say the thing because the idea is not there. It is around but you need to capture it by talking with others, in that relation and interaction with others (Esteva, 2015a: 531).

I've advocated for a Thinkery ever since – a relational way of creating thought.

Esteva, one of the key post-development thinkers of our time, has contributed a significant tome of thinking for community development theory and practice. A contributor to the *Community Development Journal* (2014, 2015a, 2015b) and author of several significant books, my favourite being *The Future of Development: A Radical Manifesto* (with Babones & Babcicky, 2013), I often return to what I find to be disrupting thought.

Yet, two things, linked to more personal interactions with him, have really sat with me over many years. First, in an invitation to Gustavo to contribute to an edited book on ethics and community development (Banks & Westoby, 2019), he asked me to await his

http://dx.doi.org/10.3362/9781788531245.014

decision for a week. With that time passing, he finally wrote words to the effect of, 'I've tried to get inside the idea of writing this chapter; I've really tried Peter, but I can't, sorry'. There was something profoundly honest and authentic about his reply, and I've learned to do the same inner work before I agree to many things. I particularly love this idea of 'trying to get inside', which I interpret as connecting thought, emotion, and passion together. If they all connect it's possible to be inside something, giving form (for example, a chapter) with spirit (living writing). If not, then what is produced will be dead/ening. This resonates with my experience of all creative processes. Second, he did send me some notes he'd written, and the substance was significant, focused on the professionalization of 'needs', and linked to his notion of being a 'deprofessionalized intellectual' (Esteva, 2015a: 529). It is this work of deprofessionalizing that I see as his gem of a wisdom for community practitioners. In our correspondence his words were:

> When I was a child the word 'need' had only one practical application: shitting. It was used when my mother told us, 'Once you arrive in your uncle's house, ask him where you can take care of your *needs*.' We took care of our needs then; we did not manufacture them as we do now. This way of talking applied to everything. Our needs were defined by our own desires, capacities, our tools, the way we used them, and were strictly personal, imponderable, and incommensurable. No one could measure or quantify my relationship with my dog, my reactions to the first novel that I read, my physical and emotional condition when I got a headache, or what I wanted to learn (personal communication, 2016).

Here was the heart and soul of his critique of professional practice, development generally, and community development particularly. If we are party to manufacturing need then we have been co-opted into a paradigm that exercises power – transforming people into the 'needy', repeating what Ivan Illich called 'disabling professionals'. It's muchlike the post-development angle that one day back in 1949, people awoke and discovered they needed 'development' and that therefore they were poor – because the US president, Truman, described much of the world as 'underdeveloped' (Esteva et al., 2013: 5).

With this critique of professional manufacturing of need, Esteva advocates for a two-fold strategy of: 'struggling against the dictatorship of the professions' (Esteva, 2015a: 532); and also de-professionalizing ourselves as practitioners/people. This latter task is exceptionally difficult, because it means un-learning how we see the world through particular language and concepts, and this unlearning means:

> losing yourself when you are deprofessionalizing ... if you are shaped with professional words, your being is a profession. You do not see that your eyes are not your eyes, they are the eyes of the profession. To dismantle that is to dismantle yourself. It is very challenging (Esteva, 2015a: 532).

His journey

Esteva's journey (in life, and this deprofessionalizing journey) has been long, and not without turmoil, and much detail can be accessed in his elegant biography by Olsen (2018). Primarily a Mexican philosopher, educator, and economist, he has dedicated his life to working in solidarity with the Mexican peasants, and in that long journey has finally, in his 80s, found himself living close to his ancestral Indigenous home, working for the university linked to the Indigenous movement, Zapatista.

He has previously worked for corporations and government; flirted with guerrilla movements (inspired by the Cuban revolution in the 1960s), considered violence as an option (joining an urban 'cell' planning violence), but re-read Gandhi, and opted for nonviolence. Now a celebrated thinker, his encounter and then long collaboration with the Austrian radical priest, Ivan Illich (who lived and worked in Mexico), transformed his thinking and practice.

But it was the 1994 Zapatista uprising that was seminal in his life, and as Olsen says,

> For Esteva, it was the beginning of what would become a long intellectual tryst with the Zapatistas. He participated in the civil society events the Zapatistas hosted in the Lacandon Jungle in late 1994. In 1996, he became an informal adviser in their negotiations with the government for the San Andres Peace Accords. And they later became a recurring subject in his voluminous social writings, such as *Grassroots Postmodernism, The Future of Development,* and the essay *The Zapatistas and Peoples Power.* Through his literary oeuvre, Esteva has made a name for himself continually seeking—much like the Zapatistas— to articulate an alternative vision of a more just social reality (Olsen, 2018).

His work is prolific and profound, and along with the wisdom already mentioned above, I'd like to foreground his views on commoning, interculturality, and hospitality.

Commoning

As a post-development thinker, much of Esteva's work has been an inquiry into 'what comes after failed development?' One of his key answers is, 'the commons', which represents the 'cell of a new society' (Esteva, 2015b: 744). Yet, his approach to 'the commons' is quite necessarily different to many. Recognizing the enclosure of the commons as a historical process, and acknowledging the movements that are reclaiming or regenerating the commons (for example commonly managed land, Wikipedia, open-access software, cooperatives, and so forth), he advocates for people to see what's already happening. His suggestion is that there is a new post-capitalist world emerging among the commons. But, importantly, it is not one form. So, he is adamantly against the idea of 'the commons' as a universal category, but is instead for a 'family of words that includes different traditions' of commoning (Esteva, 2015b: 744).

Significantly, he is highly critical of the Nobel prize winning work of Elianor Ostrom, for her work on the economizing the commons. Aligned to Vandana **Shiva**, Esteva believes that Ostrom is destroying the commons by turning it into a resource. This misses the ontological and relational dimension of communing (see Esteva, 2015: 745; and Esteva, 2014 for fuller discussions).

Interculturality

In rejecting a universal category of 'the commons', Esteva is also arguing for the key idea of interculturality (for which he is indebted to Ivan Illich). Interculturality involves dialogue across cultures, and not in the sense that the goal of dialogue is a victory, or a won argument. This victory-seeking attitude would imply (as per most of history) the 'imposition of one vision on the other; we will talk in my terms …' (Esteva, 2015a: 531). Instead, he dreams that people can be really open to one another, in a 'heart to heart … [where] we can find something' (ibid: 531). As such, crucial to dialogue is the ability to really listen, 'allowing the other to change you' (ibid), and without this shift of allowing oneself to be changed, there's no hope of a movement from colonization to interculturality.

Hospitality and 'co-motion'

This approach to interculturality and allowing the other to change you was, for Esteva, as per Illich, about 'friendship'. Disavowing a professional development paradigm of professionals and the people, and particularly professional intervention (based on those produced needs discussed above), Esteva is for a whole new paradigm of 'development', which is signposted by hospitality, friendship, and co-motion. These three ideas in one sense correspond to an alternative way of thinking about our work as community practitioners. In earlier writing, Esteva argued for 'hospitality' as an alternative to 'alternative/another development' (Esteva, 1987: 137). In this he is suggesting that 'because of the damage done by development' (ibid: 138), 'we' need to be hospitable, and that this work takes place in the midst of what has become an inhospitable world. He adds other work too, such as needing to apply 'remedies in order to repair our damaged lives and environment, and to regenerate them' (ibid: 138). Here there is the reaching for what I have come to think of as a paradigm of healing the world, much needed in these difficult times.

References

Banks, S. & Westoby, P. (2019) *Ethics, Equity and Community Development,* Policy Press, Bristol, UK.

Esteva, G. (1987) 'Regenerating people's space', *Alternatives* 12(1): 125–152.

Esteva, G., Babones, S. & Babcicky, P. (2013) *The Future of Development: A Radical Manifesto,* Policy Press, Bristol, UK.

Esteva, G. (2014) 'Commoning in the new society', *Community Development Journal* 49(5i): i144–i159.

Esteva, G. (2015a) 'Conversing on the commons: An interview with Gustavo Esteva – part 1', *Community Development Journal* 50(3): 529–534.

Esteva, G. (2015b) 'Conversing on the commons: An interview with Gustavo Esteva – part 2', *Community Development Journal* 50(4): 742–752.

Olsen, J. (2018) 'Gustavo Esteva and the Long Road to the Zapatistas', [online] Available from <https://pulitzercenter.org/reporting/gustavo-esteva-and-long-road-zapatistas> [Accessed 20 May 2019].

CHAPTER 15

Frantz Fanon: *A 'revolution in listening'*

By Peter Westoby

Frantz Fanon 1925–1961

Introduction

One of the most influential people in helping us understand community development practice in the post-colonial context is Frantz Fanon.

Though he was writing in the 1950s, in recent years, particularly in places such as South Africa – where I have spent decades working – it seems that Fanon has arisen from the dead. Like Derrida's 'spectre of Marx', we should now talk of the 'spectre of Fanon' and everyone is reading Fanon.

He appears to be vigorously alive in the present – along with the phenomena of indigenous resurgence and post-colonial struggles around the world – sparking reflection on diverse issues such as the psychology of colonization, strategies for decolonization, critical race relations, inter-sectional sexuality, and so forth.

Originally from Martinique, Fanon developed his understanding in the latter stages of European colonial rule in Algeria in the 1950s. Both his personal and professional history gave him a profound insight into the turbulent events that surrounded him. As a trained and practising psychiatrist, and profoundly influenced by the existential and phenomenological philosophies of his day, he experienced the sweep of historical events that forged the colonial legacy, along with the struggle to rectify those events in the decolonizing struggle (Cherki, 2006). His most loved works include *The Wretched of the Earth* (1968), and *Black Skins, White Masks* (1967a). I like to think of him, much like **Hannah Arendt**, as a political phenomenologist, making sense of the political phenomena they lived through as it arose – **Arendt** on Nazism and the rise of authoritarianism, and Fanon on

http://dx.doi.org/10.3362/9781788531245.015

the colonial experience and decolonizing struggles. Neither stepped back from history to try to make sense of it from a so-called objective distance. Instead, they were immersed within it, understanding it from the 'inside-out'.

The imperative to listen

In South Africa Fanon's work is linked closely to Steve Biko's Black Consciousness philosophy, and some suggest that Biko's praxis was the most accurate manifestation of a Fanonian living philosophy. In this tradition liberation is not only political and economic, but epistemological, requiring a 'decolonizing of the mind'. His work has also been aligned to Gramsci's ideas, particularly critiquing any distancing objectifying praxis by intellectuals who have 'no skin in the game'. As per Gramsci's idea of 'organic intellectuals', Fanon insists that the intellectual-activist 'class', which *could* include university-educated community development practitioners, must listen – hence my titling of this reflection 'a revolution in listening'.

Aligned to Fanon's philosophy, one that cannot be abstracted and disengaged from real historical struggles for emancipation, I have found my way into the contemporary relevance of his praxis through Nigel Gibson's *Fanonian Practices in South Africa* (2011). And particularly relevant is his interpretation of the shack-dweller activism of Abahlali base Mjondolo, who are 'doing autonomous politics' differently in the post-colonial struggle of South Africa. One of the primary calls from Fanon's work is to have:

> One's ears open to the voices and the thinking that comes from unexpected spaces, namely, the new movements from below (Gibson, 2011: 6).

Gibson has been doing that with this shack-dweller activist movement and has become a friend of the movement in active solidarity. Here is the essence of the relevance of Fanon's living philosophy for community development practitioners. There's a necessity to listen to, and learn from, new forms of revolt, particularly from the edges and margins of society. Such listening leads to accompanying and practices of solidarity.

This living philosophy is also poignant in recognizing that those who liberate then tend to domesticate, in the sense that – to take the concrete example from South Africa as a case in point – under post-apartheid rule, 'the people find out the ubiquitous fact that exploitation can wear a Black face' (Fanon, 1968: 145). A living philosophy then calls for a sensitized revolutionary listening, a 'revolution in listening', ever probing into the liberatory spaces of renewal (that of course themselves always need renewing, forever at risk of domestication). In South Africa these spaces of renewal appear to be among the student movements, the grassroots shack-dweller movements, and the so-called service-delivery protests. Globally, perhaps the places of renewal include indigenous resurgence, anti-extractivism activism, extinction rebellions, the #MeToo movement, and so on. His work then invites community development practitioners to pause, reflect on their work, and consider the question: 'Are we listening in the unexpected places'? Are we attuned to the movements from below?"

Dialectic practices and a praxis, or organizing

Another key point for practitioners is to be engaged with what Fanon understood as a key dialectic requiring first, engagement in a critique of decolonization in particular concrete contexts – a practice of dialogue between intellectuals/activists and 'the people'; and second, to stand and listen to the standpoint of 'emergent movements that challenge philosophy' (Gibson, 2011: 7). This philosophy from 'the edge, or below' will be an 'elemental philosophy of liberation ... always present in the movements of the damned of the earth' (ibid).

For Fanon, understanding the praxis that would emerge from this dialectic listening is crucial. There is the necessity of a new humanism that *begins* from the humanity and solidarity of the 'damned'. For Fanon, this beginning becomes alive in an 'event' or movement whereby the pain or suffering – what could be understood as the hidden or invisible resistances – *becomes manifest* in a historical, social, and politically visible movement.

In past writings I have understood the key Fanonian contribution as adding *the organising dimension* to Freire's social learning and dialogue praxis. It is not enough to do circle work, dialogue, and learn. There is the need for organization, linking the oppressed with the equivalent of Gramsci's 'organic intellectuals', which I like to think of as community development practitioners. Yet, like Freire, Fanon insists on organizing *and* reflection. There's no room for activism without reflection. As Gibson puts it, 'For Fanon, activity that shuns reflection and critical thought cannot lead to liberation' (Gibson 2011: 11). Learning from his concrete experience during the Algerian revolution, in *A Dying Colonisation* (1967b), he writes about the exhaustion, and indeed mindless activism and brutality that comes from a lack of reflection and critical thinking. Without reflection, organizing, and strategic dialogue between the 'damned' and the organic intellectuals, there is the danger of a spiral of violence that leads to nothing enduring and often ends up with external forces intervening – which undoes any true liberatory impulse.

The spectre of colonisation

If, as I wrote in the introduction, the 'spectre of Fanon' has arisen within South Africa, manifest as vigorous dialogue between the wretched of the earth and the organic intellectuals of those movements – then another key wisdom learned from Fanon's work is that colonization is also spectral, menacing, ever present.

Fanon appreciated that traditional life did not finish with the invasion of the colonizers, that war did not end when the shooting stopped, nor poverty when welfare came. The events of history and public policy continue their impact long after they are officially over. In this sense, the 'spectre of colonisation lives on' and, in a capillary like way, works its agony through many dimensions of life.

Take for example, in Australia, that most cruel policy of removing Aboriginal children from their families simply because of the colour of their skin. Such a policy did not die when the policy was revoked decades ago but is still alive and well in the impact trail it created, and then is somewhat re-made in contemporary forms, such as through so-called 'child protection' policy and practices. Fanon understood that the events of history and the policies that shaped the times, whether they were helpful or harmful, attached themselves and added to, and even continued, the unfolding story. Even when the hard, upward decolonizing struggle begins in earnest, all that history of hurt comes into the birth of the new nations and new organization, even though they are founded on the dreams of liberation.

What is so practical about this spectral understanding of colonization is that it helps community development practitioners understand the depth and grip of colonization in the people with whom they are working, and within themselves. This understanding gives a solid basis for a genuine dialogue between practitioners and the people – grounded in a sound and accurate analysis of colonization's impact on everyone.

In conclusion – a radical empathy

If the chosen gem of wisdom from Fanon's work is 'a revolution in listening', I'd like to finish with the accompanying insight of Fanon scholar Christopher Lee, who suggests that Fanon, somewhat like

Freire, had a profound practice of 'radical empathy' (Lee, 2015: 14). Acknowledging that **Freire** was deeply influenced by Fanon, the latter was particularly able to step out of his privileged middle-class background and elite education and consider the lives of oppressed people. As co-author Dave Palmer suggests, 'people like Fanon remind me that the profound experience "with the people" shapes empathy; and it was his own experience as a black man that shaped his understanding'. Fanon stepped into a place of deep listening, solidarity, and learning, and used his knowledge to purse social-political change. He also became a revolutionary himself, even embracing violence as almost inevitable in the struggle to overcome structural violence. His praxis is profoundly political and revolutionary. His practice is deep empathy. Both require revolutionary listening.

References and key works

Cherki, A. (2006) *Franz Fanon: A Portrait,* Cornell University Press, Ithaca, NY, & London.

Fanon, F. (1968) *The Wretched of the Earth,* Grove Press, New York.

Fanon, F. (1967a) *Black Skin, White Mask,* Grove Press, New York.

Fanon, F. (1967b) *A Dying Colonialism,* Grove Press, New York.

Gibson, N. (2011) *Fanonian Practices in South Africa: From Steven Biko to Abahlali base Mjondolo,* KwaZulul Natal Press, South Africa.

Lee, C. (2015) *Frantz Fanon: Toward A Revolutionary Humanism,* Jacana Media, South Africa.

CHAPTER 16

Paulo Freire: *Start with the people, but don't stay with the people*

By Peter Westoby

Paolo Freire 1921–1997

Generative themes, circle work, and codification

In 2018 I was visiting a Nepalese non-government organization (NGO) working in remote and difficult parts of the country. I'd been invited to come and learn about their practice, based explicitly on Paulo Freire's work, and to then offer some reflective conversations.

The NGO's approach to community development was to place two community educators in a village for two to three years to animate social change. For the first three months the educators were 'not allowed' to 'do' anything (that is, not allowed to initiate activities or projects) other than to visit households, hear people's stories, get to know the villagers, and perhaps help out in the fields. Freire had this to say about such observation process:

> It is essential that the [workers] observe the area under varying circumstances: labour in the fields, meetings of a local association (noting the behaviour of the participants, the language used, and the relations between the officers and the members), the role played by women and young people, leisure hours, games and sports, conversations with people in their homes (noting examples of husband-wife, parent child relationships). No activity must escape the attention of the [worker] in the initial survey of the area (Freire, 1970: 103–104).

In this time, other than building relationships, their main task was to listen to what Freire called the 'generative themes', that is, the key issues facing the community. Then, sometime after that initial three months, the educator/animators brought people together to do what

http://dx.doi.org/10.3362/9781788531245.016

Freire called 'circle work' – on the day I visited, this consisted of about 30 people sitting around in a circle, about 20 women and 10 men. The educators had prepared a small role-play on domestic violence (DV) – one of the key generative themes that had emerged from conversations in the previous months. This role play, in which a scene of DV was played out, was offered as what Freire called a 'codification', that is, a generative theme turned into a 'picture' that would then trigger community dialogue. I observed this dialogue over the next couple of hours as the educator-animators asked what the people had seen, what had happened, if this ever happened in the community, what could be done and so forth. The dialogue moved the group to re-consider what they had seen as 'normal' – DV as okay or invisible – to something that had been made visible and could be changed. It was as if, as Freire puts it, 'By taking some distance, they emerged and were thus able to see [their lives] as they never had before' (Freire, 2005: 39).

In this sense, the community educators led a process that is characterized by the chosen gem of a wisdom – 'start with the people, but don't stay with the people'. The generative themes, the issues shaped by language and worldview of the people, are the starting point. In the above story this was DV (and there were others too). Community educator/animators – not the NGO hosting/employing them – using the Freirean approach, do not generate the ideas or issues for change. *These come from the people* – hence 'start with the people'. However, the dialogue process, as circle work, using a process of codification for dialogue and renewed observation, *doesn't stay with the people*. It should challenge, nudge people into new understandings. It should embody what Freire called 'conscientisation' – that is, the people should move from understanding their world as 'natural' to seeing it as cultural and historical, and therefore able to be changed.

Who Paulo Freire is ...

Paulo Freire was born in 1921 in Recife, a port city of north-eastern Brazil. He said that it was his parents who originally inspired in him a love of dialogue and a respect for others, and these attitudes were to influence his approaches to adult education. Although he trained as a lawyer, Freire did not practise law, choosing instead to enter into the world of adult education and illiteracy – and it is in this domain that he has left a great legacy. In 1946, Freire was appointed director of the Pernambuco Department of Education and Culture where he began to develop an educational praxis that would profoundly influence liberation theology, literacy work, and adult education around the world. Imprisoned and exiled in the 1960s, he became a Harvard University professor. In 1970 his seminal book *Pedagogy of the Oppressed* was published, which has been hugely influential across many disciplines.

Freire also deeply influenced **Myles Horton**, as per the delightful dialogue between Horton and Freire in *We Make the Road by Walking* (Horton et al., 1990), along with **bell hooks**. At the same time Freire's thinking is profoundly indebted by others in this collection, such as the work of **Frantz Fanon**.

The art of the question – from banking to dialogue

Returning to the story, as I watched those two community educators I was particularly attentive to the questions they asked. Putting questioning in context, Freire is well-known for critiquing what he called the 'banking' method of education – when an 'expert' stands in front of people and 'teaches' – in which the banking metaphor indicates experts as teachers *depositing* knowledge into people's heads. For Freire this approach to teaching is oppressive, or domesticating, particularly training people for the capitalist world narrowly oriented to employment, bureaucratized minds, and atrophied imagination. In this approach, people do not discover knowledge that builds their freedom and a political understanding of the world.

He contrasted this 'banking' method with 'dialogue', suggesting that the real pathway to knowledge is discovery and that this occurs when people learn *with others* in conversation – hence the idea of circle work – a process of learning, reflection, and political analysis.

What then becomes central to the educator/animator's practice is the art of questioning. Real dialogue involves mutual questioning, and there is a famous dialogue of Freire's with Antonio Faundez in *Learning to Question: A Pedagogy of Liberation* (1989) where Antonio says, '… all knowledge begins with questions. It begins with what you, Paulo, call curiosity. But curiosity is asking questions' (1989: 35). Freire responds with the idea of 'castration of curiosity' in which imagination has shrunk, and 'there's not even any searching' (ibid). I watched the community educators in Nepal ask questions – they were curious, and the people became curious – and as per Freire's dialogue method, eventually people in the circle of 30 also started asking questions, which of course led to conversation, analysis, and strategies for change.

Humanisation - cultivating a capacity for love

Stepping back in time to 2007, I was travelling in India contemplating my new life that was about to start as a community development academic. I was somewhat apprehensive, almost afraid to step into a teaching role – 'did I dare to teach?' is a question Freire asserts is important for those who love teaching. I decided to use some of that time to re-read that seminal book *Pedagogy of the Oppressed* (1970), one that had shaped my life back in the 1980s as a young community development practitioner. Despite all the wisdom of the book, the striking feature of this re-reading was Freire's constant and unembarrassed use of the word 'love' in relation to his work, and more particularly in relation to dialogue. For example, he states:

> Dialogue cannot exist however, in the absence of a profound love for the world and men. The naming of the world, which is an act of creation and re-creation, is not possible if it is not infused with love. Love is at the same time the foundation of dialogue and dialogue itself (Freire 1970: 62).

In this statement Freire not only articulates a powerful method of social change, but also shows a profound understanding of humanity and the need for any development work to ultimately be a humanizing process. Community development work without love can become technical, routinized, shallow, and exploitative. Later, in *Teachers as Cultural Workers* (2005: 5) he re-stated, 'We must dare, in the full sense of the word, to speak of love without the fear of being called ridiculous, mawkish, or unscientific.'

In an era of dehumanization, of human 'resources', and social 'capital', we desperately need to rehumanize the world. This is a key to Freire's thinking. However, what is pertinent for community development workers is also Freire's particular understanding of dehumanization, which is usually loaded with the 'false generosity of paternalism' (Freire, 2005: xxi), not love. Any impulse towards humanitarianism, what I usually see embodied in the gesture of 'helping', is often captive to such paternalism. Such a community development practitioner is an 'instrument of dehumanisation' (ibid).

Praxis and politics

Not so long ago there was a string of comments linked to a provocation on the International Association of Community Development Facebook site. Proclaiming that academics and theory were a waste of time, the comments emphasized how important practice is. Childlike in this display of asserting one (practice) over the other (theory), more or less everyone had failed to remember the basics, beautifully explained by Freire:

> [We must] not follow certain traditional methods that tend to separate theory from practice and that we not engage in any sort of work or activity that essentially dichotomised theory and practice by either underestimating theory, denying its importance, by exclusively emphasizing practice as the only thing to really count. On the contrary, my intention was to have, from the very beginning, direct experimentation with the contradictions between theory and practice (Freire, 2005: 37).

For Freire, praxis emerges from the tensions that play out *between* theory and practice. People take action in the world, a form of practice, and yet reflect on that practice in the light of theory. Even Freire's theory of education for domestication versus liberation is enlightening. I teach, a form of practice, yet embedded in the keyword 'teach' is this theory of domestication/liberation, which forces me to reflect on what my teaching practice is achieving. Without the theory there's every chance my teaching will drift towards domestication, because this is more or less the goal of university administration as a neoliberal institution. So it is within community development praxis. For example, a community development practitioner aspires to support people to have 'more freedom' in their lives as a result of being involved in a community process – and the theory of 'development as freedom' versus 'development as participation in economic development' supports reflection on the aspiration. Without the theory of 'development as freedom' a community development practitioner is likely to be seduced by the power of neoliberal visions of development (the economic participant, everyone as a social entrepreneur).

A praxis that links practice with theory orients community development work towards politics, bringing people together to understand key issues in their lives – such as the politics of health care and education, the politics of public space design and urban planning, and the popular politics of division and fear. For Freire, education, and we will add community development, cannot avoid politics. Politics as a form of collective praxis sits at the heart of our work.

References

Horton, M. and Freire, P. with Bell, B., Gaventa, J. and Peters, J. (eds) (1990) *We Make the Road by Walking: Conversations on Education and Social Change*, Temple University Press, Philadelphia, PA.

Freire, P. (1970) *Pedagogy of the Oppressed,* Herder and Herder, New York.

Freire, P. & Faundez, A. (1989) *Learning to Question: A Pedagogy of Liberation,* WCC Publications, Geneva.

Freire, P. (2005) *Teachers as Cultural Workers: Letters to Those Who Dare Teach,* Westview Press, CO.

CHAPTER 17

Mary Graham: '*Place method' and custodians of land*

By Athena Lathouras

Mary Graham 1948—

Mary Graham was my teacher at university in the late 1990s. She and her good friend Lilla Watson helped prepare us for social work practice with Aboriginal and Torres Strait Islander peoples. I remember them showing tremendous graciousness as they gently raised our consciousness about Australia's damning racial context and history. We came to understand the impact of white settlement and the ensuing intergenerational trauma that persists to this day because of those government's social policies. Their teaching had a profound impact as I started to develop an understanding of my own white privilege. And like many of my class colleagues, I committed to do what I could to reduce the deleterious effects of racism and to work for justice and equality for Australia's First Peoples.

Mary Graham is a *Kombumerri* person (Gold Coast in southern Queensland, Australia) through her father's heritage and connected with *Wakka Wakka* country (South Burnett in Queensland, Australia) through her mother's people. She is an Indigenous elder and philosopher and is a lecturer teaching Aboriginal history, politics, and comparative philosophy. Mary works as a community worker and researcher, and serves on the boards and committees of many Aboriginal organizations in Australia. Her life's work has also included working to shape more just social policies for Aboriginal people.

Australian Aboriginal people are the oldest continuous civilization in the world and historically comprised in the order of 600 cultural groups and languages. Graham (2017) argues that in this long period of time Aboriginal people have learned important lessons about their association with the land and about the nature of human society. She

http://dx.doi.org/10.3362/9781788531245.017

suggests that in their long history Aboriginal people have had to try to work out answers to critical questions. These include, 'How do we live together - in a particular area, nation, and on Earth - without killing each other off?'; 'How do we live together without substantially damaging the environment?' And finally, '*Why* do we live?' (Graham, 2008: 181, my emphasis). In this sense, while a community worker and teacher, Graham is a philosopher and always comes back to core questions to do with the good life, meaning, and relationships.

With her final question posed above, she emphasizes that 'we need to find the answer in a way that does not make people feel alienated, lonely or murderous' (Graham, 2008: 181). Key to Mary Graham's contribution as a critical thinker is the idea that the land is a guide for relationships. And for a good society we would all benefit from adopting what is known in Australian Aboriginal culture as a *custodial ethic*.

Aboriginal worldviews

Graham contends that there are two basic precepts of Aboriginal worldviews. They are: *The Land is the source of the law*, and *You are not alone in the world*.

With the first precept Graham is drawing from the work of Christine F. Black (2011) who foregrounds that the land is the *source* of the law. Graham explains that 'the land is a sacred entity, not property or real estate; it is the great mother of all humanity' (Graham, 2008: 181). Significantly, the land, and how we treat it, is what determines our human-ness. Here, Graham is connecting to the second precept, explaining that 'Aboriginal people have a kinship system that extends into land … and has its own Dreaming or explanation of existence. The Dreaming is a combination of meaning – about life and all reality, as well as an action guide to living' (Graham, 2008: 182).

At the heart of this law is a relationalist ethos. Aboriginal relationality is a refined system of social, moral, spiritual, and community obligations. A relationalist ethos is one that centres on the relationship between people and the land, and importantly, *action* associated with caring for land and for people. Ethics only comes from the action of looking after something outside of ourselves. In the first instance, Graham argues (2017), this is the land.

For Graham (2017) these two precepts speak to two kinds of relations, the relationship between *land and people*, and the relationship *between people*. Importantly, she claims that the relationship between people is always contingent on the relationship between land and people. That is, land first. For Aboriginal people this relationship is also described as a custodial ethic, which is a relational ethos with land, whereby people are always thankful for it and obliged to look after it. Graham (2017) quoting Irene Watson (2017: 209), argues there is the 'law of reciprocity', one that has come out of this relationship between humans and land. The land looks after us and we look after it, repeating reciprocally, on and on.

Learning about place – a place method

The inextricable connection between 'country' and 'community' that Australian Aboriginal people have is articulated in the reflection on **Deborah Bird Rose**. Mary Graham, adding to Rose, also discusses the law of place (2009: 76–77). Aboriginal Australia's perspective on the nature of existence, referred to earlier, is that the sacred dreaming is the system of creation that brings the whole of existence into being and ensures its continuity. The Dreaming, with ancestral beings as intermediaries, brings into being place, and the law for that place. With this law comes identity, obligation, kinship, and, crucially, the template for relationships in that place.

For Aboriginal people, place informs a 'Mode of Being in the world' (Graham, 2009: 77). It shapes identity or a sense of 'being' or personhood, as well as 'belonging' and 'connectedness' (Graham, 2014: 18). It provides a coherence among individuals, family, clan, community, and networks, with spirit and human agency (Graham, 2009: 77).

Moreover, place is epistemologically and ontologically central to notions and discussions regarding action or intent (Graham, 2014: 18). Helpfully, she argues that when incorporating what she calls 'Place method' (2009: 77) into daily life, it becomes a way of seeing and a form of knowing that employs historical knowledge, reflexive reasoning, and dialectic awareness as well as providing tools to realise new potential for the emancipation and understanding of dislocated individuals and collectives. This is pertinent, especially with regard to addressing the intergenerational trauma facing Australia's First Peoples referred to earlier. By refining people's thinking abilities and moral sensibilities, those employing a place method are equipped with a new consciousness about how to approach a problematic situation; or to see what must be done about it and how to do it.

Thus, the gem of wisdom for community development is to practice a form of custodial ethics and place method – in relation to the land and its people. Graham claims (2009) we have much to gain by exploring this method with its emphases on relationality and interconnectedness with all life forces. How to do this, starts with observation. She suggests (2017) that people could learn about everything in their own area or place. They could try to replicate what traditionally Aboriginal people growing up learned about their land, where they developed sophisticated understandings of the land, the waters, the soils, insects, and all the flora and fauna on that land. Such close learning, Graham (2014) argues, elicits feelings of empathy, where people start to care for the land in their local area and create a sense of place for them. Furthermore, the empathy that is built through this process is integral also to relationality as a means of preserving positive, constructive human relations. We remember the Aboriginal worldview relates to the relationship between land and people, and the relationship between people.

Much like **Hillman's** phenomenological thinking, Graham (2008: 193) suggests that the world is immediate, not external. We are all its custodians, as well as its observers. However, she warns that:

> A culture which holds the immediate world at bay by objectifying it as the Observed System, thereby leaving it to the blinkered forces of the market place, will also be blind to the effects of doing so until those effects become quantifiable as, for example, acid rain, holes in the ozone layer and global economic recession. All social forces which has led to this planetary crisis could have been anticipated ...

In contrast she suggests that...

> What will eventually emerge in a natural, habituated way is the embryonic form of an intact, collective spiritual identity for *all* Australians, which will inform and support our daily lives, our aspirations and our creative genius (Graham, 2008: 193, my emphasis).

Conclusion

The three critical questions posed by Graham (referred to earlier) – those to which answers need to be found so that people don't feel alienated, lonely, or murderous - are critical for these contemporary times. Aboriginal custodial ethics signpost a way of thinking and acting that is hopeful. Graham's ideas about place and committing to practical action to care for land can be achieved, for example, by joining Landcare, Bushcare or Coastcare groups or defending place or territory against forces of destruction and extractivism. Graham also highlights the usefulness of citizens or people's assemblies (personal communication, 2019). Citizens' assemblies are gaining traction with governments globally as a form of inclusive citizen engagement. They are processes where ordinary citizens gather together to hear from experts, discuss in depth, and develop recommendations on public policy issues (Boswell, Niemeyer and Hendriks, 2013).

In highly politicized contexts, however, or where just transitions at a systems-level are required, other tactics are required to affect change. Concluding a recent key-note speech on earth-centred ethics, Graham (2017) presented a challenge, one that resonates with **Greta Thunberg's** stance. Referring specifically to the current climate crisis, and in Australia, cruelty associated with the Australian government's policies against Aboriginal people and against asylum seekers, Graham argues for value clarity and far more action. She is forthright that practising earth-centred or custodial ethics means we need to openly come out against these things; that we need more hard protests that seek justice; we need more organizing for collective action.

References and key works

Black, C.F. (2011) *The Land is the Source of the Law: A Dialogic Encounter with Indigenous Jurisprudence*, Routledge, New York.

Boswell, J., Niemeyer, S. & Hendriks, C. (2013) '"Julia Gillard's Citizens" assembly proposal for Australia: A deliberative democratic analysis', *Australian Journal of Political Science* 48(2): 164–178.

Graham, M. (2008) 'Some thoughts about the philosophical underpinnings of Aboriginal worldviews', *Australian Humanities Review* 45: 181–193.

Graham, M. (2009) 'Understanding human agency in terms of place: A proposed Aboriginal research methodology', *PAN: Philosophy Activism Nature* 3: 71–78.

Graham, M. (2014) 'Aboriginal notions of relationality and positionalism: A reply to Weber', *Global Discourse: An Interdisciplinary Journal of Current Affairs and Applied Contemporary Thought* 4(1): 17–22.

Graham, M. (2017) 'How Can We Build an Inspired Earth Ethics, First Nations Peoples' Perspectives', Keynote Speech at the *Inspiring Earth Ethics: Linking Values and Action Conference*, 23–24th November, 2017, Australian Earth Laws Alliance [YouTube video] <www.youtube.com/watch?v=hHYEVYqg3L8> [Accessed 3 October 2019].

Watson, I. (2017) 'Aboriginal laws of the land: Surviving fracking, golf courses and drains among other extractive industries', in Roger, N. & Maloney, M. (eds.) *Law as if Earth Really Mattered: The Wild Law Judgment Project,* pp. 209–218, Routledge, Abingdon, UK.

CHAPTER 18

Epeli Hau'ofa: *staying close to the ground*

By Peter Westoby

Epeli Hau'ofa 1939–2009

Epeli Hau'ofa, a Tongan scholar, ethnographer, and acclaimed fiction writer is well loved in the Pacific. Working for over 10 years in Vanuatu, I discovered his work on a visit to Suva, Fiji. Exploring the university book shop there I came across two of his well-known fiction pieces, *Tales of the Tikongs* (1983) and *Kisses in the Nederends* (1987), along with a collection of his anthropological musings *We Are The Ocean* (2008). Some hours later, reading and lounging on a chair in the sweltering heat, I was laughing out loud – the kind of laughing that has you in gut wrenching agony.

Known as a satirist, inspired by many cartoonists, but particularly the Australian Leunig (Hau'ofa, 1987: 168), Hau'ofa, purposefully and potently indulges in stories and wisdom that penetrates some core challenges of 'development' in the Pacific. In an illuminating interview with Subramani he suggests that, 'I almost lost my sense of humour trying to be civilised; but fortunately I never got quite civilised' (Hau'ofa, 1987: 161). This is not to say he's anti-civilization, and for 'tradition', but it is to state clearly that for Hau'ofa it is critical to maintain an ability to laugh at ourselves, and laugh generally. Aptly, he describes himself as a 'clown who likes to laugh a lot' (Hau'ofa, 1983: vii), particularly using this clowning and humour to laugh at the absurdity of much of what is going on in the world generally, and within development particularly. His twelve short stories within the *Tales of the Tikongs* focus on the particular absurdities of much development practice, offering the device of story to help penetrate more clearly the 'rocky road of island politics, love, corruption, religion, culture, truth, dependency, and foreign aid' (ibid: vii).

http://dx.doi.org/10.3362/9781788531245.018

Be an ethnographer – 'stay close to the ground'

While maintaining a capacity for humour, clowning, and satire, Hau'ofa – a speaker of seven languages – suggests that the skill of ethnography is needed more. Reflecting on his use of ethnography both as a fiction writer and anthropologist, his argument is that this skill 'keeps you close to the ground'. It's this idea that I've chosen to highlight as the gem of a wisdom. Expanding this, he explains that:

> I'm essentially a peasant albeit a highly educated one. There has been for many years a tussle between the peasant and the scholar in me. And I'm more than glad that the former has the upper hand. I like to view things from the ground up, preferably from the perspective of the Lowly Worm (Hau'ofa, 1987: 171).

In this reflection, we suggest that this worm-like, ethnographically grounded, or 'ground-up' way of seeing is crucial for community development practitioners. I often find myself discussing with my students that community development practitioners need social, emotional, and anthropological skills (along with some technical ones too). The anthropological – or ethnographic, enables practitioners to 'observe analytically the minutiae of actual behaviour and arrange them into connected social and cultural patterns' (ibid: 173). Such skill comes only with 'painstaking practice' (ibid), which in turn keeps people 'intellectually and emotionally close to the ground'. This practice ensures practitioners do not leap into their 'idea' of 'ideal' of what is happening in a social situation – a fundamental and novice mistake. This novice mistake tends to lead to working with what *we would like to happen*, as opposed to what can happen in the light of a very grounded understanding *of the actual*. An ethnographic lens ensures such grounding in the actual.

Poverty as belittlement

For Hau'ofa, getting close to the ground has required an ongoing struggle with the conditions of colonialism and small island life, and the question of what is to be done. In earlier writing he explained how, 'colonialism has isolated us … diverting us from our connections, from our traditional connections and redirected our connections to themselves … that's the beginning of belittlement' (2008: xiv). He suggests, 'the key is … the ability to overcome the psychology of belittlement and the feelings of helplessness it creates' (ibid: xix). He articulates two main strategies to do this. First, the role of the arts, particularly a new Oceanian art, that 'expands horizons in new directions' (ibid: xix). Such artistic endeavour has both personal and collective effects in the sense that people can, as he puts it, 'feel to breathe again, to dream the impossible' (ibid: xix). Second, to use the powerful metaphor of the ocean as a metaphor, that can become a 'weapon of and for the weak'. Here he is arguing for the power of a larger strategic identity that connects Pacific islands into a larger regional oceanic identity that is 'capable of affording a stronger footing in today's engagement with the forces of globalisation' (ibid: xix).

His comments and analysis remind me of a conversation from my work in Vanuatu between a leader from Vanuatu – the then General Secretary (GS) of the Malvatumauri National Council of Chiefs, and some colleagues, and myself. The GS was visiting a group of Australian colleagues in Brisbane. As a part of that visit we spent a week in retreat at a Gold Coast house, mainly learning language. And, then, one beautiful late afternoon, a few of us were walking along the beach, salivating about a possible fish and chips dinner, when the guest from Vanuatu paused and said:

> Look at all that wealth you have here [pointing at the amazing sky-line of the Gold Coast metropolis] – if we in Vanuatu decide that this is the measure of wealth, we will always be poor. The only way we can re-discover our wealth, and not feel poor, is to re-evaluate our wealth in terms of what we have. And we have a lot.

In this re-evaluation, he was referring to the wealth of natural resources such as shells, pigs, mats, *kastom*, and community resilience. This conversation was one of several triggers, which led to 2011 being the year of the *kastom* economy that was forged on Vanuatu and now there is a whole movement around this new *kastom* economy linked to explorations of Melanesian socialism (Westoby, 2010).

In a sense this leader of Vanuatu was seeing, sensing, and feeling the possible poverty of belittlement, and at the same time re-imagining life based on a revitalization of customary wealth, and linking this to a broader Melanesian identity (beyond Vanuatu).

Yet, there are dangers in this revitalization too, as Hau'ofa suggests, for he is also against what he calls, 'romantic neo-traditionalism' (Hau'ofa, 1987: 165). In being for decolonizing and yet against 'neo-traditionalism', he argues that:

> The solutions to all the major problems in our islands lie in regional and ultimately in wider international co-operation

(even if this means struggle), and not so much in our own small and narrow local efforts (ibid: 164–165).

You could say that he holds a strong commitment to a meta-level practice that links the local to the global.

The taboo place between insider–outsider

Another useful wisdom from Hau'ofa's work is the idea that many community development practitioners could well be occupying what he calls the taboo place between being an insider person – someone who is comfortable with institutions and the status quo, and the outsider – someone who feels completely alienated or outside of the conventions of society. My sense, as is Hau'ofa's, is that the in-between space, which he names as the taboo space, is where extraordinary 'power, knowledge, creativity, and freedom' can flourish (Hau'ofa, 2008: 103). It is taboo because it is a kind of no-person place, with no clear sense of how to be. Community practitioners tend to occupy such spaces, for example, as articulated in the imaginatively titled report, 'In and Against the State' (see Hoggert et al., 2008). Often community development practitioners are in the in-between space translating language, ideas, desires, to – on the one hand, the state, or those with resources and power – and on the other hand, everyday people in places with few resources and little power. Some observers of practice call this a 'brokering' role. It can be a taboo place of danger because there are significant risks, such as not being understood by either outsiders and insiders; being perceived as selling out to one or the other, and so forth. It takes highly attuned judgement and technical skills to navigate this place.

Finally, Epeli Hau'ofa, a Tongan man of blood, yet Oceania man of soul, lived a rich life. Often himself the outsider, he contributed widely in the Pacific, working many years at the University of the South Pacific in Fiji, and also founding the Oceania Centre for Arts. Mixing anthropology, sociology, and fiction writing, he has been a gifted voice for the Pacific and could give much to the world.

References

Hau'ofa, E. (1983) *Tales of the Tikongs*, University of Hawaii Press, Honolulu.

Hau'ofa, E. (1987) *Kisses in the Nederends*, University of Hawaii Press, Honolulu.

Hau'ofa, E. (2008) *We Are The Oceans: Selected Works,* University of Hawaii Press, Honolulu.

Hoggert, P., Mayo, M. and Miller, C. (2008) *The Dilemmas of Development Work,* Bristol University Press, Bristol, UK. Distributed by Chicago University Press Books, Chicago, IL.

Westoby, P. (2010) 'Dialogue and disentanglement: Navigating tensions for sustainable community economic development within Vanuatu', *Journal of Environmental, Cultural, Social and Economic Sustainability* 6(1): 81–92.

CHAPTER 19

James Hillman: *'Ensouling the world' and notitia*

By Peter Westoby

James Hillman 1926–2011

Cheryle Van Scoy

Encountering Hillman's opus

Experiencing a spiritual crisis in my late 20s, I was introduced to James Hillman's work by a Jungian analyst in Durban, South Africa. He's journeyed with me ever since, and I have more Hillman books in my personal library than any other, sitting alongside Thomas Moore's work, who, more than anyone, has popularized his work. Visiting the Hillman OPUS archive at Pacifica Graduate Institute, California in 2016, (where the archive of mythologist Joseph Campbell also sits) was one of the most enchanting moments of my scholarly life – and I will never forget piecing together letters exchanged between Hillman and David Abrams, authors of the most animating of books, *The Spell of the Sensuous* (1996). However, while journeying with Hillman has been crucial for my personal life, this journey has gradually come to shape my understanding of community work, indicated in my research and the writing of my books *Creating Us: Community Work with Soul* (Westoby, 2016a) and *Soul, Community and Social Change* (Westoby, 2016b).

Who was James Hillman?

James Hillman, one of the key inheritors of Carl Jung's work, drew deeply on the phenomenological tradition of philosophy and gifts community development practitioners with a new way of perceiving the world and their practice. Aligned to what is understood as a depth-approach to social and ecological practice (and what I have come to understand as one of the 'shadow traditions' of thinking, being, and doing[1]), he invites a way of perceiving called 'ensouling the world'.

http://dx.doi.org/10.3362/9781788531245.019

Hillman, who was handed the mantle of the Jung Institute in Zurich, or in a more enchanting turn of phrase, 'took on Jung's daimonic inheritance' (Russell, 2013: xi) as director of studies in 1959, initiated a revival of the idea of 'soul' and 'soul of the world'. This started with his seminal book in 1975: *Re-Visioning Psychology* – nominated for a Pulitzer Prize – and then his essay, 'Anima Mundi: The Return of the Soul to the World' (Hillman, 1992b).

For Hillman, Jung's notion of the soul, linked to Jung's theory of individuation, had been captured by an ever-increasing narrow psychology, which over-emphasized a *turn inwards,* towards subjectivity. In Hillman's critique of this inner turn, he was rescuing or unearthing the deeper and broader perspective of Jung's opus, *turning outwards* (and backwards, to the 'lament of the dead', a way of talking about the soul's burden of history) and making it relevant for everyone, particularly those interested in 'healing culture' (Hillman & Shamdasani, 2013: 159). And I suggest community development practitioners are deeply committed to healing culture, hence the choice of Hillman as one of our reflections.

What it might mean to heal culture

Here is a story that might help understand what I mean: I sit almost daily in what was my local Yeronga shopping village. I often walk the 100 metres from my home and settle in for a coffee. It is a semi- circle of shops – bakers, bottle-shop, butcher, fruit and vegetable store, sushi, a gorgeous Thai, and a few others. It's a quick stroll to the train station. It could be perfect. But I sit there observing, noticing, and sensing, sometimes in conversation with others, and I reach for an accurate 'seeing' of this social phenomenon of the village, one representing the gesture of our social-body. And of course, it is hard not to see what is unfolding. At the centre of these shops is a car park. It is a chaotic space of cars moving in and out, around, and through. Those of us sitting around this centre get to breathe the fumes and struggle to converse over the noise of machines. It is tough going to be in this village if you desire conviviality! The gesture is clear – a place of efficient commerce, designed for cars, quick shopping, and meagre human exchange, perhaps indicative of a broken culture, colonized by capitalist logics. That is simply what it is, a seeing. It is quite shocking to see: a true diagnosis of a society's social priorities. And only this shocking seeing, not shying away from what is, is the pathway towards healing. To see in this way requires a particular noticing too, which is explored below.

Ensouling the world

In a nut-shell, the argument for ensouling the world is that, not only are people alive, animated by the life-force or their soul's unique gift and calling (Hillman, 1999), but so is the world, the cosmos, the culture – even a shopping village. Hillman referred to this living way of perceiving the world as 'ensouling' the world (Hillman, 1992). From this ensouling perspective, as per phenomenology, 'the social' can be seen in a different way to normal habitual impulses, which tend to see in linear, reductionist, and deadening ways. Recognizing that all perception (after all, phenomenology is all about the philosophy of perception) is a form of participation – that is, humans make choices about how to perceive – at the heart of this reflection is the argument for a way of perceiving the social in ecological, organic, aesthetic, and living ways (as opposed to those habitual ways of seeing in linear, reductionist, and deadening ways).

As per this phenomenological approach to social practice, practitioners need to start to perceive the community phenomenon they are attending to in a broader way, engaging a broader array of senses than the usual rational and analytic.

Hillman wanted practitioners to re-cultivate a phenomenological – or what he sometimes called a poetic or aesthetic perception – to engage more with the world, to equip people to see the 'images in events that give rise to meaningfulness, value and a full range of experiences' (Hillman, 1989: 15). He saw a particularly powerful role for the arts, symbols, and other archetypal 'readings' of the social.

An approach that takes the wisdom 'ensouling the world' seriously leads *away from* any perspective that experiences the world in either a distant objectifying way or perceives it purely analytically (using the intellect rather than, say, imagination, usually drawing on metaphor and myth). Instead, ensouling the world insists in bringing meaning and healing to the culture, or more broadly to the world – the world as efficient ugly shopping villages, sick mono-cultural farming, deadening urban landscapes, and so forth.

Phenomenology of the social

In dialogue with Hillman's work, a significant contribution in grounding such ideas in everyday social and community practice is also made by one of the authors of *Towards Psychologies of Liberation* (Watkins & Shulman 2008), Mary Watkins, from Pacifica College, California. She also wrote the influential essay 'Breaking the Vessels:

Archetypal Psychology and the Restoration of Culture, Community, and Ecology' (Watkins, 2008).

She explicitly introduces Hillman's 'soul of the world' into the social practice field, asking social practitioners to *refrain from quick intervention*, and enter into a much longer process of observation, listening, and imaginative participation in the social sphere. In her dialogue with Hillman's work we start to see very explicit gems of wisdom for community development practitioners.

She invites community development practitioners to listen to more people connected to whatever social issue is being explored, whether it is a local social problem (homelessness, drugs) or a socio-creative challenge (such as urban design). In that listening, she insists on *more dialogue* and then the awaiting, as per discerning the 'soul of the world', for images to arise that offer deeper meaning, and deeper diagnostics about a way forward linked to an analysis that arrives from imagination, and therefore perceives the 'whole'. Of significance, Hillman also suggests that the most potent kind of listening or perceiving comes from the heart (Hillman, 1992a). In this, he resuscitates the idea of the heart as an 'organ of perception', able to perceive, and suggests that being attuned aesthetically to issues such as beauty and ugliness can tell us more about the essence of a social phenomenon than any analytical perception (ibid: 59).

Notitia

Notitia is a term of Hillman's that pushes practitioners to notice, and keep looking, listening, and noticing, but then doing it more with all their senses, with the importance of prioritizing sensing over 'feeling' (hence in the above story I used words such as observation, seeing, sensing). As Watkins suggests, the noticing needs 'the gift of careful attention that is sustained, patient, subtly attuned to images and metaphors ...' (Watkins, 2008: 6). Part of this kind of noticing also requires what Hillman called 'seeing through' and awaiting 'the imaginal'– which for Watkins represents Hillman's warning, that 'we are always in the embrace of an idea' (ibid). The point is that ideas are often abstractions, or quick leaps to interpretation and judgement. In contrast, 'seeing through' and awaiting 'the imaginal' requires social practitioners to attend to the images of the world as presented through story, or an unfolding story within a community and culture, therefore letting go of pre-determined fantasies.

Returning to the story

I finished the Yeronga Shopping Village story above by suggesting:

> The gesture is clear – a place of efficient commerce, designed for cars, quick shopping, and meagre human exchange, perhaps indicative of a broken culture, colonized by capitalist logics. That is simply what it is, a noticing. It is quite shocking to see: a true diagnosis of a society's social priorities.

In this perception of the heart, an aesthetic response, I also experienced a yearning. I yearn for something like an Italian or Spanish piazza. I long for their equivalent beauty and imagine what such a centre could induce from local residents, to have a real 'centre', a hearth, honouring the mythological Hestia figure in our collective culture (Paris, 2017: 185ff). Such honouring would be healing, re-fostering a warmth in our culture that is fractured by too much Hermes energy, mythically caught in exchange, movement, and efficiency.

In conclusion

The story suggests to community development practitioners there is a different kind of noticing or perceiving. Attuned aesthetically to issues such as beauty and ugliness, being open to images that arise that depict the 'whole', the 'essence', the 'gesture', invites a different set of feelings, longings, yearnings, and also analysis (an analysis of the heart and imagination). Such practice also eschews a view of community development practice that bifurcates the social from the aesthetic. Instead, ensouling the world tries to perceive where aliveness and beauty are present in all things – in the story, a shopping space, but, also many other places – and brings this perceiving into our work.

Endnotes

1. In the Joanna Macy reflection (in this volume), I suggest that 'shadow traditions' of practice draw on emotion, imagination, ritual, the symbolic, and the aesthetic. These are shadow in the sense that they have been repressed in a dominant scientific, materialist, rationalist, and analytical shaping of much community development thinking and practice. Such shadow traditions include the depth psychology of Jung/Hillman, phenomenology (disrupting the dominance of Cartesian deadening analytic

philosophy), Indigenous epistemology, and practice resurgence, Joanna Macy's deep ecology, and so forth.

References

Abrams, D. (1996) *The Spell of the Sensuous: Perception and Language in a More-Than-Human World,* Vintage Books, New York.

Hillman, J. (1975) *Re-Visioning Psychology,* First Harper Colophon, New York.

Hillman, J. (1989) *Blue Fire - Selected Writings By James Hillman,* Harper-perennial.

Hillman, J. (1992a) *The Thought of the Heart and the Soul of the World,* Spring Publications, CT.

Hillman, J. (1992b) 'Anima Mundi: The return of the soul to the world.' *The Thought of the Heart and the Soul of the World,* by James Hillman, Spring Publications, CT.

Hillman, J. (1999) *The Force of Character and the Lasting Life,* Random House, Sydney, Australia.

Hillman, J. & Shamdasani, S. (2013) *Lament of the Dead: Psychology after Jung's Red Book,* W.W. Norton & Company, New York & London.

Paris, G. (2017) *Pagan Meditations: The Worlds of Aphrodite, Artemis, and Hestia,* Spring Publications, Thompson, USA.

Russell D. (2013) *The Life and Ideas of James Hillman - Volume I: The Making of a Psychologist,* Helios Press, New York.

Watkins, M. (2008) 'Breaking the vessels: Archetypal psychology and the restoration of culture, community, and ecology', in S. Marlan (ed.), *Archetypal Psychologies: Reflections in Honour of James Hillman Edition,* pp. 414–437, Spring Books and Journals, Los Angeles, CA.

Watkins, M. & Shulman, H. (2008) *Toward Psychologies of Liberation,* Palgrave Macmillan, Basingstoke, UK & New York.

Westoby, P. (2016a) *Creating Us: Community Work with Soul,* Tafina Press, Brisbane, Australia.

Westoby, P. (2016b) *Soul, Community and Social Change,* Ashgate Press, UK.

CHAPTER 20

bell hooks:
We come to theory
because of our pain

By Peter Westoby

bell hooks 1952—

bell hooks is an intellectual, feminist theorist, cultural critic, artist, and writer that has sat close to my heart and practice for many years. I have re-read several of her books over and over, sat in numerous groups that have met monthly, reading and reflecting on her wisdom, and I've insisted that many of my students engage her work. She's a special one, integrating the scholarly and artistic, the activist and reflective. I think I fell in love with her work when reading an account of how she challenged **Paulo Freire's** patriarchal and sexist language (which is clear when reading *Pedagogy of the Oppressed*). His responsivity, as per his espoused dialogical ethics, was non-defensive, and in their ongoing dialogue, I could see the integrity of her (and his) work – the profound connection and integrity of theory and practice (something unusual among scholars) (hooks, 1994: 55). hooks even says, 'I loved him [Paulo Freire] in this moment for exemplifying by his actions the principles of his work' (ibid). This is a hiatus moment when scholarly work meets praxis, hence the attraction for community development thinkers and practitioners.

I came to healing because I was hurting

While tempted to focus on her 'pedagogy of healing' (challenging all dimensions of oppression in a system and society of domination), I have opted to foreground the idea of 'I came to theory because I was hurting'. This sentence in its full context says:

> I came to theory because I was hurting – the pain within me was so intense that I could not go on living. I came to theory

http://dx.doi.org/10.3362/9781788531245.020

desperate, wanting to comprehend – to grasp what was happening around and within me. Most importantly, I wanted to make the hurt go away. I saw in theory then a location for healing (hooks, 1994: 59).

This 'coming to theory' started in childhood as hooks tried to make sense of her experience of being a young black woman – predominantly understanding racism in first segregated and then desegregated schools – and then later the intersectionality of race with gender and class. This journey continued well into early adulthood as she attended university as a young African American woman making sense of that personal pain experienced as a child. This started a profound journey that has taken her into activist circles, the academy (trained in Stanford, Wisconsin and Santa Cruz), Buddhist training, the arts, and many inter-disciplinary dialogues.[1]

My rationale in foregrounding this element of her vast work is that it is tempting to think people will engage in community development processes because of 'ideas' or 'ideology', particularly if people are university trained in community development and lean towards the abstract. But, as per this 'saying', most people will come to community development processes (without even needing to know they are doing community development) because of their pain.

A collective praxis

Feeling alone, someone might decide they need to become part of a group, or share their story with someone else, hence seeding a re-weaving of connection. Feeling angry at what is going on in a neighbourhood, someone might join a local action group. Feeling confused about some phenomenon in life, a person might join a local learning circle. The point is, that it is the pain – individual, social, local – that leads to people's participation in joining with others in a group or community processes. It is, to use a common community development theory, the movement from private pain to public action, as people collectively make sense of their pain in dialogue with one another. Importantly, to avoid misunderstanding, hooks was in deep dialogue with **Freire's** work, and she clarifies that many people mistake **Freire's** concept of conscientization to be about individual transformation of attitudes and ideas. Instead, hooks, like **Freire**, argues that conscientization is always 'joined by meaningful praxis' (hooks, 1994: 47). This connects theory and practice, and for community development, the praxis (which is the joining of theory and practice) is a collective one. To re-state hooks' wisdom for community development, we could say something like:

> *we* come to theory and practice, *with others*, because *we* are hurting, and can only make sense of our hurting *with others*.

This collective element is often the 'community' dimension of community development – not community as place, as locality, as everyone in a village or neighbourhood. No, it is the forming of groups as people come together to share. It is also not the 'group-think' of ideology, of everyone agreeing on what is wrong or what should be done. Instead, it is the 'with' of people being in dialogue with one another, sharing stories, and forging an analysis and pathway of what to do together (disavowing that there is a right path).

Born as Gloria Jean Watkins in Hopkinsville, Kentucky, USA, bell hooks adopted the pen name of her maternal great-grandmother, a woman known for speaking her mind, yet used the lower-case version to distinguish from her. Post-PhD she has worked in many universities, publishing well over 30 books. Known as a feminist scholar and activist, a more recent theme – highly relevant to this book on community development – is that of *community and communion*, which for her signifies the ability of loving communities to overcome race, class, and gender inequalities. She is one of the few scholars who is absolutely unapologetic in writing of the importance of love in healing and social change work.

The practice of love

Comfortable with the idea and practice of love, she has been profoundly influenced by, among others, the already mentioned **Paulo Freire**, Peruvian liberation theologian Gustavo Gutierrez, psychologist Erich Fromm, Buddhist monk **Thich Nhat Hanh**, and African American writer **James Baldwin**, along with Malcolm X and Martin Luther King, Jr. Each has written about love in everyday life and social change work.

Her thinking and writing about love, consistent with the wisdom foregrounded in this chapter, emerged from the pain of several failed relationships. In reflecting on those experiences, she theorizes love in relation to patriarchy (e.g. how men are shaped as boys to be more or less illiterate in relation to their feelings), and also the need for people to embrace a spiritual sensibility (not promoting religion) (hooks, 2000, 2003).

In honour of her work, in 2014 the bell hooks Institute was formed, dedicated to: 'promot[ing] the cause of ending domination through understanding the ways systems of exploitation and oppression' (www.bellhooksinstitute.com/welcome/).

A culture of domination

This mission foregrounds her commitment to critical thinking and emancipatory praxis that takes intersectionality seriously. She is always reaching to understand how gender, race, class, and capitalism interact to create systems and practices of domination for all people. She uses, as she puts it, 'the complicated phrase "imperialist white supremacist capitalist patriarchy"', arguing that, 'this phrase is useful precisely because it does not prioritise one system over another but rather offers us a way to think about the interlocking systems that work together to uphold and maintain cultures of domination' (hooks, 2013: 4). For hooks this culture of domination is not so much about 'white folk' but about 'white supremacist thinking' that is an 'underlying belief system informing nearly every aspect of … culture and habits of daily life' (hooks, 2013: 12). With this understanding, 'everyone could move away from the us/them dichotomies which promote blame and prevent us all from assuming accountability for challenging and changing white supremacy' (ibid).

In conclusion, bell hooks' work is rich beyond the traditional borders of scholarly work. Riffing on themes such as love, a pedagogy of healing, a culture of domination; being unafraid to integrate autobiography with theory; contributing to feminist, media, film, and so much other literature – she is one of the gems for community development theorists and practitioners.

Endnotes

1. E.g. with Cornell West, with James Hillman, and Stuart Hall

References

hooks, bell (1994) *Teaching to Transgress: Education as the Practice of Freedom,* Routledge, London and New York.
hooks, bell (2000) *All about Love: New Visions,* USAL Harper.
hooks, bell (2003) *Teaching Community: A Pedagogy of Hope,* Routledge, London and New York.
hooks, bell (2013) *Writing Beyond Race: Living Theory and Practice,* Routledge, London and New York.

CHAPTER 21

Myles Horton: *Educators first, Organizers second*

By Athena Lathouras

Myles Horton 1905–1990

Annemarie Schwarzenbach

I was introduced to Myles Horton's significant work as a member of a Queensland Popular Education network.[1] This group of peers come together to support our attempts to 'radicalize' community development. We read relevant texts and critically reflect on our practice, bringing intellectual rigour and collegial support to our various community development efforts. When we read the book, *We Make the Road by Walking: Conversations on Education and Social Change, Myles Horton and Paulo Freire* (Horton et al., 1990), we learned about Horton's convictions and methods for educating and organizing so that groups might take control of their own destinies. Because Horton's work was primarily with poor, working class people, he set out to develop a form of education which led people to challenge unjust systems (Lewis, 1990), much like **Paulo Freire's**. For over sixty years he worked with people in labour and civil rights movements in the southern United States and Appalachia to create social change.

Horton founded the Highlander Folk School as a base for his work in 1931. Highlander taught leadership skills to thousands of people in the face of segregations laws and challenged the social, economic, and political structures of the segregated south of the United States. Working closely with labour unions, anti-poverty organizations, and civil rights leaders, Highlander ran programmes focussing on school desegregation, voter education, and civil rights action. Significantly, though, Horton emphasized that community organizing and building social movements was not the primary aim of Highlander. His dedication to improving the lives of people took place through a holistic, experiential, and democratically based education process that would support organizing and social movement building.

http://dx.doi.org/10.3362/9781788531245.021

Thus, I have chosen to highlight Horton's gem of wisdom for community development – first to be educators (albeit of the radical kind) and second to be organizers. Like **Freire**, Horton made the point that education must be linked to nascent social movements to ensure the work has a structural intention – that is, radical (as opposed to simply being reformist) (Horton et al., 1990). Horton set out first to teach people to be educators, so that any organizing that followed was highly participatory, fostered democratic decision making, and was owned by all those involved (Horton et al., 1990: 123).

Radical education

As a young man, Horton was set on this path because of his own dissatisfaction with the education profession he'd chosen. One of his concerns was that the traditional education system prevented ordinary people from learning about their own lives and problems. Mostly, they studied how other people lived, that is, people in high and distant places. He was also critical of the traditional top-down approach to education which only serviced the status-quo, where students were transformed into agents of American technology and consumerism. He believed this set individuals up to go it alone, and for competition in a capitalist system that benefits only some. Whereas radical education, he believed, starts with democratic processes for learning, and aims to replace, transform, and rebuild society, thus allowing for equal participation in society.

'Radical educators', Horton claimed (Jacobs, 2003: 249), devise a range of imaginative learning opportunities based on people's experiences so they learn how to analyse their experiences, take action, and maybe transform those experiences. Horton claimed it is a practice by which people can make education serve their needs as *they* perceive them and promote their aspirations as *they* define them. This kind of decision-making process is educational in its own right and is a means of accelerating the kind of learning people need if they are to take control of their own lives.

Horton also believed that learning is enhanced when it takes place collectively, as part of a group. Through workshops he set up mutually beneficial learning spaces where people told their stories and shared experiences. He fostered peer-to-peer learning where people developed analyses about why communities were facing challenges and difficulties. He also used conflict and contradiction to help people think critically, where groups made decisions about what to discuss and how to proceed. In effect, these processes forced people to work through differences for common action. Horton said:

> ... conflict gets the whole group involved. You don't even try to referee between two people. At this point the group takes over the discussion, since the problem being debated is everyone's problem. And when this happens, everyone discovers that the issue is not as simple as the two people have stated it, and a lot of complications surface and get aired (Horton, 1990: 47, cited in Wallace, 2006).

Radical education grows out of caring for people and having respect and trust that people have within themselves the potential, intelligence, courage, and ability to solve their own problems. It is an approach that stands counter to traditional ways of education, one where experts have the answers. As participatory education, it is a 'crucible for empowerment of the poor and powerless' (Horton et al., 1990: xv).

The Highlander Folk School

After completing his graduate education in sociology, Horton went to Denmark to study the Danish Folk High School movement. There he learned about the importance of peer learning in nonformal settings and came back to establish Highlander. Known as 'Schools for Life' (Rahimi, 2002), Folk Schools are places where people find their identity through relationships with others. Horton's hope was that students could learn to take their place intelligently in a changing world while making decisions for themselves and acting on the basis of enlightened judgment.

Highlander's achievements have been significant. In the 1930s they worked with local labour organizations and unions who were organizing and helped advance workers' rights across the entire south of America. In the 1950s and 1960s Highlander created the Citizenship Schools (which later sprung up throughout the country). These were an adult voter education school that taught thousands of African Americans and others from culturally diverse backgrounds how to read, in preparation to vote. In the 1970s and 1980s the Appalachian Self-Education Program (ASEP) modelled on the Citizenship School, worked with the rural poor in the Appalachian region on a range of environmental issues (anti-strip mining, fighting pollution and toxic dumping), as well as worker health and safety struggles. For its role in providing education on behalf of human rights, in 1982 Highlander was nominated for a Nobel Peace Prize (Rahimi, 2002).

Lesser known, is that Highlander did not want people to learn just about their political and economic problems, but to cherish their culture, art, and music. Horton's first wife, Zilphia, said, 'Music is the language of and to life. Songs of merit give people dignity and pride' (Folk Alliance International, 2012). The evening gatherings at Highlander were given over to dancing and singing – songs about people's work, life, hopes, and sorrows. During the 1960s and the civil rights struggle, Highlander became most famous for a protest song penned under its roof – *We Shall Overcome*. The song and how it was used was an ultimate expression of Highlander's values. This one unifying anthem not only said who they were, but musically expressed all the hope, determination and spirit of that social movement. It was sung during the famous civil rights marches at the time and is still used today refitted for other people's movements (Folk Alliance International, 2012).

> *We shall overcome, we shall overcome, we shall overcome, some day.*
> (Sung with 'quiet determination'[2])

Committing to the long haul

Myles Horton died in January 1990 at the age of 84. His autobiography published that same year, *The Long Haul,* is named for those people committed to long-term social change work, the so called 'long haul' people (Kohl, 1990: xiv). Horton posits that a long-range goal is one that needs to grow out of loving and caring for people, and a belief in people's capacity to govern themselves. The quality of the process you use to get to a place determines the ends, Horton argued (1990). As such, when building a democratic society, people must act democratically in every way. His reflection stemmed from a lifetime of work where he saw people's capabilities flourish when working on a small-scale issues, and also work on the larger scale such as with the labour, civil rights, and antiwar movements. He said:

> You have to have hope (in people's capabilities), when you work with people and try to help them learn – and not teach them. Then you inspire them by your belief … your belief in people's capabilities is tied in with your belief in a goal that involves people being free and being able to govern themselves (Horton, 1990: 227).

In today's fast-paced, and oftentimes shallow or disposable world, Myles Horton's commitment to the slow, purposeful, and long-lasting work is instructive. What a remarkable legacy he has, as Highlander continues today as the *Highlander Research and Education Centre in Tennessee* (www.highlander center.org) and remains a catalyst for grassroots organizing and movement building.

Endnotes

1. See the of the action research project that led to the formation of the Popular Education Network in south-east Queensland, Australia: Lathouras, A., Westoby. P & Shevellar. L. (2019) 'Reimagining and radicalizing community development practice in south-east Queensland through popular education research', *Community Development Journal,* <doi:10.1093/cdj/bsz008>
2. New words and music adapted from the hymn 'Overcome Some Day' by Charles A. Tindley, by Zilphia Horton, Frank Hamilton, Pete Seeger, and Guy Carawan, 'We Shall Overcome' – dedicated to the writers of The Freedom Movement.

References and key works

Horton, M. and Freire, P. with Bell, B., Gaventa, J. and Peters, J. (eds.) (1990) *We Make the Road by Walking: Conversations on Education and Social Change,* Temple University Press, Philadelphia, PA.

Highlander Research and Education Centre, [website] <www.highlander center.org/> [Accessed 5 March 2019].

Horton, M. (1990) *The Long Haul: An Autobiography,* Doubleday, New York.

Folk Alliance International (2012) [website] *Highlander Research and Education Centre – Folk Alliance International Lifetime Achievement Award 2012,* <www.youtube.com/watch?v=dAUCZH-r3KQ&t=6s> [Accessed 15 May 2019].

Kohl, J. (1990) 'How this book came about', in Horton, M., *The Long Haul,* Doubleday, New York.

Jacobs, D. (2003) *The Myles Horton Reader: Education for Social Change,* The University of Tennessee Press, Knoxville, TN.

Lewis, H.M. (1990) 'Introduction' in Horton, M., *The Long Haul: An Autobiography,* pp. x–xxi, Doubleday, New York.

Rahimi, S. (2002) 'Peace profile: Myles Horton', *Peace Review* 14(3): 343–348.

Wallace, J. (2006) 'The use of a philosopher: Socrates and Myles Horton', in Harvey, I., Lisman, C.D. (eds.), *Beyond the Tower: Concepts and Models for Service-learning in Philosophy,* pp. 69–90, American Association for Higher Education, Grandview, MO.

CHAPTER 22

John Keats: *Negative capability and coming into community*

By Dave Palmer

George Scharf

John Keats 1795–1821

Who was John Keats?

John Keats was born in England in 1795 and is considered amongst the brightest but briefest stars of Romantic poetry. He died prematurely at the age of 25, incredibly just four years after he started publishing his many works, in the end three full volumes. Like many great writers and thinkers, he was not appreciated during his lifetime.

Keats' poetry is famed for its sensuous and emotive imagery. In the words of the great Percy Shelley, his style was magnificent and beautiful, 'more gorgeous in its effects, more voluptuously alive than any poet who had come before him: "loading every rift with ore"'.

He is most known for his beautiful odes that evoke deep and intense emotion through their depiction of nature's gifts: the birds of the heavens, the trees of the forests, and the flowers of the gardens. Today his poems are some of the most popular and most studied in English literature. Among his most famous works are 'Ode on a Grecian Urn', 'Ode to a Nightingale', 'To Autumn', and 'Endymion'.

Another element of Keats' contribution is his collection of letters. Although directly after his death critics regarded this work as mere distraction, they re-emerged in the 20th century to become just as admired and attended to as his poetry. These letters reflect the convention of the day in that he wrote daily to his friends, family, and fellow writers. They are laden with wisdom, insight, humour, and great parody.

Perhaps his most read and well-cited letters are those to his brothers George and Thomas on the 22 December 1817, in which Keats introduced the notion of 'negative capability' (Keats, 1899) to describe a

http://dx.doi.org/10.3362/9781788531245.022

state, a way of being in the world – perhaps even a particular gait – where one positions oneself to be able to deal with the uncertainties, unfamiliar conditions, changeable circumstances, and mysteries of a new environment.

On negative capability

Like many of his insights, Keats reveals more about negative capability through his poems, only quietly mentioning the idea in a letter or two. It seems that what he means is one's capacity to exist in moments that might otherwise be uneasy, perhaps even confusing or unknown. He puts it like this:

> I mean Negative Capability, that is, when a man is capable of being in uncertainties, mysteries, doubts, without any irritable reaching after fact and reason (Keats, 1899: 277).

Against the wisdom of many poets and philosophers of his time, Keats rallied against an obsession with truth, reason, order, and dogma. In a letter to close friend J.H. Reynolds in February, 1818, he made clear his disdain for writing that seeks to influence and convince the reader of a particular moral or intellectual position:

> We hate poetry that has a palpable design upon us—and if we do not agree, seems to put its hand in its breeches pocket. Poetry should be great & unobtrusive, a thing which enters into one's soul, and does not startle it or amaze it with itself but with its subject (Keats 1899: 314).

Although referring specifically to the art of poetry, Keats' notion has been since used by philosophers, business intellectuals, and arts practitioners to describe the ability of people to come to know, to perceive, think, and operate without the need to impose presupposition of a predetermined set of intellectual, political, or cultural lenses to a situation. Keats calls us to adopt the gait of one who is receptive to experience and emotion rather than those who search for facts, reason, truth, or a solution to a problem. To use more popular parlance, Keats encouraged an attitude of openness of mind, particularly an openness to affect, emotion, and experience without the need for unambiguous analysis or explanation.

Here it seems that he is offering a counter to a thing we tend to take for granted in our modern lives and much of the community development canon. In particular, he seems to be challenging the dual faith we seem to have in effort and rationality, suggesting that these practices are often counterproductive to being human and attaining wisdom. This approach too often sees us quickly coming to conclusions, seeking definitive analysis, keeping possible new ideas and feelings to a minimum, invoking prior knowledge and conceptual ideas taken from elsewhere, rushing into interventions, seeking to break down problems into bite-size chunks, and resorting to policy clichés (Edmonstone, 2016).

Arguably, in his notion of negative capability, Keats offers us a different way to come into a 'community'. This he says involves us training ourselves to put our ego and self-identity on hold and submit ourselves to the experience of being in a community. Rather than setting out a clear plan, as we are often expected to have, he, almost counter-intuitively, might say that our first gesture when we arrive at new communities is to empty our mind of what we think are certainties. 'The only means of strengthening one's intellect is to make up one's mind about nothing – to let the mind be a thoroughfare for all thoughts. Not a select party' (Keats in Mishra, 2011: 50).

How is this to be achieved? How can we rid our minds of previous thoughts? How will this liberate and make it possible to learn? These are all great questions that, lamentably, Keats did not have the time to elaborate on. However, some of those who write after him provide hints. For example, in applying Keats to the practice of action learning, Edmonstone (2016) uses a number of metaphors to help understand how to adopt a stance of negative capability. The first is the notion of a building a 'container' or space. He describes the practice of momentarily celebrating the state of going to places where we experience not knowing, or being in a state of paradox. The second is the metaphor of a dinner plate. The opposite of negative capacity involves already having a 'full-plate', being an expert with all the necessary knowledge. Emptying the plate makes it possible for new taste sensations to be enjoyed, novel stimuli to be relished, and fresh palates to be savoured.

This attitude of openness of mind involves embracing uncertainty and doubt and treating our mistakes as experience. It asks us to move into uncertain situations whilst practising a state of not-knowing and holding back from conclusions. For community workers, this would mean slowing down, speaking less, listening more often, waiting and humbly standing ready to contemplate, rather than acting.

Here Keats is using the word 'negative' not in the pejorative sense that it so often appears in popular Western organizational theory or social policy. Instead he suggests that our lives (and community work) can be shaped by what we do not possess in knowledge. It perhaps also signals Keats' attempts to counter the Western idea that we fix things by introducing positive energy, resolving challenges by injecting electricity from outside the system. One might suggest that there is some good reason for those involved in community development to share his scepticism of the faith we often have in outside solutions that come as interventions from above and the past successes of clever and determined social planners.

Against the adoption of careful plans, targeted interventions, and precision blueprints, Keats might advocate that community workers adopt the posture of a poet: a certain passivity, a keenness to embrace the mysterious, doubt about the wisdom of intervention, and drop their relentless search for knowledge and certainty. Instead, he calls us to contemplate the beautiful and the mysterious, to seek experience and draw upon intuitive appreciation. Importantly, the peculiarities of a particular locale, the colour of a unique community, the social textures of each set of circumstances, offer us the most striking insights into what might be possible.

As an advocate for creativity Keats reminds those interested in community work that it is the tools of the poet that set us up for our work. If we adopt his insight on negative capability, we will see community as an uncertain place that can give rise to a wide array of experiences, perspectives, and possibilities. We would then say that only when we can stay open-minded as community workers can we find creative solutions with community.

References and key works

Edmonstone, J. (2016) 'Action learning, performativity and negative capability', *Action Learning: Research and Practice* 13(2): 139–147.

Keats, John (1899). *The Complete Poetical Works and Letters of John Keats, Cambridge Edition*, Houghton, Mifflin and Company, Boston, MA, and New York.

Mishra, P. (2011) 'A Deconstructive stylistic reading of Keats' "Ode on a Grecian Urn"', *Language, Linguistics, Literature: The Southeast Asian Journal of English Language Studies* 17(2): 49–58.

CHAPTER 23

George Lakoff: *Don't think of an elephant!*

Mikethelinguist

By Dave Palmer

George Lakoff 1941—

Who is George Lakoff?

George Lakoff was born in the USA and is a cognitive linguist, philosopher, political consultant, and 'activist'. Since 1972 he has taught at the University of California at Berkeley. He has also been an academic at Harvard and the University of Michigan and is now Richard and Rhoda Goldman Distinguished Professor of Cognitive Science and Linguistics at Berkley. Since the 1980s he has studied political institutions, campaigns, and the way language and 'framing' are used to convince the public to support particular political agendas. He has also acted as a consultant for a range of prominent Democratic figures in US politics, advising them on how to combat powerful and well-resourced Republican interests who invest heavily in polling how the public responds to messaging and loaded language. From 2003 to 2008 Lakoff worked with the progressive think tank the Rockridge Institute, carrying out research to help liberal candidates re-frame their message using political metaphors.

Speaking in pictures

In the 1970s Lakoff started researching the way language is used figuratively, and challenging the idea that metaphors – or figures of speech that describe an object or action in a way that isn't literally true, but helps explain an idea – are mere ornamental devices in language. Instead he used his background as a cognitive linguist to show how important metaphor is in our processing of complex ideas. He argued that metaphors are embedded deeply in our

http://dx.doi.org/10.3362/9781788531245.023

minds in the form of 'frames', hence giving the brain a powerful way to process ideas and abstract concepts.

His ideas follow the logic that: 1) In order for our mind to process ideas they must first take the form of pictures or images. In other words we need to 'see' ideas before they can be understood; 2) Language and facts on their own are not necessarily helpful in achieving this; 3) Indeed often we find that concepts and 'data' are irrelevant or not cognitively digested until they are turned into images; 4) There are a number of ways of processing ideas including using narrative (where the mind can imagine the story through images), figurative language, poetry, and metaphor; 5) This happens because a metaphor allows us to associate the abstract idea with something we know from elsewhere.

For example, we often talk about a community as if it were a body. Our community development practice should have heart, strength, and result in a breath of fresh air, combating drug, suicide, or crime pandemics. At other times we use building metaphors, talking about healthy communities standing on a solid foundation, doing the groundwork before projects, setting up structures of support, and finding concrete solutions that are underpinned by local people who act as architects of their own destiny.

In everyday practice and experiences inside communities we rely heavily upon metaphors. People routinely talk about development as involving people in a shared journey. In this way, the metaphor of pilgrimage is evoked. Often, we talk about community work as a means of countering 'society's ills', 'helping make communities healthy', 'building from the ground up' and creating 'grass roots' movements. Here medical and biological terms are being invoked. It is also common to use war metaphors. We 'fight for the community', 'confront the enemy within', 'attack social problems head on', or talk about our 'battles' with various groups. Not only do these metaphors create a set of pictures that help us understand in particular ways, they also structure how we act. For example, powerful in war and sport metaphors is the strong presupposition that we 'win' or 'lose' by taking on an oppositional approach or build a strategy that is adversarial. According to Lakoff this is not simply being pedantic. Rather, metaphors shape the way we think and act in deep ways offering us 'mental structures that shape the way we see the world'.

Importantly for Lakoff, these frames are so powerful, so embedded within our cognitive processes and life histories, that data, facts or information that is grounded in solid evidence are often rejected by us if they do not match the frames we use. In other words, he challenges the very modernist assumption that humans are principally rational beings who respond when a logical argument is put to us. Indeed, Lakoff says that when confronted with a rational argument that is inconsistent with our framing the brain mostly responds by casting aside the facts. We need look no further, says Lakoff, than the present global fascination with political figures who routinely take a position in stark discord with the scientific evidence.

Equally, says Lakoff (Lakoff and Johnson 1980: 4), it is possible to reconfigure our relationships through 'reframing' the metaphors we use. Take for example an exchange that draws upon the language of war so that the discussion includes phrases like 'their claims are indefensible', 'the criticism is right on target', and the need to 'demolish the argument'. Imagine if these war frames were replaced with softer metaphors so that people talked about 'setting sail together on a new journey', 'creating community harmony', 'seeking pearls of wisdom from the community', 'encouraging ideas to blossom', and 'building fruitful engagement'; thus drawing on the language of travel, music, jewellery, botany, agriculture, and marriage.

In the mid-1990s Lakoff began to explore how this might work in relation to politics and the way ideas influence our voting behaviour. In his 1996 book, *Moral Politics*, he put forward the view that people unconsciously relate to political ideologies and the 'messaging' of political interest groups, through metaphors of the family. He posited that there are at least two mega metaphors that all of us know and respond to. The first he called the frame of the strict father figure. The second he called the frame of the nurturing parent. Conservative interests, he suggests, are more drawn to the frame of the strict father figure, the directive leader who protects, provides safety, lays down definitive rules and sees to it that his family is raised within a strict moral order. Liberal or progressive interests, he suggests, are more drawn to the frame of the nurturing parent, who also protects and provides safety, but instead approaches change through careful and gentle instruction, care, considerable flexibility, and with joy and compassion.

Most of us he says have enough experience of these two parental frames to result in the synapses of our brains (what some call our brain wiring) recognizing both strict father figure and nurturant parent metaphors when they are offered to us. In other words, because of our previous experiences most of us are susceptible to having either frame 'activated', depending on the language, stories, and metaphors that are presented to us by public figures or their marketing minders.

Perhaps the most useful element in his science of metaphor is that people are most likely to be convinced of the merits of a progressive agenda if individual issues or policy ideas are tied together by the larger frame of the nurturant parent. Lakoff observed that if we do not understand this then we risk constantly responding to the central messages of the conservatives who have invested considerably in creating language and political messaging that targets the strict father figure frames that are so powerfully entrenched in our minds and stories.

In arguing against the position of conservatives we can run the risk of supporting their message. This, says Lakoff, is because in order to argue against something we need to start with the message itself, accepting or setting out our counter position using the framing that we stand against. As he puts it 'when we negate a frame, we evoke the frame'. Using the powerful account of President Richard Nixon, Lakoff reminds us that when Nixon addressed the country after the Watergate affairs had become public he said, 'I am not a crook'; he thus associated his image with that of a crook so that people only thought of the word 'crook'. In this way, Nixon tried to counter the claims of Democrats by framing himself in terms of crookedness. It mattered not that he was denying his wrongdoing, it was that he framed this in terms already framed by his opposition.

Importantly for Lakoff the solution to challenging the power of the popularity of conservative policy solutions is not in speaking to the conservative audience, or challenging them by using 'education', reason, or countering with facts. Rather it is in 'reframing' or changing the metaphors we use. In other words, when confronted by those who speak to the strict father figure 'story' we should reconfigure our response drawing the audience to their experience of the nurturant parent metaphors.

In making these observations Lakoff offers much to community development practitioners who deal daily with the stories of community, the stories of government, and the framing of debates and policy. In considerable measure, the art of community development involves framing. Too often the communities with whom we work have had the core frames that relate to their lives set out by others. Many have been framed as dysfunctional, disadvantaged, troubled, or poverty stricken. The metaphors used frequently depend on strict father frames that set out an argument for hard intervention by strong and capable outsiders. These call for heavy-handed solutions often using criminalizing, medicalizing, and militaristic metaphors to legitimize the 'help' of others. These frames can be very hard to counter and are often very seductive. On the other hand, most of us respond to the language of the nurturant parental with its call to care, sensitivity, growth, and wisdom. Lakoff's ideas may go some distance to both helping us understand strict policy frames that impose solutions and allowing us to reframe them towards more nurturant and collegial responses.

References and key works

Lakoff, G. and Johnson, M. (1980) *Metaphors We Live By*, University of Chicago Press, Chicago, IL.

Lakoff, G. (1996) *Moral Politics: How Liberals and Conservatives Think.* University of Chicago Press, Chicago, IL.

Lakoff, G. (2005) *Don't Think of an Elephant: Know Your Values and Frame the Debate*, Scribe, Carlton North, Melbourne, Australia.

Lakoff, G. (2006) *Whose Freedom?: The Battle over America's Most Important Idea* Farrar, Straus and Giroux, California, CA.

Lakoff, G. (2016) 'How to Help Trump' [website] https://georgelakoff.com/2016/12/15/how-to-help-trump/[Accessed 1 September 2019].

CHAPTER 24

Rosa Luxemburg: *Are you willing to go to prison?*

By Peter Westoby

Rosa Luxemburg 1871–1919

Luxemburg and 'international' capitalism

In early 2016, visiting Berlin, I had meetings with the Africa desk staff of the Rosa Luxemburg Foundation. I'd been doing action and solidarity-related research in Uganda for several years and the Foundation was funding some of the activist work of the Indigenous NGO, the National Association of Professional Environmentalists (NAPE). In Berlin, sitting under the shadows of Red Rosa's (which she is sometimes called) legacy, I was attuned to the links of her thinking and the work I was observing and learning about. NAPE's community educators are working across Uganda using **Freire's** popular education approach to support communities to organize. The education and organizing work is *against resource extraction companies* in cahoots with local elites doing mining activity, petroleum exploration, palm oil plantation expansion, and more (see Westoby & Lyons, 2016). This resource extraction work is resulting in significant human displacement.

Reading Luxemburg's oeuvre now for this reflection, I am reminded of the people I've sat with in Uganda. They were often trying to connect the dots of their lived experience (displacement, confusion, rage) and the activities of these companies, and their government.

Luxemburg astutely recognized that capitalism's ongoing endurance would be sustained through its *imperial international* dimension. She is internationally known for her theory of imperialism. Capitalism would either create new 'needs' or desires within 'local' populations or move into 'new' non-capitalist territories to create new markets. She was spot on, and there, in 2014–2016, I was watching it unfold in Uganda. Most of these communities lived off the commons and

http://dx.doi.org/10.3362/9781788531245.024

practised some kind of non-capitalist commoning (see **Esteva** and **E.F. Schumacher**). Yet, international capitalism's extractivist practices had arrived. David Harvey, one of the key interpreters of Marx today, has made a case for 'Luxemburg's grasp of the connections between ecology, class and empire' (Evans, 2015: 217).

Are you willing to go to prison?

I also listened to those Ugandan subsistence farmers who'd lost their land, tell their stories of going to prison, fighting what was happening in their communities. Reminded that Rosa Luxemburg went to jail three times in her life – and on release from her third term, was murdered by so-called comrades, with her body being thrown into a canal – I am also reminded of the tradition of a willingness to go to prison in the struggle for justice. Reading and reflecting on her life, and particularly the activist traditions of community development work, I have pondered how important it is to be willing to go to prison as part of the struggle. Hence, this is my chosen gem of a wisdom. Rosa, perhaps like Gandhi, saw it as an inevitability. She was not afraid of it and wrote what were to become her inspiring *Prison Letters* (see Luxemburg, *Complete Works: Letters*, forthcoming). Not overwhelmed by these prison experiences, she writes of her companion, a bird, that would visit daily, and overflowed with gratefulness for life. Holding prison as a reality and demonstrating gratefulness seem like profound practices.

Who was Rosa?

Constantly exhausted, yet invigorated by living her deep calling, Rosa Luxemburg paid the ultimate price. Murdered at the age of 47 by fellow socialists who saw her as too radical, she lived a very full life. Her death was precipitated mainly by her attacking the German socialists in parliament who voted for World War I – that is, nationalism trumped international socialism and solidarity of the workers.

Born in Poland in 1881, she became a leading protagonist within Germany's social democratic party, known as the SPD. Advocating for non-parliamentary activist work she was often at odds with those leaders within the SPD who believed capitalism could be reformed from within parliament – that is, whose aim was to gain more votes, more seats in parliament. She is famous for two key questions: 'socialism or barbarism?' and 'reform or revolution?' She wanted revolution, not parliamentary evolution.

There has been an enduring intrigue about her work for scholars, but often it has been linked more to her life as a female trailblazer challenging the patriarchy of the SPD. As Bill Blackwater suggests, her thought has been overlooked by 'the compelling narrative of her life-story', particularly as a woman (Blackwater, 2015:72). Her thought has often been marginalized – by the centre-left for being too revolutionary, and by the Soviet authorities for critiquing Lenin. Yet now, with the ongoing crisis of financial capitalism and social-ecological dangers, her work is experiencing a resurgence. You could say that the barbaric nature of contemporary financial hyper-capitalism is now being 'seen' in its full 'splendour'.

In 1915, Rosa and some comrades formed the Spartacus League in opposition to the SPD, and this League eventually became the German communist party. With the League advocating a 1919 uprising – she was a strong believer in the mass strike – Rosa was arrested, beaten, and shot dead in custody.

Ideals, analysis, yet not an ideologue

Rosa had a deep integrity. She believed deeply in international socialism, and 'the international' was central to her ideals and analysis. Her infamous *Junius Pamphlet* of 1916 raged against the capitalist 'orgy of chaos'. Recognizing that capitalism is intricately connected to imperial expansion – as explained above – she saw nationalism as a deep threat to the global project of international socialism.

At the same time, she is celebrated within circles of Marxism for taking on Berstein, who argued for an evolutionarily rather than revolutionary praxis for change. Luxemburg never believed capitalism was redeemable and argued that it needed to be cleared out at its roots. In a sense, she was a 'true believer' – always scary to the establishment.

Yet, her beliefs did not so much come from an abstract cognitive theorizing, but from ongoing close observation of the phenomenon of capitalism, and particularly seeing its impact on the workers/poor. For example, although a strong theorist, she says, 'If sophisticated theory purposes to make a clever dissection of it, it will not perceive the phenomenon in its living essence … but kill it altogether' (Evans, 2015: p75). In a sense, then, her theorizing was constantly linked to the observing phenomenon, and to thinking, much as **Arendt** suggests. Having read much of her work and about her life, I often ponder her love of nature and observational attitudes – her original aspiration was to become a botanist or zoologist – and wonder if this love is what really equipped her to be such a potent theorist. In the same way, like Leonard Cohen's admonishment to avoid slogans, Luxemburg argues that, '[t]he secret is to live the subject-matter in one's heart. Then one finds words that are fresh, rather than the old familiar phrases' (Evans, 2015:59).

A socialist imaginary

Freire argues that our imaginations have shrunk, and one of the consequences of this is not being able to imagine anything beyond capitalism. And while history suggests Luxemburg is both right (capitalism does appear to be barbaric) and wrong (revolutionary socialism has been somewhat discounted), perhaps she can again awaken our imagination to the possibilities of socialism. Advocating uniquely for *both* democracy *and* socialism, her work is still well placed to disrupt the taken-for-granted concession that 'there is no alternative' to capitalism. Clearly, the barbaric ecological (extinction) and social (inequalities, displacement) consequences indicate that disruptive change to the current capitalist economic and liberal political order is a necessity.

Well-known evolutionally oriented contemporary thinkers such as Thomas Piketty (2014), or Erik Olin Wright (2010) prod and probe into new territory about the crises of capitalism and the possibilities of socialism. Wright in particular examines the history of different theories of social change leading to the possibilities of socialism, naming them as 'ruptural, interstitial and symbiotic' (Wright, 2010) but makes the key point that we must hold onto an emancipatory utopia – and his is un-apologetically democratic socialism. Luxemburg would sit clearly in the ruptural camp, demanding a revolutionary transformation from the capitalist order. She saw clearly enough to be disappointed with what she saw unfolding in Russia under Lenin, yet she truly hoped for huge change in the post-World War I confusion.

Focusing on the contradictions of consumption and credit

At the heart of her critique of Marx and others of her time was their focus on production rather than consumption as the key driver of expansionist capitalism. Re-orienting her Marxist analysis towards consumption, she recognized that capitalism could keep expanding only if it created new markets of consumers – outlined in her key works *The Accumulation of Capital* and her posthumously published *The Accumulation of Capital: An Anti-Critique*. The main source of this expansion would be foreign countries (such as the Uganda story at the beginning) or less-developed places 'at home' (e.g. integrating new groups into consumption habits). However, she advocated that this expansion would eventually hit a limit – capitalism could not expand indefinitely, particularly on a finite planet. Hence, she saw hope that capitalism would eventually collapse under this profound contradiction. Notwithstanding capitalism's potential to support expansion and extraction to other planets, we are probably at a historical moment where the contradictions are becoming clearer.

Credit, another key element of her thesis – understood more clearly in this era of financialization of the economy – is yet another source of expanding consumption (Blackwater, 2015: 82ff). Yet even this source of growth is starting to become problematic as the 2008 financial crisis showed the true limits of an economic bubble created by credit growth and financialization as opposed to the 'real economy'.

In conclusion, I'd suggest that community development practitioners can foreground this Luxemburg focus on consumption and credit, and create spaces of dialogue that enable people to reverse the consumption and credit-use habits that sustain expansive imperial capitalism. Refusing to 'be what we've become' – hyper-consumers – resistance insists in putting our energies back into reweaving the social fabric of community, while re-shaping how we consume and accumulate wealth, with recognition that such resistance cannot be achieved alone. Community has a significant role in supporting people in conversations about an art of living that affirms contestation and flourishing.

References

Blackwater, B. (2015) 'Rediscovering Rosa Luxemburg', *Renewal* 23(3): 71–85.

Evans, K. 2015. *Red Rosa: A Graphic Biography of Rosa Luxemburg,* Verso Press, New York.

Luxemburg, R. (1916) *The Junius Pamphlet.*

Luxemburg, R. (1963) *The Accumulation of Capital,* Routledge, London.

Luxemburg, R. (1972) *The Accumulation of Capital - An Anti-Critique,* Monthly Review Press, New York.

Luxemburg, R. (Forthcoming). *Complete Works: Letters,* Verso Press, London.

Piketty, T. (2014) *Capital in the Twenty-First Century,* The Belknap Press of Harvard University Press, Cambridge, MA.

Westoby, P. & Lyons, K. (2016) '"We would rather die in jail fighting for land, than die of hunger": A Ugandan case study examining the ambiguous deployment of corporate-led community development in the green economy', *Community Development Journal* 51(1): 60–76.
Wright, E. O. (2010) *Envisioning Real Utopia,* London: Verso Press.

CHAPTER 25

Wangari Maathai: *Plant trees and protect genuine democracy*

By Athena Lathouras

António Cruz, Agência Brasil

Wangari Maathai 1940–2011

Wangari Maathai was a Kenyan environment and democracy activist, most well-known for her visionary work through the Green Belt Movement. In 2004 she was the first African woman to receive a Nobel Peace Prize which, significantly, resulted in environmental issues being propelled into the global limelight (Scott, 2013).

'I was born to an old world that was passing away'

In her 2006 memoir, *Unbowed,* Maathai describes the changing context that shaped her thinking and activism. She was born to subsistence farmers in 1940 in the small village of Ihithe in the central highlands of what was then British Kenya. During her childhood the land around Ihithe was still lush, green, and fertile; rain fell regularly and reliably. To her community, Mount Kenya was a sacred place. They believed everything good came from the mountain including abundant rains, rivers, and clean drinking water, and they wanted for nothing (Maathai, 2006b: 5).

She laments that those beliefs and associated traditions have virtually died away, recounting her country's history of British colonization (2006b: 7–10), the forcible relocation of local people, and their subsequent trauma from displacement. Echoing the story of Achebe's famous novel *Things Fall Apart,* the worldviews of European Christian missionaries had their influence and within two generations many people had lost respect for their own beliefs and traditions. Traders and administrators followed the missionaries and introduced new methods for exploiting rich natural resources through logging, clear

http://dx.doi.org/10.3362/9781788531245.025

cutting native forests, establishing plantations of imported trees, hunting wildlife, and undertaking expansive commercial agriculture. Maathai explains that their 'hallowed landscapes' (2006b: 6) lost their sacredness and were exploited as local people became desensitized to destruction, accepting it as a sign of progress.

Acknowledging the unalterable change that ensued with colonization and development, she highlights her own privilege associated with her opportunity for a Westernised education introduced by the colonial administration. In early adulthood, subsequent membership in civic organizations exposed her to environmental issues and those faced by women. She met rural women who lacked firewood, clean drinking water, balanced diets, shelter, and income. She learned of the causes of environmental degradation – deforestation, devegetation, unsustainable agriculture, and soil loss – and how they contribute to malnourishment and poverty. These were the 'tributary of knowledge' (2006b: 123) that influenced the direction of her activism.

The Green Belt Movement - 'Foresters without diplomas'

Responding to the inextricable link between the health of the land and health of the people, in 1977 when Kenya hosted the United Nations Conference on Desertification in Nairobi the Green Belt Movement (GBM) was launched as a non-government organization focussing on environmental conservation and development (Maathai, 2006b). The GBM empowers communities, particularly women, to conserve the environment and restore degraded watersheds of catchments to improve the livelihoods of local communities. Their integrated approach supports and diversifies sustainable sources of income from tree planting activities as well as promoting alternative and profitable use of the forest, but with a clear view of the forest as a 'commons'. Maathai refers to GBM members as 'foresters without diplomas' (2006a: 130), signalling that ordinary people can develop skills associated with food security and water harvesting at the household level, as well as skills for sustainable farming methods.

An early GBM goal was to plant a tree for every person in Kenya – 15 million people. They created tree planting communities, sourced funds from a range of donors, and set up seedling nursery sites. They used the slogan 'One person, one tree' (2006b: 134). Since 1977, over 51 million trees have been planted in Kenya, creating green belts on public and private land (www.greenbeltmovement.org). They increased their impact by structuring their work beyond the local level, replicating the approach across Africa through the Pan-African Green Belt Network (2006a: 103). As Maathai's reputation grew, she was invited to speak at conferences and summits across the globe, and other countries took up the GBM model, or adapted it to suit their local contexts.

Endogenous-led community development

The philosophy of the GBM is to develop people's understanding of the link between good governance and conservation – a critical consciousness about how an environment that is well managed helps to sustain a good quality of life. Maathai (2005: 198) states that initially the work was difficult because historically people have been persuaded to believe that because they are poor, they lack not only capital but also the knowledge and skills to address the challenges they face. They were unaware that a degraded environment leads to a scramble for scarce resources, or of the injustices flowing from international economic arrangements. Moreover, people were conditioned to think that solutions must come from outside. Significantly, her approach was endogenous led, that is, originating from within the community itself. Maathai passionately argues 'for African communities to discover the value of embracing their *own* destiny and determining their own *futures,* rather than solely and passively relying on outside forces' (Maathai, 2009: 22, her emphasis).

Consequently, the GBM evolved from a tree-planting programme to community education programmes, much like the radical education work of Paulo **Freire** and Myles **Horton**. People sought to identify the root causes of poverty and environmental degradation and take ownership of the problems and solve them. She states:

> They realize their hidden potential and are empowered to overcome inertia and take action. They come to realize that they are the primary custodians and beneficiaries of the environment that sustains them (Maathai 2005: 198).

The GBM critical consciousness-raising process eventually mobilized citizens to challenge widespread abuses of power, corruption, and environmental mismanagement (Maathai, 2005). The tree became a symbol for the democratic struggle in Kenya, where trees of peace were planted to demand the release of prisoners of conscience and a peaceful transition to democracy.

Practicing good governance using the three-legged stool metaphor

In 2002, the courage, resilience, patience, and commitment of GBM members, other civil society organizations, and the Kenyan public culminated in Kenya's peaceful transition to a democratic government and a more stable society. Maathai directly appealed to development practitioners and the part they play in the good governance of a democracy. She warned that the term 'democracy' (2009: 55) can just become a bromide during times of voting in general elections, as opposed to the political systems, institutions of the state, and cultural values that encourage basic freedoms, human rights, and individual and collective well-being. Genuine democratic values and processes always need protecting and maintaining, she argued (Maathai, 2009: 56).

Maathai's wisdom can be seen as applicable to all contemporary democracies when she names a number of crucial features for a genuine democracy including: an informed and engaged citizenry; an effective and truly representative parliament; an independent judiciary; and an independent fourth estate (Maathai, 2009: 56). Community development practitioners have a significant role to play in working to create an informed and engaged citizenry when working to create democratic spaces with groups and when forming democratic community organizations.

To explain her work and philosophy she uses the metaphor of a traditional African stool, comprised of a seat with three legs. These represent three pillars for a just and stable society. The first leg represents *democratic space*, where rights – human, women's, children's, environmental – are respected. The second leg symbolizes *sustainable and accountable management of natural resources* for people living today, especially those at the margins of society, and for future generations. The third leg stands for '*cultures of peace*' (Maathai, 2009: 56, my emphasis), and takes the form of fairness, respect, compassion, forgiveness, recompense, and justice.

She argues that 'it is crucial to approach development from this perspective, in which an environment is created for citizens to engage productively' (2009: 58). When citizens feel secure and where these three legs are in place, they can be educated, productive, and creative. In these types of situations, the spirit of citizenry not only welcomes development, but drives it itself, because individually and collectively people feel they have an opportunity to contribute; for the benefit of the many, not just the few.

Sustain yourself and stay committed to justice work

It is now widely accepted that climate justice is the defining issue and challenge for the 21st century. We also know that choosing to engage in environment justice and its associated democracy justice work is not easy. Maathai writes of her own experiences of personal and professional vilification and abuse, as well as periods of imprisonment because of her efforts (Maathai, 2006b: 184-205). She acknowledges, 'There are moments when you will become discouraged and disheartened ... and committing yourself to be of service can be emotionally and spiritually taxing' (Maathai, 2009: 188). It seems crucial that we mitigate our own fatigue, and thus inertia.

Be that as it may, in her last book published before her death, she presses us to take up the challenge for justice work (Maathai, 2010: 24). She sets out spiritual values for healing ourselves and the world, insisting that addressing the ecological crisis requires both a physical response – to transition to new sustainable practices – and, perhaps harking back to her childhood experience where landscapes were considered 'hallowed', she also calls for a spiritual response – to develop a new level of consciousness based on spiritual values. Much like Mary **Graham,** she calls for us 'to be custodians of the planet and do what's right for the earth, and in the process, for ourselves' (Maathai, 2010: 24-25).

We can learn from Maathai, too, a lesson about how to sustain ourselves for the long haul of social justice work. She says that the core lesson she has learned over the many years of activism is 'to be patient, persistent and committed ... like a seedling, with sun, good soil, and abundant rain, the roots of our future will bury themselves in the ground and a canopy of hope will reach into the sky' (Maathai, 2006b: 289).

References and further reading

Achebe, C. (2002) *Things Fall Apart,* Penguin Books Ltd, London.

Maathai, W. (2005) 'Nobel Peace Prize Speech: Nobel Lecture, Oslo, 10 December 2004', *Meridians* 6(1): 195–201.

Maathai, W. (2006a) *The Green Belt Movement: Sharing the Approach and the Experience.* Lantern Books, New York.

Maathai, W. (2006b) *Unbowed: One Woman's Story,* Arrow Books, London.

Maathai, W. (2009) *The Challenge for Africa,* Random House, New York.

Maathai, W. (2010) *Replenishing the Earth: Spiritual Values for Healing Ourselves and the World,* Doubleday, New York.

Rakoczy, S. (2013) 'Wangari Maathai: Discerning a call to environmental justice', *Journal of Theology for Southern Africa* 145: 75–91, March 2013.

Scott, K. (2013) 'Peace profile: Wangari Maathai and the Green Belt Movement', *Peace Review: A Journal of Social Justice* 25(2): 299–306.

The Green Belt Movement, [website] www.greenbeltmovement.org [Accessed 5 November 2019].

CHAPTER 26

Joanna Macy: *Life comes from reconnecting*

By Peter Westoby

Adam Shemper

Joanna Macy 1929—

Introduction

In preparing to write this reflection, I re-read Joanna Macy's memoir *Widening Circles* (2000) for the third time in my life, and then I quickly dipped into the published version of her doctorate, *Dharma and Development* (1983). Also before me are the two books of hers that have been prized resources for many years – *Coming Back to Life: Practices to Reconnect Our Lives, Our World* (1998), and *Despair and Personal Power in the Nuclear Age* (1983). How does one synthesize such wisdom down to even several, let alone one 'key gem of a wisdom'? I await insight, practising her practices, trying to settle into seeing the patterns and relationships within her work, not the parts. What is it that connects all her work? Clearly, it is this imperative that 'life comes from reconnecting' in every sense of the words, and it's this very easily written 'every sense' that needs to be explored.

An agile life

Macy, a US citizen, is well known as an environmental activist, author, scholar of Buddhism, general systems theory, and deep ecology (she forged a deep friendship with the Australian deep ecologist, John Seed, of the International Forest Alliance). Her journey from home took her, with her then alive partner, to live in India, Sri Lanka, Tunisia, and Nigeria.

Returning to the USA, she found her way into integrating spirituality with social action, along with experimenting in intentional community (her family lived in a cooperatively run household for a few years).

http://dx.doi.org/10.3362/9781788531245.026

In this journey, she has remained very alive, in the sense of maintaining an agility to keep responding to invitations, new learning, and opportunity. Being open to the world, in that way the Buddhist Dharma invites, seems to have led organically to spaces of deep learning. That openness and learning took her illegally to Tibet, to the communities affected by Chernobyl, to protests against nuclear armament, and many other places.

In the late 2000s I spent six days in a workshop at the Northern Rivers area of NSW, Australia, designed on Macy's ideas. Mornings were spent in meditative silence, afternoons in activist-oriented reflection, finally returning to evenings of silence. The Dharma of spirituality and social action were connected, enabling each of the participants to find their way into reconnection. The thinking, feeling, sensing, and intuition functions were all legitimated and activated and I remember leaving the space ready to engage 'the world' in my own unique Peter way – living from 'the inside out' as I have come to imagine it (not the outside in, meeting the outside expectations of others, ideology, or religion). I felt like I had reconnected with my body, my emotions, and my vision for a sustainable world.

An ethic – to choose life

At the heart of Macy's contribution is the insistence that at this historical moment, people must make a conscious choice *for life*. By this, she means for a life-sustaining future that is attuned to the planet, which also resonates with Arturo Escobar's more recent reflections on 'futures that have a future' (Escobar, 2018: 9). As she and Molly Brown say, 'we can meet our needs without destroying our life-support system' (Macy & Brown, 1998: 16). Linking this simple ethical choice with reflections on living systems theory, Buddhist understandings of life, deep ecology, and psychology, Macy provides a holistic understanding of what's needed.

A story: The great turning

Part of what is needed is a 'story'. Linking to our reflections on **Lakoff's** work (in this volume), the story offered, as metaphor or a picture is 'the great turning'. Linked to the large social movements unfolding around the world – what post-development thinker Escobar refers to as 'transitions' (2015) – the great turning is indicative of the generative choices of countless individuals, groups, and movements that are working *for life*. In turn, this discourse of transitions represents a significant shift away from the language of 'crisis'. Grounding 'the great turning' in everyday practice, Macy also provides a particularly useful three-fold framework enabling practitioners to 'see' the landscape of strategic activity.

The first part of the framework involves seeing the work of people who are doing 'analysis of structural causes and creating of alternative institutions' (Macy & Brown, 1998: 19). This requires understanding the dynamics of the current military-industrial growth system. Macy and Brown pose questions such as, 'What are the tacit agreements that create obscene wealth for a few, while progressively impoverishing the rest of humanity?' and 'What interlocking causes indenture us to an insatiable economy that uses our larger body, Earth, as supply house and sewer?' (ibid).

The second element calls for a 'change to hearts and minds' (1998: 21). This requires careful and honest dialogue with ourselves and with other people around the concern of earth care. Dialogue should be gentle, so as to draw people in, enabling them to overcome fear, apathy, selfishness, and ignorance. For Macy and Brown, such dialogue is aimed at shifting 'perceptions of reality, both cognitively and spiritually' (ibid).

Macy and Brown's third strategy is that of 'holding actions' in which some people mobilize around the issue of protecting environmental sites that others are still trying to utilize in unsustainable ways (1998: 17). This strategy requires still more radical action, which will probably mean confrontation.

A warning – apatheia – numbing

One of the ever-present ideas in Macy's work is that people can also numb themselves into a state of despair. She calls this state *apatheia,* a Greek word that quite literally means 'non-suffering'. Macy's suggestion is that to participate in 'the great turning' requires a 'response-ability', that is, an ability or capacity to act when suffering is experienced or seen. And of course, for anyone with eyes open there is plenty of suffering to see.

However, if suffering is not felt, if pain is blocked, there is little capacity to respond. In lieu of this, Macy makes the case that many people cope with their despair about the 'futures without a future' (those Escobar words) through disconnecting from their bodies, their grief and rage, and their ability to pause and take stock of the pain. The danger, then, is either the *apatheia* of non-responsiveness, or a kind of obsessive non-reflective, or disembodied form of activism. People in a state of non-suffering numb themselves with various forms of addiction. Or people in pain, without reflection, run head-long into wilful non-strategic activism.

A method – reconnecting

In response to her observations about this kind of numbing, or state of non-suffering, Macy has co-created 'practices to reconnect our lives, our world' (Macy & Brown, 1998). For her, such practices enable people to transform the *apatheia* into energies on behalf of life. Representative of what I have started to call 'shadow traditions' of practice – Macy's work draws on emotion, imagination, ritual, the symbolic, and the aesthetic. These are shadow in the sense that they have been repressed in a dominant scientific, materialist, rationalist, and analytical shaping of much community development thinking and practice. Such shadow traditions include the depth psychology of Jung/Hillman, phenomenology (disrupting the dominance of Cartesian deadening analytic philosophy), the resurgence of indigenous epistemology and practices, and Joanna Macy's deep ecology.

Developed over the past thirty-plus years with colleagues around the world, hundreds of thousands of people have participated in what was initially called 'despair and empowerment' work, but now are known as 'Practices to reconnect our lives, our world'. These practices include group workshops and ritual practices, all of which aim to reconnect emotion, passion, ideas, and practice.

In Conclusion

With profound synchronicity, the week I was writing this reflection a woman from Brazil wanted to meet with me and discuss the plight of the Amazon and her activist work there. She started the story telling me of her discovery of Joanna Macy's work at a moment in her life when she needed to reconnect spirit and activism, slowness and strategy, a love of the forest as well as a capacity to 'fight' those intent on destroying it. Now trained in Macy's approach to reconnecting, she is working to support activists around the world to reconnect with the deeper parts of themselves, animated by love, life, and a dream.

References

Escobar, A. (2015) 'Degrowth, postdevelopment, and transitions: a preliminary conversation', *Sustainable Science,* 10: 451–462.

Escobar, A. (2018) *Designs for the Pluriverse: Radical Interdependence, Autonomy, and the Making of Worlds,* Duke University Press, Durham & London.

Macy, J. (2000) *Widening Circles: A Memoir,* New Catalyst Books, Canada.

Macy, J. (1983) *Dharma and Development,* Kumarian Press, West Hartford.

Macy, J. (1983) *Despair and Personal Power in the Nuclear Age,* New Society Publishers, Gabriola Island, BC.

Macy, J. & Brown, M. (1998) *Coming Back to Life: Practices to Reconnect Our Lives, Our World,* New Society Publishers, Gabriola Island, BC.

Photo Credit – Photo of Joanna Macy by Adam Shemper ©

CHAPTER 27

Manfred Max-Neef:
Poverties, not poverty

By Peter Westoby

Manfred Max-Neef 1932–2019

Olga Berrios

Max-Neef's story and 'my language as an economist … was useless'

Emma Kidd in her wonderful book, *First Steps of Seeing: A Path to Living Attentively (*2015), quotes Max-Neef:

> I was standing in the slum. And across from me, another guy was standing in the mud. And well, we looked at one another, and this was a short guy, thin, hungry, with five kids … And I was the economist from Berkeley, having taught in Berkeley and so on. And we were looking at one another, and then suddenly I realized I had nothing coherent to say to that man in those circumstances, that my whole language as an economist, you know, was absolutely useless (Kidd, 2015: 145).

The quote is indicative of Max-Neef's journey, from an economist with Shell, to a Berkeley academic, a practitioner with various UN organizations, and then finally, after winning the 'alternative Nobel Prize' – known as the Right Livelihood Award – he set up CEPAUR (Centre for Alternative Development) in Chile. Max-Neef, along with many colleagues, used this Centre as a base to explore poverty from the ground up. At the heart of the journey was a move away from explanations about poverty, to a living inquiry into the experience of poverties, from which key concepts emerged that *could allow the poor to make sense of their experience.*

Personally, I love his work, and the two books, **Schumacher's** *Small is Beautiful* and **Max-Neef's** *Human-Scale Development*, are the two books I set all students in my community community economics course to read.

http://dx.doi.org/10.3362/9781788531245.027

Needs and satisfiers

One of those key concepts that emerged from a living inquiry into the experiences of poverty is his matrix of needs and satisfiers, whereby Max-Neef and his team, through many years of exploration with communities, identified nine universal needs *common to all,* regardless of culture, financial status, education, and so on. These needs included: subsistence, protection, affection, understanding, participation, creation, idleness, identity, and freedom.

Importantly their team then identified what they called 'satisfiers', which, contrary to the universal needs, are *culturally and contextually specific.* Such satisfiers are ways people's needs are met, and synergistic satisfiers are key ones that meet multiple needs at once (e.g. a democratic trade union meets the needs of understanding, participation, and identity, or breast feeding meets the needs of protection, affection, and identity).

This needs–satisfiers matrix is well-developed in *Human-Scale Development: Conception, Application and Further Reflections* (1991), and includes stories of how communities have then hosted multiple-day methodologies of dialogue and analysis to identity their needs and possible synergistic/satisfiers via the matrix (Max-Neef, 1991: 39). For example, this methodology was picked up by communities in South America and Max-Neef himself notes that:

> We used to arrive in Andean communities to be approached by local leaders with a photocopy of a photocopy of a photocopy, almost unreadable, ready to discuss whether their interpretation was correct and whether their projects satisfied the philosophy of Human-Scale Development. It was moving to witness how such marginal communities adopted the principles and designed local development projects that conventional experts would have been unable to conceive of. Many of those projects have survived and flourished (Smith & Max-Neef, 2011: 176).

Poverties, not poverty, which generate pathologies

Part of the challenge of thinking about needs is how we think about poverty. In the light of this, my chosen gem of a wisdom is Max-Neef's insight that we should be thinking about *poverties, not poverty.* This is a way of decolonizing the idea of poverty as traditionally seen through a purely economic lens. Thinking instead of poverties as powerlessness, Max-Neef suggests we should think about the *many faces of powerlessness* – economic, social, political, emotional, cultural, spiritual, and so forth – also as the face of unmet needs. For example, someone might be stuck economically when they cannot get out of debt, at the mercy of a money-lender charging high interest rates; or they are stuck socially – feeling isolated, or cut off, or they have a mental illness and there is need of a friend or affection to accompany them on their journey towards social connection. Maybe they are stuck culturally in that they don't fit in with the mainstream culture and its norms of behaviour, so they feel excluded, hidden, with no validated identity and stuck on the margins. Or they are stuck politically, seemingly unable to influence or participate in decision-making – it's done behind the closed doors of the powerful, and resources are always allocated elsewhere. The point is that poverty is multi-faceted and best thought of as poverties.

At the same time, Max-Neef also suggests that:

> … most of the social problems we identify today, such as depression, alcoholism, eating disorders, unemployment, racial conflicts and disaffected youths, can be seen as *pathologies* (Kidd, 2015: 151).

Linking to the earlier discussion, this means that:

> If we look carefully, each 'problem' can be traced back to an array of fundamental needs which are not being met. … paying attention to the array of unmet needs of individuals and groups of people makes it possible for us to resolve the problems that we perceive in the world around us at the root of the matter (Kidd, 2015: 151).

Such a framework helps in not focusing on the 'problem' or pathology per se, but working with communities to identify the unmet needs and potential satisfiers.

Self-reliance

As would be clear by now, Max-Neef's *human-scale development* is a methodology for communities to make sense of their own pathologies, needs, and possible satisfiers. Within this community methodology, Max-Neef also argues for community self-reliance. By this, he understood communities, 'in terms of a horizontal interdependence and in no way as an isolationist tendency' (Max-Neef 1991: 58). At a fundamental level it means that communities are capable of 'promoting participation in decision making, social creativity, political self-determination, a fair distribution of wealth and tolerance for the diversity of identities' (ibid). He adds that:

> It is only by generating self-reliance, where people assume a leading role in different domains and spaces, that it is possible to promote development processes with synergetic effects that satisfy fundamental human needs (Max-Neef, 1991: 57–58).

But he then adds something very important, arguing that:

> Self-reliance becomes the turning point in the articulation of human beings with nature and technology, of the personal and social, of the micro with the macro, of autonomy of planning and of civil society and the state (ibid).

This connecting of the idea of self-reliance and articulation is Max-Neef's way of thinking about, and discussing, the often dis-connected domains of:

> human beings, nature and technology; personal and social; micro and macro; and autonomy of civil society and the state. Whereas conventional development paradigms assert the primacy of one over the other, Max-Neef brings them into a coherent interconnected relationship whereby the relationship itself must become a key focus for development processes.

He was particularly interested in the micro-macro articulation, explored further now.

Micro-macro articulation

Community development is often thought to be a locally focused practice. However, a key wisdom of Max-Neef's is that our work needs to be attuned to what he called this *micro-macro articulation* issue. That it, what we do locally – at a micro level – ideally needs to also have a macro impact. This impact could be through a policy change or catalysing a broader social movement. In his delightful book *Outside Looking In: Experiences in Barefoot Economics* (1981) he tells the story of a project, known as ECU-28, set in the Andean region of Ecuador that demonstrates the process of micro-macro articulation.

The methodology of the project was to mobilize a participatory process of *horizontal communication* between villages that rarely had the opportunity to meet together. In coming together these villages created a shared understanding of their problems through building a *regional consciousness.*

In doing this, the project avoided the more orthodox process of peasants from different villages talking to the 'vertical structures' of the state only *as individual villages* – that is, each village making its own representation about its 'village problems'. Instead, through a series of grassroots processes supported by the project, village committees were brought together to formulate a regional analysis of their state of affairs – which they could then take to the relevant state authorities *as a whole.*

Through the process of 'provincial encounters', which consisted of village committees meeting together, learning from one another, and building a shared community analysis, they formed a *regional structure*—a Regional Peasants' Congress. Such a Congress was still rooted in the local (people represented their local villages and reported back to the whole village), yet it created a regional analysis and regional people's power-base (Max-Neef 1992: 25–117).

This story highlights some important processes for building regional structures that enabled the possibility of micro-macro articulation. As a regional structure with a regional consciousness the people had a power-base to tackle more substantive issues than they would have been able to do as an individual village. To do this, the project initiated key practices, including:

- building horizontal relationships between people who have similar experiences, but have not been able to share with one another;
- strengthening these horizontal relationships to the point where people could build more formal structures;
- maintaining clear lines of communication and accountability between the local and the newly forming regional structure;
- nurturing participatory leadership where the emergent leaders remain committed to an ethos of ongoing participation rather than accumulation of power;
- recognizing that while larger structures require some kind of role definition, the key ethos should remain relational rather than role-oriented; and
- spending time on building a strong sense of shared values and vision.

As per this story and identification of key practices, community development as a praxis can be challenged by Max-Neef to consider the micro-macro relationship from the beginning of the process, as part of the design itself.

In conclusion

I almost managed to meet Max-Neef. I was planning a visit to Chile in 2016 as part of a sabbatical journey of reflection, and Max-Neef and I were in email conversation. I was more excited than words on paper can convey. Yet, life intervenes, as if often does when we're making plans, and I was unable to get there. It's one of the great regrets of my engaged scholarly life.

References

Kidd, E. (2015) *First Steps of Seeing: A Path to Living Attentively,* Floris Books, UK.

Max-Neef, M. (1981) *From the Outside Looking In: Experiences in Barefoot Economics,* Dag Hammarskjöld Foundation, Sweden.

Max-Neef, M. (1991) *Human-Scale Development: Conception, Application and Further Reflections,* The Apex Press, New York & London.

Max-Neef, M. (1992) *From the Outside Looking In: Experiences in Barefoot Economics,* Zed Books, London.

Smith, P.B. & Max-Neef, M. (2011). *Economics Unmasked: From Power and Greed to Compassion and Common Good,* Green Books, Totnes, UK.

CHAPTER 28

Chandra Talpade Mohanty: *Pay attention to silence and erasure*

By Dave Palmer

Chandra Talpade Mohanty

Chandra Talpade Mohanty 1955—

On our overreliance upon identity and categorization of community

My early education in youth and community work was influenced heavily by teachers who were strongly committed to a 'radical' tradition where power was understood as a global and imposing force exercised from above upon the powerless. This, we were told, provided us with excellent tools of analysis, particularly for working with groups of young people from poor backgrounds, the blue-collar classes, young women, and those from 'communities of colour'. Many of our discussions were fierce, and often involving competitions on which groups experienced the most 'oppression'. In retrospect, often our debates and some of our plans for work with young people were a little simplistic and misguided ... but education should allow students to test things out and experiment with ideas.

Two of my colleagues seemed not very willing to participate in these debates and not so enamoured with much of this 'radical' way of working. One was a Noongar (Indigenous man from the southwest of Western Australia) and the other a Malaysian-born woman who was raised in a public housing suburb. My Malaysian-born friend frequently remarked that she could rarely recognize in what she read anything 'that resembled what happened in my suburb'. I recall my Noongar friend telling me that 'I keep hearing that I have been oppressed as an Aborigine ... but my family were never poorfella, blackfellas [an Aboriginal English phrase for those with a deep experience of poverty] ... we have always been hard workers, we cleared

http://dx.doi.org/10.3362/9781788531245.028

the bush, built the fences and ran all the shearing contracts.' Their experience in the lectures and tutorials was of being talked about, not being invited to talk to *their* lives. Too often this is what happens to people who are subject to the interventions of community workers.

Who is Chandra Talpade Moharty?

Chandra Talpade Mohanty is an academic, postcolonial writer, and anti-capitalist and anti-racist activist. She was born and raised in Mumbai, India, spending time in Nigeria, London, and the United States, where she now lives. Her early education occurred in India, with postgraduate studies taken in the USA. Like other postcolonial writers such as **Homi Bhabha** and **Trinh T. Minh-ha**, the experience of moving from their home communities to the US gave Mohanty a profound set of insights into how westerners go about constituting and imagining 'Other' communities.

She is perhaps best known for the publication of her 1984 essay, 'Under Western Eyes: Feminist Scholarship and Colonial Discourses', where she offers a critique of Western feminist work, in particular the reliance on categories such as 'Third World woman' and the part this plays in legitimizing the need for Westerners to save those who have been constituted as powerless victims.

In a similar critique as **Bhabha's** she reminds us that the ideas, knowledge construction, and storytelling of the West (the intellectual work) is highly implicated in the history of imperialism, government, theft, and military acquisition of land. She observes:

> Contemporary imperialism is, in a real sense, a hegemonic imperialism, exercising to a maximum degree a rationalized violence taken to a higher level than ever before – through fire and sword, but also through the attempt to control hearts and minds (Mohanty, 1984: 335).

While her critique is specifically directed at Western feminism, Mohanty's work could equally apply to much community work practice, particularly those who describe people with whom we work as somehow powerless, in need of empowerment and outside intervention.

Pay attention to silence and erasure

According to Mohanty (2003: 124) the business of thinking about community, home, belonging, nation, and identity are becoming profoundly complicated. This is particularly so since the unlocking of global borders and the consequent impact on people's lives where relationships have become more complex, connected, multilayered, and interdependent. At the same time, she says, the lives and voices of many have been left neglected with these groups being talked about rather than listened to. This is particularly so for communities (such as those defined as 'Third World women'), who have become the subject of 'experts', policy boffins, the media, and research.

Importantly for Mohanty, the process of the making of 'Third World women' is very similar to the process of making community as 'disadvantaged', 'marginalized', 'at risk' and 'in need'. She points out that in subtle but powerful ways the way we talk, the way we construct, the way we treat people categorized in this way often results in erasure of the identities and lives of those women described as non-Western. This is replaced with one-dimensional ideas about those who are weak, incapable of agency and action, and therefore, silent. Thus she says that when we think of women in 'under-developed' communities we rely on conceptions of: 'an essentially truncated life based on her feminine gender (read: sexually constrained) and being "third world" (read: ignorant, poor, uneducated, tradition-bound, domestic, family-oriented, victimized, etc)' (Mohanty 1984: 337).

This stands in stark contrast to the way Westerners represent, or see themselves, 'as educated, modern, as having control over their own bodies and sexualities, and the freedom to make their own decisions' (Mohanty 1984: 337). This distinction, she says, is driven by a way of thinking that privileges those 'telling the story', those who see themselves as the norm or referent. In other words, she points out that this storytelling about non-Western communities presupposes that the ideal and healthy community is one where men are involved in waged labour, are productive to the global economy, are well educated, have modern health systems available, are empowered, and autonomous.

In relying on such simple binary and oppositional ideas (such as women in contrast to men, the West in contrast to Third World, dysfunctional community in contrast to healthy community) we lose sight of the agency of people and the many and complex situations within which they live. Such simple and reductive formulations make it difficult to see what these 'Other' communities bring to the table. So rather than opening up our knowledge of what is happening in specific communities Mohanty observes that it silences and erases the experience of those we variously classify as 'community', 'third world', 'Indigenous', and 'dysfunctional'.

Radicals are made not born

Mohanty is also suggesting that useful work is grounded in conscious decisions to quietly ally oneself with those who get talked about and acted upon. We ought to assume we do not know and must learn. Central to this is the decision to move to specific places to listen to the specific experiences and ideas, acknowledging that particular people have particular stories, histories, identities, and experiences. To counter the practice of universalizing processes that dehumanize people one needs to be 'contextual, place-based and attentive to the way power works within the structure and culture of our diverse institutional spaces' (Mohanty, 2016: 88). For example, the way Indigenous Australian groups from Central Australia respond to the current approach by government to not provide income security to large numbers of families is very different to the way that citizens in Chile respond to the 2019 raising of Santiago Metro's subway fares. Both groups have been subject to government neglect, economic impoverishment over generations, and the longstanding forces of colonizing practice. The voice and lives of both groups have seen their stories silenced and erased. However, the specific conditions, experiences, histories, and strategies are different.

This approach to becoming an ally demands time, patience, and familiarity with culture, language, and history (considerable commitment). Mohanty is thus clearly making the point that 'radicals are made not born' (Mohanty 2016: 89). To paraphrase her, there is nothing natural or internal to the human condition that guarantees we work with communities in a way that respects their specific circumstances. Rather the practice of respectful recognition is 'forged 'in conjunction with particular communities. This happens over time and only, much like the raw iron-ore that must endure the massive heat of the forge, when we have felt and understood the heat that communities face.

A useful insight from Mohanty in this regard is that we need to step outside of our experiences, institutions, and organisational roles if we are to build these 'radical' relationships. Speaking about her own circumstances Mohanty (2016: 89) sees as central her conscious decision to 'NOT allow the academy to be the only space of struggle for [her]'. This demands that she has one foot planted in a university setting and another outside with the community.

Mohanty's contribution to community work

In setting out the features of a radical ally Mohanty suggests four key features. In my view this directly speaks to those interested in community development with each feature equally applicable to work with community.

The first feature in our practice, she says, ought to include a commitment to question what appears to be normative. She calls this denaturalizing and demystifying power. Here we need to nurture our capacity to imagine how communities are different from how they have been constituted in the media, in policy, and by the 'experts'.

The second feature of a radical practice is to support and help build communities of dissent both in the institutions we inhabit and the communities outside of our experience. She calls this, refusing 'the isolation that neoliberal, commodified cultures thrive on and to actively cultivate mentors, teachers and guides who inspire us (Mohanty, 2016: 90).

The third feature is to seek out and build coalitions between groups who may not 'naturally' appear to be allies. This involves encouraging what **Angela Davis** calls 'unlikely coalitions' to fight against different forms of injustice. Like the long-standing radical traditions in community development this demands we are constantly on the look out to bring otherwise distant communities together to share their stories, make friendships, and build coalitions that can take action together.

The fourth feature involves a warning against assuming our work is new and that we have 'discovered' the art of work with community. As she puts it, those of us working radically with community are not the first to do so. Rather, the work 'stands on the shoulders' of generations of people who were here ahead of us, respectfully listening, noticing the unique circumstances of others, and supporting social and political movements.

In this way she provides counsel on the dangers of arriving in communities with abstracted and preconceived ideas and projects already built without due consideration to the specific histories of those with whom we ally ourselves. Here Mohanty reminds us of the long traditions in community development of seeking relationships where we avoid domesticating the people with whom we work, listen first, seek emancipation, and notice the wisdom, talent, and unique capabilities of others.

References

Mohanty, Chandra T. (1984) 'Under western eyes: feminist scholarship and colonial discourses', *Boundary 2* 12 (3): 333–358.

Mohanty, Chandra T. (2002) '"Under Western Eyes" revisited: Feminist solidarity through anticapitalist struggles', *Signs: Journal of Women in Culture and Society* 28(2): 499–535.

Mohanty, Chandra T. (2003) *Feminism Without Borders: Decolonizing Theory, Practicing Solidarity,* Duke University, Durham, NC.

Mohanty, Chandra T. (2016) 'Editor's interview with Chandra Talpade Mohanty', *Journal of Narrative Politics* 2(2): 86–90.

CHAPTER 29

Fran Peavey: *Questions are the art of gentle revolution*

By Athena Lathouras

Frances Peavey 1941–2010

The American political activist, Fran Peavey, visited Australia many times in the late 1980s–1990s. I was fortunate to hear her speak about her approach to compassionate politics. Her philosophy and practice profoundly impacted me and propelled me into the Heart Politics movement. *Heart Politics* (1986) is the title of Peavey's first book and the name given to networks in Australia, New Zealand, and the United States which support activists' personal development. As a member of the Maleny Heart Politics group I also started my own experiments with integrating personal and social change work.

People who have written about Fran Peavey have given her many labels – political activist, pacifist, feminist, nuclear disarmament pro-testor, environmentalist, social change catalyst, and comedian. She was a professional comedian and used humour in her story telling as an aide to help people confront the absurdities and tragedies going on in the world. Her social change actions were varied – from ending homelessness, opposing wars and nuclear proliferation, to cleaning up rivers. For 16 years she travelled regularly to the holy Indian city of Varanasi to support local groups in addressing the horrendous levels of gastrointestinal diseases caused by parasites in the Ganges River.

Peavey is known most for developing the social technology 'strate-gic questioning', which is a special type of questioning and listening to create change, or 'the skill of asking questions that will make a difference' (Peavey in Green, Woodrow & Peavey, 1994: 92). Peavey claimed that strategic questions create a resonant field into which your own thinking is magnified, clarified, and new motion can be created (Vogt, Brown & Isaacs, 2003).

http://dx.doi.org/10.3362/9781788531245.029

Heart Politics

One school of thought suggests that an effective social change activist requires practitioners to have a toolbox of technical skills and knowledge. Another school of thought assumes that effective social change is more directly influenced by and dependent upon values and feelings, the ability to understand oneself and understand society. The Heart Politics approach emphasizes the latter and prioritizes personal growth, relationships, and spirituality (Whelan, 2002). There may be wisdom in adopting elements of, or integrating, both schools.

The purpose of Heart Politics 'gatherings', as they are known, is to support social change agents to bring about social, political, cultural, environmental, and economic change through 'compassion', and through a tuning of the heart to the world's affairs (Lesser, 1989). This philosophy is political to the extent that it challenges the norm, affirms the possibility of a just and humane future, and emphasizes the links between the personal and political action. The term 'gatherings' suggests pedagogic intentions promoting informality and social interaction rather than rigid structures and one-way communication, which might be typical for other types of conferences where practitioners gather (Whelan, 2002).

At a Heart Politics gathering in Australia in 1989 Peavey said:

> People often ask about the term 'heart politics' and what it means. It seems like an oxymoron. An oxymoron is a phrase that is self-cancelling, stupidly contradictory like 'military intelligence'. Instead 'heart politics' might be called an 'oxysavant' – brilliantly contradictory. Putting the two words next to each other in our minds creates a spark of a new dream, a collision of old expectations of rigid politics and of dreams of the heart – and a light of that spark, a vision for a new way of seeing both heart of power and strength, and politics. It is a politics of openness, instead of closedness (Peavey, 1989 cited in Whelan, 2002).

As a social change philosophy, underpinning Heart Politics is the presumption that people generally share many positive values and visions for the future, and a conviction that these ideals can be achieved cooperatively (Whelan, 2002). Peavey used this non-adversarial and culturally sensitive change philosophy throughout her lifetime in a myriad of actions to bring coalitions of people separated by race, culture, and class together.

A [North] 'American Willing to Listen'

After years of local activism, Peavey wanted to know what the rest of the world thought about some of the more pressing issues for the times. She travelled on an around-the-world ticket with a sign saying '[*North*] *American Willing to Listen*'. She met people in public spaces by arrangement and at random and asked open-ended questions such as – 'What are the biggest problems you see affecting your country or region?' and 'How would you like to things to be different in your life?' (Peavey, 1986: 75). These served as springboards for opinions and stories as well as the opportunity to refine her interviewing technique. She gained an acute sense of the social and historical currents around the world by visiting scores of countries and conducting thousands of interviews. Peavey concluded that, despite cultural differences, people universally shared a desire for a peaceful, safe, and sustainable world (Whelan, 2002).

Significantly, her philosophy stresses the need to respect those whom we oppose, as much as those we support. It endorses the idea that the common good can be realized best by people operating from their hearts as well as their heads (Lesser, 1989: 91). Those working for social change, Peavey argues (1986: 146), tend to view their adversaries as enemies, to consider them unreliable, suspect, or of lower moral character. The Heart Politics disposition stands in stark contrast to a self-righteous 'us' and 'them' approach (Peavey 1986: 141). It is coming from a strong humanist philosophy, incorporating a generosity of spirit (Whelan, 2002). She argued that demonizing one's adversaries costs greatly and is a strategy that tacitly accepts and helps perpetuate a 'dangerous enemy' mentality. Fear and hatred can thrive in the abstract, she claimed, and it's easier to be prejudiced against people never met. But most of us, if given a protected situation and a personal connection to the people feared or hated, will demonstrate they are compassionate human beings (Lesser, 1989).

Lesser (1989: 92) provides an example to illustrate this. During the Vietnam War Peavey met with the head of a napalm factory. Along with other peace activists, she was trying to get the factory to shut down. Prior to the meeting she researched every aspect of the company's activities and investigated the background of the company president. She wanted a profile on her 'true enemy' before looking him in his eyes. The last thing she expected to find was a 'human being'. The man had a loving family and church community; and he was valued by his community. After several hours of conversation, Peavey urged the company president to desist from 'the business of burning people'. A few months later when a new contract was drawn up for the production of napalm, the president declined the bid. He'd decided to put the factory to another use. Peavey says she does not know if their discussion prompted a change of heart, but she knows the process enabled them to discover each other's humanity.

Strategic questioning and the art of gentle revolution

The aforementioned 'listening project' helped Peavey to develop the interviewing technique of 'strategic questioning' documented in her book *By Life's Grace: Musings on the Essence of Social Change* (1994). The book title signifies why her questioning approach might be contributing to a gentle revolution – the gem of wisdom for community development. When one thinks of all the social, political, and economic injustice in the world, it naturally fuels righteous anger. Yet with grace or goodwill, the desire to change 'others' is tempered in generosity and forgiveness. Peavey emphasizes that treating adversaries as potential allies need not entail uncritical acceptance of their actions. The challenge, she claims, is to call forth the humanity within each adversary, while at the same time preparing for the full range of possible responses – a path to be found between cynicism and naivety (Peavey, 1986: 149).

Strategic questioning supports this process and could well be worth learning for all community development practitioners. It promotes deep reflection and change, and helps uncover actions, dreams, and strategies buried under fear and helplessness (Green, Woodrow & Peavey, 1994: 2). The process supports change for both the listener and the questioner. By opening oneself up to another point of view, our own ideas shift to take into account new information, new possibilities, and new strategies for resolving problems.

To briefly touch on the process: Peavey divides the types of questioning into two levels. The first level of questions are those that describe the issue or problem, which provide facts and points of view for all the main players in order to frame the strategic questions that follow. The second level of strategic questions enable the community practitioner to dig deeper, to envision, consider alternatives, evaluate possibilities, and foster a commitment to action. These are the so-called 'long-lever' questions (Peavey, 1994: 95). She suggests:

> Questions can be like a lever you use to pry open the stuck lid on a paint can … If we have a short lever, we can only just crack open the lid on the can. But if we have a longer lever, or a more

dynamic question, we can open that can up much wider and really stir things up ... If the right questions is applied, and it digs deep enough, then we can stir up all the creative solutions (Peavey in Vogt, Brown & Isaacs, 2003: 3).

This form of listening and questioning is the heart of Peavey's political practice. She argues that asking questions and listening for the strategies and ideas embedded in people's own answers can be the greatest service a social change worker can give to a particular issue (Peavey, 1994: 87).

Endnotes

1. I am grateful to Tracy Adams, Jill Jordon, Tony Woodhouse, and Robin Clayfield for 'holding' the Maleny Heart Politics network locally over many years, and for supporting my and others' efforts for social change.

References and key works

Green, T., Woodrow, P., and Peavey, F. (1994) *Insight and Action: How to Discover and Support a Life of Integrity and Commitment to Change,* New Society Publishers, Philadelphia, PA.

Lesser, D. (1998) *Fran Peavey and the Politics of the Heart,* The Whites of Their Eyes series [online] Available from: <http://davidleser.com/articles/> [Accessed 18 June 2019].

Peavey, F. (1986) *Heart Politics,* New Society Publishers, Philadelphia, PA.

Peavey, F. (1994) *By Life's Grace: Musings on the Essence of Social Change,* New Society Publishers, Philadelphia, PA.

Peavey, F. (2001) *Strategic Questioning: An Experiment in Communication of the Second Kind,* Crabgrass, San Francisco, CA.

Vogt, E., Brown, J. and Isaacs, D. (2003) *The Art of Powerful Questions: Catalysing Insight, Innovation and Action,* Whole Systems Associates, California.

Whelan, J. (2002) *Education and Training for Effective Environmental Advocacy,* PhD Thesis, Griffith University, Brisbane, Australia.

CHAPTER 30

Arundhati Roy: *Do not fragment solidarity*

By Peter Westoby

Arundhati Roy 1961—

Jean Baptiste Paris

World famous for her Booker Prize winning novel *The God of Small Things* (1997), I particularly love Arundhati Roy's non-fiction. Passionate and fierce, Roy, a political, human rights and environmental activist born in 1961, speaks to power globally – but mostly Indian state and corporate power – with integrity and potency. For this, she is not loved by the powerful. There has been a huge backlash against every piece of writing, leading to endless court cases, legal notices, death threats, and even a short jail sentence (Roy, 2019: xviii).

She first became well-known to the international activist world through her stand with the Kothie tribespeople fighting against the Narmada Valley Development Project Dam in Gujarat, India. Her account of the tribespeople's displacement written in 1999 as 'The Greater Common Good' (Roy, 1999) has stood the test of time, and only in 2017 did the prime minister of India, Narendra Modi, inaugurate the Sardar Saraovar Dam. With that, as Roy says, 'the government reneged on every promise it made to [the Kothie people]' (2019: xiv).

Since writing against the dam in 1999 she has produced a significant oeuvre of work – standing up against India's commitment to entering the nuclear weapons club, the building of the Statue of Unity (four times taller than the Statue of Liberty, and costing $430 million), endemic corruption, and the neglect of the poor.

Rarely winning friends, she has lived and walked with the Maoists in the state of Orissa so as to understand the plight of forest people being displaced due to bauxite mining. I have wondered if her great contribution is foregrounding the phenomenon of development-induced displacement (DID); that is, the displacement of people due to 'development projects' – dams, mines, roads, and so forth. Such

http://dx.doi.org/10.3362/9781788531245.030

DID is more prolific than displacement by war-related conflict, such is the insidious expansionist extractivism of hyper-capitalism.

But other than highlighting this displacement phenomenon, there are some key wisdoms that community development practitioners can learn from her work. My chosen 'gem of a wisdom' is, 'do not fragment solidarity'.

Do not fragment solidarity

There is a particular passage that has stuck with me from reading **Paulo Freire**, in which he argues that:

> One of the characteristics of oppressive cultural action which is almost never perceived by the dedicated but naive professionals who are involved is the emphasis on a *focalised* view of problems rather than seeing them as dimensions of a *totality*. In 'community development' projects the more a region or area is broken down into 'local communities', without the study of these communities both as totalities in themselves and as parts of another totality (the area, region, and so forth) – which in turn is part of a still larger totality (the nation, as part of the continental totality) – the more alienation is intensified. (Freire, 1970: 111).

In this tradition of **Freire**, in her book *Capitalism: A Ghost Story* (2014), Roy, in two passages, also explicitly critiques community development. She takes aim at community development in the context of non-government organization (NGO) funding, along with an attack on the discourses underpinning community development:

> Armed with their billions, these NGOs have waded into the world, turning potential revolutionaries into salaried activists, funded artists, intellectuals, and filmmakers, gently luring them away from radical confrontation, ushering them in the direction of multiculturalism, gender equity, community development – the discourse couched in the language of identity politics and human rights (Roy, 2014: 34).

She then engages critically with the way funding regimes lead to siloed work, which 'fragments solidarity'. It is a pretty scathing critique:

> In the NGO universe, which has evolved a strange anodyne language of its own, everything has become a 'subject', separate, professionalized, special-interest issue. Community

development, leadership development, human rights, health, education, reproductive rights, AIDS, orphans with AIDS – have all been hermetically sealed into their own silos, each with its own elaborate and precise funding brief. Funding has fragmented solidarity in ways that repression never could (ibid: 37).

I can see exactly where **Freire** was coming from some 50 years ago (his book was written in 1970), and also where Roy is coming from now. What is clear to me from pondering is that somehow community development practitioners, educators, managers, and policy makers need to heed these critiques in a way that ensures we learn; to ensure particularly that in 50 years' time someone cannot make the same critique.

For Roy, a fundamental issue is that poverty is framed as an identity problem as opposed to a structural problem. From her perspective, poverty as an identity issue can be solved when an NGO armed with the latest social technologies of 'development', or in this case 'community development', can lift people from poverty in a localized, or as **Freire** puts it, a 'focalized' intervention. Translated into action it would suggest that if an NGO comes to an impoverished community with its (using contemporary community development lingo): 'sustainable livelihood initiatives', social and economic 'innovations', 'human-rights-based work', 'micro-finance', and so forth, then a group of people – based on the identity of place/ethnicity and so forth – can be lifted out of poverty (or at least alleviated from it). For Roy this is a huge fallacy and ignores the historical and globalizing structural elements creating poverty – see for example, **Luxemburg**. It seems that Roy's critique of the identity orientation of community development (and human rights work) resonates with **Freire's**. The problem is a focus on the local only, often supported by a de-contextualized analysis of the challenges/problems at hand, and the possible solutions available.

Of course, situated behind this critique of poverty as an identity issue is Roy's critique of NGOs and their good intentions to intervene in the lives of the poor. This critique includes a swipe at professionalization, aka **Esteva**, siloed practices, specialist knowledge, and the bureaucratic regimes of development funding. In a sense, her analysis builds again on **Freire**'s, where each 'problem' is seen through a lens that is unable to see, or purposefully ignores, the whole/totality – maybe because the whole or totality is so complex.

Fundamentally, Roy's critique is towards NGOs' willingness to be part of the apparatus of pacification – *undermining the solidarity of the poor*. As per the analysis embedded within her first quote, the poor are 'bought off', and become part of the architecture of the NGO world, or the paid activist world. At the same time, this willingness for NGOs to intervene into the world of the poor with services, or programmes, undermines poor people's capacities to 'see' or view the forces and fields of oppression in their lives. 'Alienation is intensified' as the poor become agents of their own upliftment, supported by NGO interventions. Within this critical purview social solidarity is fragmented as the poor become agents who focus on assimilation into NGO initiatives and global capitalism, rather than active agents themselves who work in collective solidarity and work to make sense of their world, motivated by their imagination of what the good life is.

Walk alongside the poor

Re-orienting from community development as a service-oriented or fragmenting practice, Roy's life and writing represents an alternative way. She first and foremost walks with, listens to, and learns from the poor. Back in 2011 when I first read her account of walking with the Maoist rebels in the state of Orissa, India (Roy, 2011a) – which meant literally taking the time to live for several weeks in the forests with the Maoist freedom fighters and tribespeople they were fighting with – I was reminded of this profound practice of 'walking alongside' rather than intervening into. It implies foregrounding the work of observation and listening as opposed to intervention, a polarity of practice ever present in the social field (Kaplan, 2002). From that walking with, and listening too, Roy becomes entangled in the profoundly real and difficult choices the poor have – to align with the Gandhians or take up arms like the Maoists, reform or revolution, peaceful or militant (Roy, 2011b: 207). To sit with people, to listen and learn from them is to cloud any easy professional or ideological certainties with the real complexities of resistance to globalizing capitalism. Yet that listening too, expressed beautifully by Roy, suggests:

> Another world is not only possible, she's on her way. Maybe many of us won't be here to greet her, but on a quiet day, if I listen very carefully, I can hear her breathing (Roy, 2019: 283).

Make it impossible for them to pretend

Reading her most recent work, the foreword from *My Seditious Heart* (Roy, 2019), it becomes clear what Roy herself would like people to remember from her work. Returning to her initial solidarity work with the people of the Narmada Valley, she suggests it is that, 'we must make it impossible for those in power to pretend' (Roy, 2019: xiv). Stated more fully:

> Even as they went down fighting, the people of the Narmada taught the world some profound lessons – about ecology, equity, sustainability, and democracy. They taught me that we must make ourselves visible, even when we lose, whatever it is that we lose – land, livelihood, or a worldview. And that we must make it impossible for those in power to pretend that they do not know the costs and consequences of what they do (ibid: xiv).

In some ways this is to concede defeat strategically and tactically. Often the powerful win, as they did against the Kothie tribespeople. Yet, in defeat, there is a moral and archival imperative. The work of memory is to 'not forget' what has been done and at the same time make any pretence of hypocrisy visible.

Reference and key works

Freire, P. (1970) *Pedagogy of the Oppressed,* Herder and Herder, New York.

Kaplan, A. (2002) *Artists of the Invisible,* Pluto Press.

Roy, A. (1997) *The God of Small Things,* Random House, New York.

Roy, A. (1999) 'The Greater Common Good', India Book Distributors, Bombay, India.

Roy, A. (2011a) 'Walking with the Comrades' in *Broken Republic,* Hamish Hamilton, London.

Roy, A. (2011b) *Broken Republic,* Hamish Hamilton, London.

Roy, A. (2014) *Capitalism: A Ghost Story,* Verso, London and New York.

Roy, A. (2019) *My Seditious Heart,* Hamish Hamilton, London.

CHAPTER 31
Deborah Bird Rose:
Community as the 'shimmer of life'

By Dave Palmer

Chantal Jackson

Deborah Bird Rose 1946–2018

Who is Deborah Bird Rose?

Deborah Bird Rose was born in the USA and educated at the University of Delaware and Bryn Mawr. Sadly, in late 2018, while we were preparing this book, Deborah left those of us who still live and joined the 'old people' and 'country' as part of the interspecies of living past and present.

Deborah worked in several university settings (including the Australian National University and Macquarie University) in Australia and was, at the time of her passing, an Adjunct Professor in Ecological Humanities at the University of New South Wales, Australia. Deborah spent much of her working life as a consultant anthropologist for various community-controlled organizations and bodies representing the interests of Australian Aboriginal groups. This included the Aboriginal Land Commissioner, Northern Land Council, Central Land Council, NSW Parks and Wildlife Service, and the Aboriginal Areas Protection Authority. She described herself as being 'animated by years of learning from Aboriginal people, and by my love of earth life' (Rose, 2014).

Her early research work and intimate relationships were with Aboriginal people from the Mak Mak clan (the Victoria River area) in northern Australia, and this turned her to writing about deep philosophical questions such as why are we born, why do we live, why do we die?

http://dx.doi.org/10.3362/9781788531245.031

On the inextricable connection between 'country' and community

Deborah's many beautiful contemplations include examining the entangled relationships between people, human community, ecological community, the ethics of love, contingency, and how we can act 'in the face of almost incomprehensible loss' (Rose, 2014). In considerable measure, her work is a response to longstanding and deep connections with Aboriginal friends and family, and her love and intimate acquaintances with what many too distantly describe as 'nature'. Her own poetic writing takes us to the heart of her contribution to thinking about an interspecies 'community'. Talking about what she calls 'creature languages' or the many and varied ways the living world communicates, she said that these ways of 'speaking':

> draw the full sensorium into the communicative matrix of country. The sight and smell of flowers, the pain of the march fly bite and the sensation of blood running down the leg, the sight of swifts in the sky or flower petals drifting in the river, fireflies winking and the interminable racket of cicadas: these are multi-faceted creature-languages, and smart creatures take notice. (Rose 2013, p. 104)

In her work with Aboriginal Australians the connection between people and 'country' is paramount. Largely this reflects the fact that in traditional Aboriginal law and culture there exists an irrepressible link between people, family, other species, and 'country'. This contrasts with many taken-for-granted binary and oppositional ideas about a split between humans and nature, animate and inanimate, the rational and the emotional. Indeed, to think about the future of a community without reference to 'country' for many Aboriginal groups is akin to talking about the future of a child without reference to its mother (Rose 2004: 153). Deborah further explains that in Aboriginal ontology and everyday life practice, 'country' is an extension of family, the place where living people, ancestors, and yet unborn children dwell. As a consequence of the intimate relationships all share with 'country', much as a member of one's family does, it demands care. In turn, once nurtured 'country' offers care. To visit 'country', to travel through it, hunt on it, make fire on it, and sing to it is much like visiting an older relative. In both acts one maintains relationships, obligations, and 'keeps alive' one's family. In this way, keeping 'country' healthy (by visiting it, dancing on it, and warming its soul by fire) also involves the act of keeping the community healthy (Collard, 2008).

Deborah puts it beautifully when she says:

> In Aboriginal English, the word 'country' is both a common noun and a proper noun. People talk about country in the same way that they would talk about a person: they speak to country, sing to country, visit country, worry about country, and grieve for country and long for country. People say that country knows, hears, smells, takes notice, takes care, and feels sorry or happy. Country is a living entity with a yesterday, a today and tomorrow, with consciousness, action, and a will toward life (Rose et al. 2002: 14).

In another observation, Deborah (2004) sets out how speaking to and about 'country' is critical to the health of community. Indeed, the process of travelling to 'country' not only involves people sharing stories and 'going along together', it also animates their relationship with specific places and spaces. As many of Deborah's older friends acknowledge, going back to 'country' allows them to maintain their relationship with ancestors long passed away but still living as spirits. Important here is the conception for many elders that the dead are an integral part of the maintenance of life and experience of the young and living. In other words, the practice of walking on 'country' and telling stories (often about their ancestors) implicitly involves communion between the young (the living) and the old (the dead). It involves 'paying dues' to the ancestors, respecting the cycle of life in death and death in life and learning about their obligations to pass this on to those who 'come behind' (Muecke, 1997 and 2004). These opportunities to 'return to the old people and reconnect with "Country"' have become all the more urgent in the last one hundred years because so many have become truncated and removed from their traditional lands (Palmer et al 2006: 322). Distance from 'country' has meant distance from culture. This in turn equates with distance from health and wellbeing. The symbolic act of visiting, spending time with, and nurturing 'country' is then fundamental to community healing and wellbeing.

In part this is because 'country' is seen as something that lives and moves. It is something that creates rhythms and maintains a (heart) beat. Like a rich and many-instrumented orchestra 'country' holds a communicative system rich in rhythms and beats, as well as cycles and returns. Operating in this cultural time and space then demands that one finds the beats, paying attention to the tempo of 'country'.

It demands the embodiment of an interspecies sensibility where we move in tune with other beings who share in our diverse ecological community.

Deborah (2004) observes that this process of being on-country and singing for 'country' not only involves the young and their living elders 'going along together', but it also demands a shared relationship with elders and ancestors long passed away. She recounts the guidance received from her friend and teacher Jessie Wirrpa, about the need for those being on-country to be guided by the presence of ancestors who, if respected and asked for guidance, would lead and care for the living walkers. Deborah (2004) describes what Wirrpa taught her about 'singing out to country':

> When she took me walkabout she called out to the ancestors. She told them who we were and what we were doing, and she told them to help us. 'Give us fish', she would call out, 'The children are hungry'. When she was walking through country she was always with a group, and that group included the dead as well as the living (Rose, 2004: 167).

In a lecture Deborah describes the Yolngu idea of the 'shimmer'. Here she offers a wonderful metaphor for thinking about the importance of cross-species relationships in keeping alive what others have called community. She notes that the shimmer, or soft wavering light that brings the eye and mind to life, is central to an Aboriginal sensibility, particularly when we think about people's relationship to 'country' and other species. She points out that in Aboriginal systems the shimmer occurs throughout life, activating and appealing to the senses, evoking or capturing feelings and action. For example, many insects have shimmering responses to attract food. Flowering plants have shimmering colours and smells that lure, entice attention, and offer rewards to those species who notice. Deborah cites the arts anthropologist Howard Morphy who, in his essay 'From Dull to Brilliant', refers to the Yolngu term *bir'yun*, which translates as 'brilliant' or 'shimmering'. According to Morphy, a Yolngu painting starts with a rough or 'dull' shape, at which point the work is coming into being. From this 'dull' outline the artist works in crosshatching. This quickly shifts the look of the painting to 'brilliant', creating a shimmering effect with light coming to life, moving across the canvas so that it captures the eye. *Bir'yun* is the word used for this effect of creating a shimmer, 'the brilliance, a kind of motion that brings you into the experience of being part of a vibrant and vibrating world, the ephemeral dance of it all' (Morphy, 1989: 21, in Rose, 2014).

In a similar but somewhat different way, Deborah spent much time with people involved in ritual performance, where their bodies and 'country' connected through dance and song. In the act of dance the human body moves like the pollinating flower enticing the flying fox, shimmering in the light, moving and pulsating with the music in a way that allows the performance to come to life. These dances are important in a range of ways, sometimes activating conditions that 'open up' law and culture, other times producing desire, at other moments bringing people into important community business.

The moment of *bir'yun*, in both nature and culture, brings into being an encounter between those involved in 'a lively, pulsating world, not a mechanistic one – a world not composed of gears and cogs but of multifaceted, multispecies relations and pulses' (Rose, 2014). To encounter and then respond to such moments, particularly as they involve other species and other people is to participate in what Deborah called 'the shimmer of life'. Perhaps, this act of 'shimmering' stands as a more poetic way of describing 'community development'.

References and key works

Collard, L. (2008) 'Kura, Yeye, Boorda from the past, today and the future', in S. Morgan, M. Tjalaminu, & B. Kwaymullina (eds.), *Heartsick for Country: Stories of Love, Spirit and Creation*, pp. 60–80, Fremantle Press, Fremantle, WA, Australia.

Morphy, H. (1989) 'From dull to brilliant: The aesthetics of spiritual power among the Yolngu', *Man* 24(1): 21.

Muecke, S. (1997) *No Road: Bitumen All the Way*, Fremantle Arts Centre Press, South Fremantle, WA, Australia.

Muecke, S. (2004) *Ancient and Modern: Time, Culture and Indigenous Philosophy*, University of NSW Press, Sydney, Australia.

Palmer, D., Watson, J., Watson, A. Ljubic, P. Wallace-Smith, H. Johnson, M. (2006) 'Going back to country with bosses': the Yiriman Project, youth participation and walking along with elders. *Children, Youth and Environments*, 16(2): 317-337.

Rose, D.B. (1991) *Hidden Histories*, Aboriginal Studies Press, Australian Institute of Aboriginal and Torres Strait Islander Studies, Canberra, Australia.

Rose, D.B. (1992) *Dingo Makes Us Human*, Cambridge University Press, Cambridge, UK.

Rose, D.B. with S. D'Amico, N. Daiyi, K. Deveraux, M. Daiyi, L. Ford and Bright, A. (2002) *Country of the Heart: An Indigenous Australian Homeland*, Aboriginal Studies Press, Australian Institute of Aboriginal and Torres Strait Islander Studies Canberra, Australia.

Rose, D.B. (2004) *Reports from a Wild Country: Ethics for Decolonisation*, University of New South Wales Press, Sydney, Australia.

Rose, D.B. (2011) *Wild Dog Dreaming: Love and Extinction*, University of Virginia Press, VA.

Rose, D.B. (2013) Val Plumwood's philosophical animism: Attentive interactions in a sentient world, *Environmental Humanities* 3: 93–109.

Rose, D.B. (2014) *Shimmer: When All You Love is Being Trashed* [video on website] <https://vimeo.com/97758080> [accessed 1 April 2019].

CHAPTER 32
Bertrand Russell: *Community and the value of idleness*

By Dave Palmer

Dutch National Archives

Bertrand Russell 1872–1970

Who was Bertrand Russell?

Bertrand Russell was a British-born philosopher, mathematician, antiwar activist, and Nobel laureate. He was a prolific writer whose works span such intellectual fields as analytic philosophy, linguistics, artificial intelligence, politics, computer science, logics, history, and nuclear disarmament.

Born into the British aristocracy, with a family tree ripe with lords, ladies and prime ministers, Russell also came from decidedly liberal stock. His parents had asked the great political philosopher John Stuart Mill to be their son's secular godfather, and though Mill died shortly after Russell's birth, his writings became a powerful influence on the young Bertrand. Along with fellow members of the elite and intellectual classes he was educated at Cambridge, studying mathematics.

In Russell's writing he argues the value of a liberal and moderate form of socialism, the evils of war, the value of free speech, the importance of a scientific society shaped by reason and rationality, the legalising of same-sex relationships, and the pursuit of beauty, gentleness, and creativity.

On the value of idleness

Perhaps Bertrand Russell's great gift to those interested in community work is his wisdom on surviving the raging rapids of busyness and workaholism. In his 1935 essay *In Praise of Idleness* Russell elegantly challenges the taken-for-granted idea that to be a responsible citizen

http://dx.doi.org/10.3362/9781788531245.032

(community member) one must be busy. In his essay, which seems to stand against the wisdom of modern business gurus and popular ideas about how to run organisations, he writes that:

> A great deal of harm is being done in the modern world by belief in the virtuousness of work, and that the road to happiness and prosperity lies in an organized diminution of work (Russell, 1935: 10–11).

This is perhaps more salient now than in the 1930s when Russell wrote about the merits of more leisure time. Indeed, today it seems as if 'are you busy?' has replaced 'how are you?' as the casual greeting of the café queue. Whether we work in business, government, community organizations, or universities, the mantra of productivity – that driving force in the doctrine of consumerism – measures our movements, our achievements, our driving pulse, against what brings profits and 'outcomes'.

Largely relying on his powers of logic, Russell put paid to this idea with the clear observation that:

> Broadly speaking, it is held that getting money is good and spending money is bad. Seeing that they are two sides of one transaction, this is absurd; one might as well maintain that keys are good, but keyholes are bad. Whatever merit there may be in the production of goods must be entirely derivative from the advantage to be obtained by consuming them. The individual, in our society, works for profit; but the social purpose of his work lies in the consumption of what he produces. It is this divorce between the individual and the social purpose of production that makes it so difficult for men to think clearly in a world in which profit-making is the incentive to industry. We think too much of production, and too little of consumption. One result is that we attach too little importance to enjoyment and simple happiness, and that we do not judge production by the pleasure that it gives to the consumer (Russell, 1935: 18).

Much to the horror of many political scientists and organizational change experts, Russell mischievously suggests – in what at first glance appears counter to the truth – that today there is far too much work being done and our faith that work is noble and good is one of the most harmful risks to a healthy future. In other words, for Russell the more work and accumulation of wealth that is carried out, the greater the cultural and moral poverty for communities.

The logic for him was clear: too much work diminishes our capacity for leisure and for interesting thought, both vital ingredients for the healthy and imaginative mind of a citizen.

Writing in the early 1930s, Russell was convinced that modern economies were able to support large amounts of leisure time so that no one need work more than four hours per day. He painted the following picture of the future:

> In a world where no one is compelled to work more than four hours a day, every person possessed of scientific curiosity will be able to indulge it, and every painter will be able to paint without starving, however excellent his pictures may be. Young writers will not be obliged to draw attention to themselves by sensational potboilers, with a view to acquiring the economic independence needed for monumental works, for which, when the time at last comes, they will have lost the taste and the capacity (Russell, 1935: 20).

The consequences on civil and community life would be remarkable. Free from exhaustion, time-rich citizens would be able to commit themselves to other interests and pursuits. Idleness, as he described the product of time free from work, makes people happy and creates the conditions for people to become light-hearted, playful, more inclined towards education and, above all else, more creative. As Grieve (2015: 29) puts it, Russell concluded that this direct relationship between leisure and creativity is often 'the key to breakthrough ideas, and thus the path to genius and joy … and … happy people are generally kinder people'. Thus, limiting the work of a community (or encouraging idleness) will result in both more generous treatment of one another and more creative activity. We might say that an idle community is a healthier and imaginative community.

> Above all, there will be happiness and joy of life, instead of frayed nerves, weariness, and dyspepsia. The work exacted will be enough to make leisure delightful, but not enough to produce exhaustion. Since men will not be tired in their spare time, they will not demand only such amusements as are passive and vapid. At least 1 per cent will probably devote the time not spent in professional work to pursuits of some public importance, and, since they will not depend upon these pursuits for their livelihood, their originality will be unhampered, and there will be no need to conform to the standards set by elderly pundits. But it is not only in these exceptional cases that the advantages of leisure will appear. Ordinary men and women, having the opportunity of a happy life, will become more kindly and less persecuting and less inclined to view others with suspicion. The taste for war will die out, partly for this

reason, and partly because it will involve long and severe work for all. Good nature is, of all moral qualities, the one that the world needs most, and good nature is the result of ease and security, not of a life of arduous struggle (Russell, 1935: 20–21).

So, what might Russell's gift of idleness thus offer the community worker?

First, his observations are a sobering reminder that adding to the burdens of an overworked community by calling for yet more effort, more projects, more action, more work is bound to have ill-effects. This is a particularly useful riposte given the propensity of community workers to work themselves to the bone and measure their level of commitment against their degree of exhaustion.

Second, if Russell is right about the relationship between idleness and kindliness, then he offers community workers some deeply profound insights into how to encourage social connections amongst community members. This logic stands in direct contrast to the default position that most social policy architects adopt: that communities in poverty and communities in crisis are in this position due to their lack of skills, resources, and efforts.

Finally, Russell's clarity on idleness offers community workers the seeds of a logic and methodology where creativity is at the heart. Rather than accepting idleness as a passive and unproductive pastime Russell beseeches us to replace it with the notion that idleness can be active, especially in giving a community time to contemplate, drift clear of the burdens of everyday life, and imagine new ways of doing and being. This community work methodology might seek to energetically set up opportunities for a community to rest from the weightiness of overwork, stress, and chaos, and instead experience unburdened contemplation, stillness, and gentle communion with that which exists around us.

References and key works

Grieve, B.T. (2015) *In Praise of Idleness: A Timeless Essay / Bertrand Russell*, Black Ink Books, Collingwood, Australia.

Popova, M. (2018) 'In praise of idleness: Bertrand Russell on the relationship between leisure and social justice' *Brain Pickings* [website], <www.brainpickings.org/2018/12/27/in-praise-of-idleness-bertrand-russell/> [Accessed 22 December 2019].

Russell, B. (1935) *In Praise of Idleness and Other Essays*, Allen and Unwin, London.

CHAPTER 33

E.F. Schumacher: *Small is Beautiful*

By Athena Lathouras

E.F. Schumacher 1911–1977

Practical Action

My connection to E.F. Schumacher and the community economies tradition commenced in the 1990s when a Brisbane-based NGO, Community Living Association (CLA), hosted one-day gatherings called 'Community Futures' to help people think about the relationship between the community and the economy – a conversation about the community economies tradition. In the community economies tradition, 'community' and the 'economy' are two terms that have been long understood as mutually exclusive (Morrow et al., 2019). The modern capitalist economy has been seen as an expanding and unitary system that is dominating and shaping the social and has often been a force displacing and undermining local community. Whereas, at the heart of the community economies tradition is an activist agenda to 'take back the economy' (Gibson-Graham et al., 2013) for communities and the environments upon which people depend.

At the CLA gatherings I learned about alternative economic systems from which local communities benefit. For example, Savings and Loans Circles or money co-operatives, and L.E.T.S. (Local Energy Transfer) Schemes, which are bartering systems where members trade goods and services through a locally created currency. It has been inspiring to participate in these kinds of community development processes.

Seminal to this community economies tradition is E.F. Schumacher's expansive vision that 'small is beautiful', and this is his gem of wisdom for community development.

http://dx.doi.org/10.3362/9781788531245.033

Small is beautiful

Ernst Friederich (Fritz) Schumacher, an economist-philosopher, was born in Bonn, Germany in 1911. He has become the unlikely pioneer of the green movement. He began his career thinking like all market economists, dedicated to economic growth and the idea that to stagnate or to become smaller was death to an economy. This school of thought is that the development of production and the accumulation of wealth is the primary goal – the philosophy of materialism. However, Schumacher went on to reinforce the critique that the modern economy is unsustainable, and that there are 'limits to growth'. As his thinking changed, his call was to shape our economics around the needs of communities, not corporations, and these actions needed to be informed by scale. 'Bigger is better' is the typical approach to scale, but Schumacher's (1973) book, *Small is Beautiful: Economics as if People Mattered,* heralded a vision of contemporary economics based on human-scale, decentralized, and appropriate technologies.

This seminal book articulates what millions worldwide subconsciously believed, that unlike any previous culture or civilisation, twentieth century (and beyond) Western society, both agricultural and industrial, is living artificially off the Earth's capital rather than its income. Schumacher's ideas ensured human wellbeing, as well as all aspects of environmental sustainability, were at the centre of economic decision-making.

Intermediate or appropriate technology

Schumacher's quest for patterns of sustainability took him all over the world, and a trip to Burma in 1955 as an economic advisor to the United Nations consolidated his philosophy. There he witnessed the local people, with very low income per capita (tantamount to poverty from a Western view), going about their daily lives apparently happy and content. Whilst living in Burma, Schumacher became aware of the inadequacies of a growth-based conventional development strategy. These included the use of capital-intensive technology from the industrialized societies, which was having a harmful consequence on the local people. These and other observations led Schumacher to the conclusion that the 'problems of economics do not have any final solution, because they are human problems, that can be 'solved' only within a particular set of circumstances for a particular time and particular place' (Cornish, 1979: 276–277).

Schumacher's quest to better understand human-scale technology progressed in 1965 when he and others started the London Intermediate Technology Development Group. The group's purpose was to make known technologies appropriate to the needs and resources of poor people in poor communities, which are tools and equipment deliberately designed to be relatively small, simple, capital-saving, and environmentally non-violent (McRobie, 1980). In using the term 'intermediate technology', Schumacher envisioned a technology for the Global South that was midway between, for example, a hand hoe and a tractor (Akubue, 2000). As Schumacher described it, 'Such an intermediate technology would be immensely more productive than the indigenous technology … but it would be immensely cheaper than the sophisticated, highly capital-intensive technology of modern industry' (Schumacher, 1973: 180).

The central tenet is that such technology should be designed to fit into and be compatible with its local setting. For example, passive solar design; active solar collectors for heating and cooling; small windmills to provide electricity; roof-top gardens and hydroponic greenhouses; permaculture; and worker-managed craft industries – activities which support the goal of self-reliance of people on a local level (Rosenland in Schumacher, 1999: 146).

The approach has been taken up by community development theorists and is seen as a complete systems approach to development that is self-adaptive and dynamic, because its users become wealthier, more skilled, and able to afford and use more expensive technical means (Dunn, 1978).

Buddhist economics

Schumacher spent all his free time in Burma studying Buddhism, which then profoundly shaped his economic philosophy. His essay 'Buddhist Economics' was first published in 1966 and is widely understood as a call for an economics of peace. This approach distinguishes between 'misery, sufficiency and surfeit' (McRobie, 1999: 37). It argues that economic growth would be good only to the point of sufficiency, and limitless growth and consumption would be disastrous. Moreover, a Buddhist economics is based squarely on renewable resources: an economics of permanence. This stands in contrast with Western economics based on the ruthless exploitation of non-renewable resources and recognizing no limits to productions and consumption – a non-sustainable system.

O'Brien (2017) writes about Schumacher's prophetic ideas at this time in our history, when prevailing 20th century economic models are now falling apart. As economists scramble to explain what has gone wrong, she comments, 'Schumacher was the first to argue that economic production was too wasteful of the environment and non-renewable resources'. Schumacher argued that an economy should exist to serve the needs of people, but in a materialist economy, people exist to serve the economy (O'Brien, 2017).

Decades before human-induced global warming and the climate change crisis has become globally recognized, Schumacher was arguing for a Buddhist economy as one that distinguishes between renewable and non-renewable resources, and that a superior civilization is one built on renewable resources. He argued that, 'To use [non-renewable materials] heedlessly or extravagantly is an act of violence, and while complete non-violence may not be attainable on this earth, there is nonetheless an ineluctable duty on man [sic] to aim at the ideal of non-violence in all he [sic] does' (Schumacher, 1966).

His legacy

After Fritz Schumacher died in 1977, Satish Kumar and others founded the E.F. Schumacher Society to promote the ideas of the decentralist tradition and to implement practical programmes for local economic self-reliance, stewardship of natural resources, and community renewal (Schumacher, 2011). This Society and a myriad of other organizations, coalitions, and networks continue to advance or draw from Schumacher's guiding beliefs and ideals in various forms. See, for example, new economy networks; the transition towns movement; post-growth and post-capitalist politics movements; and the fair-trade movement. Practical local-level examples include workers' co-operatives as social enterprises aiming to distribute wealth from labour more equitably, and commoning, or the commons, to re-think how property, products, and resources are created, cared for, used, and shared.

Community economic theorists argue the need for both macro-level change and local-level change. That 'small' or alternative economic efforts need to be foregrounded, have their stories told, and technological supports developed to count them and measure their value. And, that these efforts also need to be meshed into larger networks, so a critique of larger systems that cause harm or are not supporting human wellbeing are known, and pressure can be put on decision-makers for regulation that supports more ethically sound economic practices (Gibson-Graham et al., 2013).

Conclusion

Schumacher's provocations have inspired many people to question what they want out of life. They are questioning the future and the values of a market-led consumerist society, and making radical changes in their own lifestyles. In his epilogue to *Small is Beautiful* Schumacher emphasizes the need for the philosophy of materialism to take second place to ideas such as justice, harmony, beauty, and health. He implores us to rely on 'people power' and our own mental and physical inventiveness, rather than basing our futures on imported capital and energy-intensive technologies that reduce the need for the human workforce.

References and key works

Akubue, A. (2000) 'Appropriate technology for socioeconomic development in third world countries', *Journal of Technology Studies* XXVI (1): 33–43 Winter/Spring 2000.

Cornish, E. (1979), 'Think small', *The Futurist* 8(6): 276–280.

Dunn, P.D. (1978) *Appropriate Technology – Technology with a Human Face,* Schoken Books, New York.

Gibson-Graham, J.K, Cameron, J. and Healy, S. (2013) *Take Back the Economy: An Ethical Guide for Transforming Our Communities,* University of Minnesota Press, MN.

McRobie, G. (1980) 'Preface' in Schumacher, E. F., *Good Work,* Abacus, London.

Morrow, O., St. Martin, K., Gabriel, N. and Heras Monner Sans, A.I. 'Community Economy: Community Economics Collective', [website] <www.communityeconomies.org> [Accessed 27 July 2019].

O'Brien, B. (2017) 'Buddhist Economics: E.F. Schumacher's Prophetic Ideas' [website] <www.thoughtco.com/buddhist-economics-e-f-schumacher-449728> [Accessed 13 April 2019].

Schumacher, D. (2011) *Small is Beautiful in the 21st Century: The legacy of E.F. Schumacher,* Green Books Ltd, Cambridge, UK.

Schumacher, E.F. 1966, *Buddhist Economics* [website] <www.centerfor neweconomics.org/publications/buddhist-economics> [Accessed 13 April 2019].

Schumacher, E.F. 1973, *Small is Beautiful: A Study of Economics as if People Mattered,* Harper & Row, New York.

Schumacher, E.F. (1980) *Good Work,* Abacus Sphere Books, Ltd., London.

Schumacher, E.F. (1999) *Small is Beautiful, 25th Anniversary Edition: Economics as if People Mattered, 25 years later ... with commentaries,* Hartley & Marks Publishers, Vancouver.

CHAPTER 34
Richard Sennett: *Respect*

By Dave Palmer

Richard Sennett 1946—

rubra, Ars Electronica

Respect offered first as a gift

Frequently I find myself on 'back to country' trips where senior Indigenous Australians are joined by members of their extended families, including the middle-aged, young people, and children on visits to the traditional homelands of their ancestors. Community-based organizations such as youth diversionary programmes or community-led land management teams routinely arrange these kinds of trips to support a multitude of goals including health and wellbeing, education, land care, and cultural development. Often those attending will travel for days and over hundreds of kilometres to return to visit the 'spirits' of those who have since passed away, and to help regenerate and in turn be regenerated by 'country' with their presence. A key feature of this work is making sure that there are members of different generations so that *kanyirninpa* (the holding, carrying or transfer of knowledge) to young people can occur. According to McCoy, this important cultural practice of *kanyirninpa* helps maintain the health of Indigenous communities (2008: 22). McCoy claims that *kanyirninpa* is central to the maintenance of cultural life and language, creating social bonds and social obligations to reciprocate the generosity of others (2008: 28). One Kukatja woman expresses it in this way, 'if you hold that person, that person will return that respect to you' (cited in McCoy 2008: 18, 28). *Kanyirninpa*, says McCoy, 'includes nurturance but also involves older people taking responsibility and offering protection for those they hold'. Often the English word used to describe this is 'respect', made manifest in relationships that involve passing on knowledge in ways where older people help young people 'grow up the right way'.

Often when on country, the word 'respect' gets used with young people to convey what is, to members of these communities, a central

http://dx.doi.org/10.3362/9781788531245.034

element in traditional law and culture. Indeed, I have been on trips where the word 'respect' has been painted on the side of a vehicle to express the importance of visits to the 'old people' (those who have passed away). Eager to better understand this practice I turned to the work of American sociologist and advocate for improved social ties Richard Sennett, who has much to say about respect and its part in community making.

Who is Richard Sennett?

Sennett is a sociologist, writer, urban planner, and designer who was born in Chicago and raised in the infamous Cabrini Green housing project by his mother, who was a sole parent. In his youth he trained in music, becoming a child virtuoso of the cello. When a hand injury put a stop to his career as a musician he went to university where he studied sociology. Since the late 1960s he has become one of the world's most gifted scholars on the development of cities, civics, and mature social and cultural life. His book called *Respect: The Formation of Character in an Age of Inequality* (2003) examines how modern work, social relations, and practice can be reformed to support the welfare of those on the margins, and to establish a healthy community. In it, he reminds us of the crucial link between respect, shared social bonds and the gift economy. As a lover and scholar of music he notes that the practices of musicians' have much to offer our understanding and forming practices of respect and community making.

Respect and the gift economy

In *Respect* Sennett sets out to make important observations about how depth of character and strength of community can be forged through our treatment of those who possess less resources and influence. Without directly talking about community development it is one of the most helpful books on the part that the practice of respect can play in community work. Sennett's main critique of modern ideas about respect is that, like individualism and market-driven philosophy, it is too often grounded in the notion that others less worthy and successful need to show they deserve respect before it can be acknowledged. This is a fundamental misreading of respect, he says, arguing that we should instead understand it as a practice that begins with it being offered as a gift. In other words, says Sennett, respect is not something to be earned so much as something to be offered. He helps illustrate this with Marcel Mauss' comparison between social relationships under market economies with social bonds produced by a gift economy.

In contrast to a market economy, where equal value exchange relieves those involved of any relationship as soon as items have been paid for, a gift economy obligates us to one another, producing conditions that see people reciprocating their debt. According to Mauss (2002), the gift creates an economy not of altruism but of debt, so that gifts must be eventually returned and their value matched. However, the key here is that the gift may not return precisely to the original giver. Rather, a gift moves in a circle, with at least three people needed for the gift economy to work. In a classic gift economy, the gift travels in complex directions, moving 'from one hand to another with no assurance of anything in return' (Hyde 1983: 11). In this way, the gift draws us into a mutual dependence upon those involved in the exchange, a formal give-and-take that forces us to acknowledge our participation with and dependence upon each other. It also requires us to respond to those around us, those who are 'other' but with whom we are bound, as part of ourselves, not as a stranger or alien. At its most basic level, by offering respect as a gift to others we encourage its reciprocity.

The art (and music) of respect

As Sennett so poetically reminds us, the act of offering respect (so crucial to making and sustaining a community) is similar to the act of making music. Both demand impeccable timing and the ability to produce dominant notes, silences, the minor, and harmony. Sennett likens this to the performance of the classic Brahms Clarinet Quintet in B Minor, observing that it takes the balancing of dominant and subordinate voices by various musicians. As in this kind of labour, the work of community demands that the various performers 'learn to play as one, in unison, but also by learning how to hold back or how to dominate' (Sennett 2003: 213).

He suggests that the Quintet, rich, complex, and challenging as it is, will sound like a 'mushy soup' if played by either a group of amateurs or a group made up of skilled egoists who insist on exhibiting their full talents. It can be played with beauty only when the musicians demonstrate artfulness and respect for one another by being prepared to hold themselves back at some points, play together at other points, and dominate the performance only when the time demands. His analogy is particularly worth citing for its relevance to the practice of community development.

> In theory, holding oneself back keeps one at a distance from others. In performing the quintet, avoiding the danger of swelling out instead achieves distinction and articulation within a whole. By holding back we make our presence felt – which is reserve's most subtle and more positive side.

> As in all expressive labor, there is an objective problem to be solved: the soup of notes. The performers together will have to solve that problem by learning to play as one, in unison, but also by learning how to hold back or how to dominate. The gestures in sound they create become rituals which orient them to one another and speak together.

> Rituals in social life are equally complicated acts of knitting people together - with the great difference that the 'social text' is not a written musical score; it emerges through trial and error, and then becomes engraved in memory as tradition. The hold of tradition comes from this knowing already how to express oneself to others; whereas for chamber musicians, performing traditions can help, but the real social glue occurs when the performers have to work things out for themselves (Sennett 2003: 212–213).

In conclusion: Respect and community development

Sennett not only offers an illustration from classic music but also direct insights into how we can 'hold' (*kanyirninpa*) ourselves as practitioners.

Sennett claims that over the past twenty years, social policy in the West has taken a turn so that now we tend to deny the poor, marginalized groups and welfare recipients respect, instead demanding they earn respect for themselves and show they are worthy of support and even the most basic human rights. He points out that even if our leaders maintain this position on ideological grounds, that simplistic prescriptions for more self-motivation are not enough to elevate people. He argues that we cannot expect people to build esteem if institutions neglect them, are cruel, and accept the culture of market and competition.

Rather than adding to the demands of marginalized citizens, Sennett says we are better to reinvigorate an ethic of reciprocal respect for people. Reminding us of the observations of social scientists such as Malinowski and Mauss he counsels us to build more gift relationships (where the gift prompts reciprocity) rather than market-driven ones where the social bonds cease once a transaction is complete (Sennett 2003: 212). Such a practice of respect has long roots in communities where the gift economy obligates people to one another.

References and key works

Hyde, L. (1983) *The Gift: Imagination and the Erotic Life of Property*, Vintage Books, New York.

Mauss, M. (2002) *The Gift*, Routledge, London.

McCoy, B. F. (2008) *Holding Men: Kanyirninpa and the Health of Aboriginal Men*, Australian Institute of Aboriginal and Torres Strait Studies, Canberra, Australia.

Sennett, R. (2003) *Respect: The Formation of Character in an Age of Inequality*, Penguin, London.

Sennett, R. (2008) *The Craftsman*, Allen Lane, New York.

Sennett, R. (2011) *The Foreigner: Two Essays on Exile*, Notting Hill Editions, London.

Sennett, R. (2012) *Together: The Rituals, Pleasures, and Politics of Cooperation*, Yale University Press, New Haven, CT.

CHAPTER 35

Vandana Shiva: *Be a Seed Saver*

By Athena Lathouras

Vandana Shiva 1952—

Augustus Binu

My connection to Vandana Shiva's activism can be traced to the Gandhian tradition of community development, a philosophy to which I was exposed during my undergraduate studies. Gandhi's fundamental analysis was that, if he pursued the truth of the matter (known as *satyagraha* – the force of truth), he would find that exploitation and dominance create poverty. In the Gandhian tradition, the development process is based on truth, not power, as a force of liberation for the 'poorest of the poor'.

As a young woman Shiva drew from Gandhi's philosophy, becoming politicized by the threats to the planet's biodiversity and subsequent environmental and human consequences when she became a volunteer in the Chipko movement, or *Chipko Andolan*. The movement started in response to the 1972 Alaknanda flooding disaster in northern India and raised awareness about the impact of logging in creating landslides and floods, and of the scarcity of water, fodder, and fuel. Women activists in India were practising Gandhian methods of non-violent resistance in response to the large-scale deforestation taking place in the Garhwal Himalaya (Shiva, 2013). *Chipko* means 'to hug', 'to embrace', and the women in the movement declared that they would hug the trees to protect them from the loggers. They were prepared to be killed before the trees were felled.

This commitment to environmental activism has continued throughout her life. In the book, *Why Women Will Save the Planet* (Friends of the Earth & C40 Cities, 2018), Vandana Shiva is named as one of the pioneering women who is leading the charge to address the greatest challenge humankind has ever faced – climate change. In the book's foreword, Hidalgo (2018) argues that the severity of climate impacts is inextricably linked to economics, public health,

http://dx.doi.org/10.3362/9781788531245.035

inequality, and gender. Thus, Shiva's conjoined work for women's empowerment and environmental sustainability is seen as crucial to solving our current global crisis.

Born in India in 1952, Vandana Shiva is a physicist and philosopher of science whose life's work has been about the ecological, social, and economic struggles of subsistence farmers in India. A world-renowned environmental activist, thinker, and prolific author, her interdisciplinary work draws on Indigenous knowledge systems, feminist gender studies, philosophy, physics, environmental studies, and postcolonial theory.

Ecofeminism

Shiva's philosophy has its roots in ecofeminism. This is a field of critical theory that brings together critiques of patriarchal science and a concern with the degradation of 'nature'/the environment, and makes links between these and the oppression of women (Molyneux & Steinberg, 1995). Environmentalism (the 'eco' part of ecofeminism) is understood as a movement opposed to the harm and degradation of non-human beings and entities. And the feminism element of 'ecofeminism' signals the importance of seeking to end not just the subordination, inferiorization, and oppression of women, but also of other social groups (Mallory, 2013).

In the 1993 book she co-authored with Maria Mies, *Ecofeminism,* Shiva argues that humans are governed by the convergence of two extremely powerful forces – the idea that money mutated into capital as a creative force which can take and use life from the Earth and from people, and that patriarchy is the natural order of things where men dominate women. When capitalist-patriarchy becomes one, it aggravates violence against the Earth and against women. In order to ensure the survival and flourishing of all life systems on the planet, ecofeminists argue that life-sustaining feminist values of nurturance, care, and reciprocity need to replace more patriarchally identified values of domination, exploitation, and control that condition Western attitudes toward nature (Mallory, 2013).

This capitalist-patriarchy critique has been given voice with Shiva's stances against the chemicalization of agriculture, and the engineering of biological processes. Dumble (2001) argues that central to Shiva's arguments in this realm is the theft of natural biodiversity and food security by Eurocentric science and economics; knowledge systems which women have traditionally safeguarded over centuries. Shiva challenged the accepted wisdom of the Green Revolution, which integrated farmers from the Global South into the global market of fertilizers, pesticides, and seeds. Whether farmers owned or leased their land, biotechnology's genetically programmed seed was corporate property. The lifespan of the new age seed was regulated by corporations rather than by farmers guided by generations of traditional wisdom (Dumble, 2001). Shiva's fearless activism against corporate giants like Monsanto and their patents has highlighted how poor people have been prevented from saving seeds. With a monopoly established and promises of higher yields, Monsanto's agents sell Monsanto seeds, and their pesticides and fertilizers, on credit causing more and more personal debt for farmers. This cycle of high-cost seeds and rising chemical requirements is what Shiva argues is a debt trap, one which has driven thousands of Indian farmers to suicide (Shiva, 2014).

Shiva and her allies launched ecofeminism as a global political movement in 1991, when Shiva convened a seminar on 'Women, Health and the Environment'. The movement opposes environmental degradation, economic exploitation, cultural globalization, institutionalized gender, and Indigenous discrimination (Dumble, 2001). Their efforts have grown to influence global policy on environmental and social justice, human and women's rights, Indigenous knowledge, human and women's health, and world trade regulations.

Navdanya eco farm and Bija Vidyapeeth (Earth University)

The lessons about diversity Shiva learnt as a younger woman in the Himalayan forests have been transferred to the protection of biodiversity at the Navdanya eco farm in the Dune Valley of Northern India. Inspired by Gandhi's Salt Satyagraha, in 1987 Shiva established the Navdanya Seed Satyagraha, or the Seed Freedom movement. When Shiva first heard of corporations talking about owning seeds through Intellectual Property Rights (IPR), so did her commitment to seed saving take root. She committed to not cooperate with IPR systems that make seed saving and seed exchange a crime.

Bija Vidyapeeth (Earth University) is the name of Navdanya's learning centre. It draws inspiration from Rabindranath **Tagore** (another of our critical thinkers in this book), who created Shanti Niketan, an Indian university based on living in and learning from nature. In **Tagore's** writings, nature is not just the source of knowledge and freedom, but also the source of beauty and joy, of art and aesthetics, of harmony and perfection (Navdanya, 2019).

Navdanya is known today as the hub of a movement for biodiversity conservation through community seed banks and organic farming, and thousands of visitors have travelled to Navdanya for live-in retreats, to learn organic farming practices and skills, to cultivate a sense of community, and to witness Shiva's values in action.

Since 1991, Navdanya has organized more than 500,000 farmers, and the widows of those driven to suicide, through the Bija Satyagraha movement. The Bija Satyagraha pledge farmers take says:

> We have received these seeds from nature and our ancestors. It is our duty to future generations to hand them over in the richness of diversity and integrity in which we received them. Therefore, we will not obey any law, or adopt any technology that interferes in our higher duties to the Earth and the future generations. We will continue to save and share our seeds (Shiva, 2018: 165).

Together, they are finding hope and alternatives to the indebtedness and complete desperation caused by corporate exploitation by the GMO (genetically modified organism) industry. They have conserved more than 3,000 rice varieties from across India, 60 seed banks have been established in 16 states, and Indigenous knowledges of farming and food production have been saved. They are making the transition from fossil fuel and chemical-based monocultures to biodiverse ecological systems nourished by the sun and the soil. Shiva (2019) argues that this work is supporting agricultural traditions and right relationships with the Earth.

Be a Seed Saver

Shiva (2019) argues that as the colonization of life on Earth is taking place through genetic engineering and patenting, farmers are made to believe they must buy seed every year. But what is available is chemically bred seed, cultured in neonicotinoids and genetically engineered. The food from such hybridized seed is not designed for our health, but for long-haul transportation, a long shelf-life in the supermarket, and to look unblemished and therefore more appealing to the consumer. She calls this seed and food 'slavery'.

As an ethical response to enforced uniformity and monocultures created by the GMO industry, Shiva's gem of wisdom is for us all to become seed savers. She says it is the most important thing to do in our times. Food needs to be grown in healthy soil, so it is nutritious with vitamins and vitality for our health. When we grow our own food at home and save seeds, we are taking back some of the power to actively create our futures. The nature of seed is to 'go to seed', to multiply and to be shared despite all the new laws designed to prevent us from saving seed. Thus, learning to grow our own food and save seeds means we become scientists in service of the life of the Earth. She calls for us to sow our freedom, to know our seeds and to save them.

References and key works

Dumble, L. (2001) 'Vandana Shiva' in Palmer, J.A (ed.), *Fifty Key Thinkers on the Environment,* pp. 313–321, Routledge, London.

Hidalgo, A. (2018) 'Foreword' in Friends of the Earth Trust Ltd and C40 Cities, *Why Women Will Save the Planet, Second Edition,* pp. xv–xvii, Zed Books, London.

Mallory, C. (2013) 'Locating ecofeminism in encounters with food and place', *Journal of Agricultural and Environmental Ethics* 26: 171–189.

Mies, M. & Shiva, V. (1993) *Ecofeminism,* Zed Press, London.

Molyneux, M. and Steinberg, D. (1995) 'Mies and Shiva's "ecofeminism": A new testament?' *Feminist Review* 49: 86–107 (Spring 1995).

Navdanya (2019) 'Bija Vidyapeeth – Earth University' [website] <www.navdanya.org/navdanyas-biodiversity-conservation-farm/bija-vidyapeeth-earth-university> [Accessed 25 August 2019].

Shiva, V. (1989) *The Violence of the Green Revolution: Ecological Degradation and Political Conflict in Punjab,* Natraj Publisher, New Delhi.

Shiva, V. (2013) 'The Uttarakhand disaster: A wake-up call', *Fair Observer,* <www.fairobserver.com/region/central_south_asia/uttarakhand-disaster-wake-call/> [Accessed 25 August 2019].

Shiva, V. (2014) 'Seeds of truth – A response to the *New Yorker*' <https://web.archive.org/web/20180826092608/http://vandanashiva.com/?p=105> [Accessed 11 August 2019].

Shiva, V. (2015) *Soil Not Oil: Environmental Justice in an Age of Climate Crisis,* North Atlantic Books, Berkeley, CA..

Shiva, V. (2018) *Oneness vs the 1%: Shattering Illusions, Seeding Freedom,* Spinifex Press, North Geelong, Victoria, Australia.

Shiva, V. (2019) 'Saving seeds at home with Vandana Shiva', [website] <www.youtube.com/watch?v=Xar4vixyzUs [Accessed 29 August 2019].

CHAPTER 36

Georg Simmel:
The importance of the triad and the stranger in making 'community'

Julius Schaarwächter

By Dave Palmer

Georg Simmel 1858–1918

Who was Simmel?

Georg Simmel was an early sociologist, interested in method, intimate social relationships, the metropolis, the philosophy of money and, much to our interest, the importance of the stranger and the social consequences of numbers. He was born in Germany in 1858 and passed away in 1918, allowing him to experience first-hand many profound changes in European social and political life.

Like many profound contributors to European thought in early modernity Simmel was raised in a Jewish family, arguably giving him intimate insights into the experience of being a 'stranger' or outsider. Unusually, his father converted to Catholicism, giving the young Georg some unique appreciation of the process of moving in and out of a community. This tension was played out for Simmel in his career as an academic. For much of his life he failed to gain acceptance from his sociologist peers. Partly this was because of his Jewish heritage and the popularity at the time of anti-Semitism in the academy. Additionally, many were critical of his decision to try and write in a style that made his ideas available to a general audience, refusing to accept his work as serious unless written in the technical and elite language of philosophy and sociology.

http://dx.doi.org/10.3362/9781788531245.036

On the stranger

The stranger, remarks Simmel, is one of the most important contributors to the process of community making. This involves considerable irony and, for many, appears antithetical. As Simmel might ask, how can we know what it means to have close alliances, a sense of mutuality and the shelter of community without a clear and strong sense of those who stand to threaten us?

Hence one of Simmel's great contributions to thinking about community development is to recognize that community is a highly ambivalent thing, demanding the creation of outsiders in order to produce the conditions that build safety.

Simmel's interest in social distance is important here, identifying a stranger as a person that is far away and close at the same time.

> The Stranger is close to us, insofar as we feel between him [sic] and ourselves common features of a national, social, occupational, or generally human, nature. He is far from us, insofar as these common features extend beyond him or us and connect us only because they connect a great many people. (Simmel, 1971: 147).

This stranger figure needs to be far enough away to create a mix of mystery, incongruity, and otherworldliness but close enough that it is possible to clearly see that they are not 'one of us'. In this way the stranger, as the opposite of 'us', helps us identify what 'our' community looks like, stands for, and does.

At the same time the stranger offers those 'inside' a clear chance to reinvent themselves, building new identities and creating fresh adventures. As Simmel observes, if everyone and everything is known then there is no-one who can bring something new and invigorate community. Think for a moment about our reliance in community development on the 'enemy' or threat to the community. This may be in the way immigrants are constructed as outside the nation or community, the thief in gated communities, or entities such as government, capitalism, or climate denial in activist communities.

In addition, the stranger, who is sometimes allowed to enter the community (e.g. as tourists, traders, exotic performers), regularly plays an important role in giving people a chance to lose their inhibitions, confess their inner-most frustrations, and unburden themselves from the constraints of too much community. This is because we are more likely to let down our guard, open-up, and release our inhibitions around a stranger without fear or threat of reprisal. Think for a moment about our love of going on a holiday to distant places and meeting people with whom we can share openly and build a sense of intimacy without serious investment.

What happens when we form triads?

Simmel has at least one other important contribution to make to community development, as he was amongst the earliest to understand that when one moves from a relationship between one other (what he calls a dyad) to one between at least two others (what he called a triad), one begins to see the establishment of conditions for a fundamentally different set of social relationships. For example, in a dyad the individuality and established identity of the social actor (individual or organization) is more likely to be preserved and less likely to be challenged or transformed. This is because 'each of the two feels himself confronted only by the other, not by a collectivity above him' (Simmel, 1950: 60). A dyad is also dependent on each of its members for its continued survival. As it depends on two participants the withdrawal of either means the destruction of the whole. As Simmel (cited in Coser 1971: 186) said, 'a dyad depends on each of its two elements alone—in its death though not in its life: for its life it needs both, but for its death, only one'.

Simmel observed that when a third person or third social element enters a relationship to form a triad or transform a dialogue into a three-way relationship they bring to it the potential for qualitatively different sets of social dynamics that cannot be reduced to individuals or dyads (Kitts and Huang, 2010). This is partly because in Simmel's view a triad is made up of at least three different and complex sets of interests, three identities, and three ways of doing things. This fact demands that negotiation must occur if the parties are to enter and remain a part of the triad. As Simmel points out, in the triad each individual is confronted with the possibility of being outvoted by a majority so that their interests will become secondary to those of the group. In a dyad the relationship relies on both parties immediately and clearly reciprocating, agreeing to the demands of the other or at least one person submitting to the wishes of the other. By contrast in the triad the will of two can be imposed upon one member through the formation of a coalition between the other two.

To put it another way, in contrast to a dyad a triad is more likely to develop a structure and set of interests independent of the individuals in it. Therefore, built into the very form of the triad is the means by which the group as a whole can achieve domination over its constituent members. This means that when we have a triad we have the early conditions for 'community'. Thus, in a three-way relationship we see the simplest form of a sociological drama being played out, with those involved being forced to get used to moving back and forth between freedom and constraint, at one moment enjoying autonomy while ever conscious of the need to contend with heteronomy. As Kitts and Huang (2010: 873–874) point out, this substantially alters the dynamics of the relationship:

> For example, among three parties A, B, and C, party A may have a dyadic relation to C but also may have an indirect relation to C through B. Party B may then serve to alter the strength or the nature of the relation between A and C, such as solidifying an alliance or mediating a conflict. If A and C do not interact directly, party B may broker a transaction between them and may derive power from this intermediary position.

When a third member joins a dyad, it becomes possible for one to take on the role of mediator, acting as a go-between, reconfiguring the relationships of the other two. In this way a triad makes it possible for one person (or a third party such as an organization or group) to use their impartial status to moderate, restrain, or even generate passions, conflicts, or barriers.

Alternately, the third party can act in more sinister ways, undermining, exploiting, or turning to their own advantage disquiet and dispute between the other two. The popular political strategy of divide and rule can be carefully orchestrated so that a third party can gain the dominant or upper hand for self-interest.

Simmel offers a range of examples, including instances where two men compete for a woman, the way that a child 'plays off' one parent against the other, and how political parties form coalitions to shift the balance of power or achieve particular political interests (Coser, 1971).

Triads also make possible their own survival. Because the identity and interests of the triad are relatively independent of its members, if one person leaves, the group is capable of staying alive. Indeed, the etymology of the word reflects the idea that it is a group capable of outliving its members. In this way, triads create conditions for their continued existence. To use rhetoric that has recently become popular, triads help create sustainable community (Coser, 1971).

In his work, Simmel reveals the limits of simple and often taken-for-granted ideas about power and social relations. He also demonstrates the dangers of psychological reductionism, with its propensity to claim that political influence comes from the character, intelligence, and capability of the individual.

In this way, Simmel also provides insights for those keen on working with what has come to be known as 'community development'. His observations remind us that the apparently peripheral third person or third organization, when thrown into the mix, opens-up possibilities; they can create the conditions for action and can be used to get things happening. Not only is this important in reminding us of the limits of individuals and individual organizations, it also uncovers the kind of properties and methodological devices that 'community' organizations might put to use.

References and key works

Coser, L. A. (1971) *Masters of Sociological Thought: Ideas in Historical and Social Context*, Harcourt Brace Jovanovich, New York.

Kitts, J.A. and Huang, J. (2010) "Triads", *Encyclopedia of Social Networks*, George Barnett, Editor, Sage Publications, New York.

Simmel, G. (1908) 'The Stranger', originally published in 1908 in *Soziologie*, Untersuchungen uber die Formen der Vergellschaftung, Duncker and Humblot, Berlin.

Simmel, G. (1950) 'The dyad and the triad', in *The Sociology of Georg Simmel*, Compiled, edited and translated by K.H. Wolff, The Free Press, Glencoe, IL.

Simmel, G. (1950) 'The Stranger' in *The Sociology of Georg Simmel*, Compiled, edited and translated by K. H. Wolff, The Free Press, Glencoe, IL. Originally published as Simmel, G. (1908) 'The Stranger', in *Soziologie*, Untersuchungen über die Formen der Vergellschaftung, Duncker and Humblot, Berlin.

Simmel, G. (1971) 'The Stranger, in *On Individuality and Social Forms: Selected Writings*. Chicago University Press, Chicago, IL.

Wolff, K. H. (ed.) (1964) *The Sociology of Georg Simmel*, Free Press, New York.

CHAPTER 37
Linda Tuhiwai Smith: *Listening to old knowledge*

By Dave Palmer

Linda Tuhiwai Smith

Linda Tuhiwai Smith 1950—

Listening to the old knowledges of Indigenous groups

Many years ago, a Nyungar (an Indigenous man from the southwest of Australia) colleague and I were sitting down to one of those 'light' discussions about the ethics of working with communities. The discussion took shape after I, in an intense and considered way, asked my friend what he thought to be 'ethical behaviour' or the 'right way to go about working with Indigenous people'. My friend's reply went something like this:

> *Noonook nyidiyang noonook yoowalkoorl yeye kidji nyin boodjar djinang kidji ni kaitijin Nyungar wangkiny kidji karnarn ngalang koorlangka.*

I was a little embarrassed, uncomfortable, and confused by this response and so repeated myself. I again asked what I should really keep in mind when trying to work with Indigenous communities. Unperturbed my friend repeated himself:

> *Noonook nyidiyang noonook yoowalkoorl yeye kidji nyin boodjar djinang kidji ni kaitijin Nyungar wangkiny kidji karnarn ngalang koorlangka.*

It was some years before I understood that he was saying something like: 'You non-Aboriginal man, you need to come along and sit down on my country and listen to my old and knowledgeable people talk with respect about our young people'.

I wasn't able to appreciate the magnitude of his answer to my question. Not only did I not acknowledge that I could not hear it until I learnt his language, I failed to appreciate the deep conceptual ideas

http://dx.doi.org/10.3362/9781788531245.037

that sat in his response about the important connection between *quop weirn* (healthy spirit), *gnulla koorliny moort* (time spent with family), *boordjar nyin* (sitting on country) and *koorankurl kaitijin* (becoming learned). This was because I expected the serious answers to come from English and be framed in the knowledge systems with which I was familiar.

I was first given to read Linda Tuhiwai Smith's work on decolonizing practice by the same Nyungar colleague, who is now a very close friend and family member. It seems that Indigenous philosophers routinely have to deal with well-meaning but ignorant community workers.

Who is Linda Tuhiwai Smith?

Linda Tuhiwai Smith is a Māori *mana*, an intellectual of high standing, a Professor of Māori Education and scholar of research practice. In her book *Decolonizing Methodologies* (1999), Smith sets out a deep critique of Western systems and practices of research and knowledge acquisition from a position of one who has been subjected to the often cruel, demeaning, and erroneous knowledge traditions of those involved in the colonizing project. Her interest is mostly in the research methodologies and traditions of the West as they go about their business of studying the Indigenous Other. However, almost all of her observations are equally pertinent to students of community development for at least two reasons: 1) as Said (1978) observes, the practice of research about the Indigenous Other is intricately tied up with processes of colonizing and subjugating Indigenous communities; and 2) so much of Western research ontology and method frames how 'developmental' workers come to the task of working with Indigenous communities. As Smith so poignantly puts it:

> the term research is so inextricably linked to imperialism and colonialism. The word itself 'research', is probably one of the dirtiest words in the indigenous world's vocabulary. When mentioned in many indigenous contexts, it stirs up silence, it conjures up bad memories, it raises a smile that is knowing and distrustful ... The ways in which scientific research is implicated in the worst excesses of colonialism remains a powerful remembered history for many of the world's colonized peoples ... Just knowing that someone measured our 'faculties' by filling the skulls of our ancestors with millet seeds and compared the amount of millet seed to the capacity for mental thought offends our sense of who and what we are. (1999: p. 1)

Smith's work could be understood as having two central aspirations. The first is understanding the history of Western interventions into the lives of Indigenous people and critiquing the vast body of deep cultural assumptions that Westerners bring with them. The second part focuses on setting a new agenda for Indigenous groups both as researchers and those being researched. As part of a growing group of Māori scholars, Smith has been involved in revisiting the strength of Māori knowledge and practices and setting out (in *Māori)* what this looks like.

Decolonizing practice

For Smith (1999: 10) the project of decolonizing, of speaking back and against the interests of so much work in communities, is the principal objective of those who seek to work with Indigenous communities. She posits several key questions to ask at the outset of research (and we might say community development) work:

- Whose work is it?
- Who owns it?
- Whose interests does it serve?
- Who benefits from it?
- Who has designed it and framed its scope?
- Who will carry out the work?
- Who will write up the work, and in whose language(s) will it be disseminated?

Furthermore, outsiders working in these settings need to subject themselves to other questions that come from the culture, language, and interests of Indigenous communities. They should not be surprised if these questions are not initially answerable or appear to not be relevant to the work. For example, Smith (1999: 10) tells us that we ought not be surprised to be asked:

- Is your spirit clear?
- Do you have a good heart?
- What baggage do you carry with you (literal and metaphoric)?
- Are you useful to us?
- Can you fix a generator?
- Can you actually do anything practical?

Using Indigenous language and 'theory'

The words, the names, and the conceptual devices that colonizers inscribe into places and onto communities are the first and most powerful acts of conquest. Smith aptly describes the processes of imperialism thus: 'they came, they saw, they named, they claimed' (Smith 1999: 80). Drawing on the work of African writer Ngugi wa Thiong'o, Smith notes that to write in the language of the colonizers is a subtle way of paying homage to them. On the other hand, to encourage local Indigenous people to write in the language of their families is a powerful way to support anti-imperialist and decolonizing struggles. This is because, as language carries culture, the language of the colonizer becomes the means by which the 'mental universe of the colonised' is dominated. Conversely to speak, write, and conceptualize in one's first language allows members of a community to reformulate the way they carry out their lives.

Smith has been central in the development and re-activation of *Kaupapa Māori* theories and tools for work in education and community development. She argues that these distinctly Māori conceptual devices are necessary because they help make sense of reality, enable Māori to 'make assumptions and predictions about the world in which we live', contain within them methods for selecting, arranging, planning, prioritizing, and legitimating what can be seen and done, and enable communities to deal with contradictions and uncertainties, and to take control (Smith 1999: 38).

Kaupapa Māori

Other Indigenous groups have been making similar points when they talk about research. Along with many of her contemporary Māori scholars, Linda Tuhiwai Smith has spent much time fleshing out how to carry out what she calls *kaupapa Māori* research and practice, research that starts from a Māori philosophical base. This approach takes *tikanga Māori* (a Māori way of doing things) as its first order of analysis and method. Critical here is that practitioners use *te reo Māori* (Māori language) as their means of communicating, research practice, ethical frame, and means of analysis (Smith, 1999).

Respectfully learning language can also be an important way for non-Indigenous researchers to find an ethical place for themselves. When asked whether a non-Indigenous researcher should carry out *kaupapa Māori*, researchers Bishop and Glynn (1999) answer in the affirmative – particularly if the researchers position themselves as allies and invest in building their *te reo Māori*.

Smith implies that language also holds deep clues about how we can go about the business of working respectfully with a community. The work of *Māori* scholars Angus and Sonja Macfarlane helps elaborate on Smith's earlier calls for the use of *te reo Māori*. In setting out what an ethical practice looks like, they posit that our work should be shaped by the following six practices from *tikanga Māori*:

1. *Whanaungatanga* – building and maintaining strong relationships grounded in mutual trust, protection of Māori knowledge and care between those involved.
2. *Whaiwāhitanga* – ensuring participation, co-design of the research, and that power and benefits are shared.
3. *Tātaritanga* – listening; thinking; shared meaning-making, careful analysis of the data, and checking of conclusions.
4. *Manaakitanga* – affection towards others and ensuring the welfare and *mana* (status and position) of people is maintained through respectful interaction and acknowledgement of the source of knowledge.
5. *Rangatiratanga* – supporting people to maintain autonomy and control over their involvement in the research.
6. *Aroha* – maintaining the connection to the *kaupapa* (knowledge system) and approaching work with an intention of love, kindness, and respect (Macfarlane & Macfarlane, 2013; Macfarlane, 2012).

In conclusion

Although Smith is more concerned about the act of research with First Nations groups, many of her observations are equally applicable to the business of community development. Here she reminds those interested in community development that we are likely to continue colonizing practice unless we explicitly and consciously foreground the language, cultures, and knowledge systems of communities. For example, she draws on old practices to establish a set of principles for coming into a research relationship with *Māori* communities. These are highly applicable to those involved in community work and are not so much prescribed in a code of ethics as enacted by communities who expect the following:

- *Aroha ki te tangata* (a respect for people).
- *Kanohi kitea* (the seen face, that is present yourself to people face to face).
- *Titiro, whakarongo ... korero* (look, listen ... speak).
- *Manaaki ki te tangata* (share and host people, be generous).
- *Kia tupato* (be cautious).
- *Kaua e takahia te mana o te tangata* (do not trample over the *mana* (power) of people).

- *Kaua e mahaki* (don't flaunt your knowledge).

Smith observes that for many *Māori*, it is common to introduce yourself by naming the mountain, the river, the tribal ancestor, the tribe, and the family from whence you came. This is not possible unless you can speak the language of your own community and learn the language of the community with whom you seek to work. Her work offers some sobering challenges to those of us reliant upon the language of the colonizer.

References and key works

Bishop, R., & Glynn, T. (1999). *Culture Counts: Changing Power Relations in Education*, Dunmore Press, Palmerston North, New Zealand.

Macfarlane, S. (2012) *In pursuit of culturally responsive evidence based special education pathways in Aotearoa New Zealand: Whaia ki te ara tika*. PhD Thesis, University of Canterbury, Christchurch, New Zealand.

Macfarlane, S. L., & Macfarlane, A. H. (2013) 'Culturally responsive evidence-based special education practice: Whaia ki te ara tika', *Waikato Journal of Education. Te Hautaka Mâtauranga o Waikato* 18(2): 65–78.

Macfarlane, A.H., Macfarlane, S.L. and Webber, M. (2015) *Sociocultural Realities: Exploring New Horizons*, Canterbury University Press, New Zealand.

Said, E. (1978) *Orientalism*, Routledge and Kegan Paul, London.

Smith, Linda Tuhiwai (1999) *Decolonizing Methodologies: Research and Indigenous Peoples* (2nd ed.), Zed Books, London.

Smith, Linda Tuhiwai (2015) 'Kaupapa Māori research: Some Kaupapa Māori principles' in L. Pihama and K. South (eds.) *Kaupapa Rangahau A Reader: A Collection of Readings from the Kaupapa Maori Research Workshop Series*. pp. 46–52. Te Kotahi Research Institute, Waikato, New Zealand.

CHAPTER 38
Rabindranath Tagore: *Discovering the invitation*

By Peter Westoby

Visva Vharati Archive

Rabindranath Tagore 1861–1941

A key contemporary of Mahatma Gandhi, Rabindranath Tagore spent most of his life living in Calcutta, India. Concerned with the big issue of Indian independence from British colonial rule he spent significant time reflecting on the links between love and force (Hill, 2014: 58), suggesting that 'when love and force do not go together, then love is mere weakness and force brutal' (Hill, 2014: 58). For Tagore, such coming together is reflected in his commitment to bringing the social and soul together, holding both an aesthetic and a social-political sensibility. In this reflection I will explore this bringing together of the social and the soul, along with a couple of key wisdoms, including 'see what the people see' and 'discovering the invitation'.

'See what the people see'

Introduced to Tagore's work in 1992 by my community development teacher Anthony Kelly, I keep returning to his opus (Gupta, 2006). Echoing in my head is the Tagore wisdom Kelly taught all his community work students over a 30-year period: 'see what the people see' (Kelly & Westoby, 2018: 62). This wisdom sits with me whenever I approach a new group or community; *how do I see their world*, or try to get inside the world as they see it? Recognizing this is almost impossible, for how people see the world is shaped by deeply ingrained lenses and leanings; to be asking the question at least invites a pause, a renewed realization that, 'I really don't have a clue'.

I find this wisdom particularly important as I become more experienced, because there's a heightened risk of thinking experience

http://dx.doi.org/10.3362/9781788531245.038

enables practitioners to understand more quickly. Perhaps it does. But, perhaps quite the opposite. Experience can lead to hubris, quick assumptions of 'knowing'. Hence, the importance of returning to, check and, 'see what the people see'.

For life and your song

It has been tempting to see this wisdom – 'see what the people see' – as the gem for this reflection, and it was equally tempting to focus on Tagore's view of soul, and the need to be 'for life' and 'finding one's song'. As Alam and Chakravarty put it in their most beautiful tome, *The Essential Tagore* (2011), Tagore was 'a great poet of the will to live' (2011: xxix), which they denote as 'the irrepressible Tagorean energy, the irresistible will to arrive …' (ibid), and then perhaps more insightfully, they cite Das, a contemporary of Tagore, who said, 'in the midst of this, I find myself – I so, surprised, my song awakens' (ibid). What would it be for each community development practitioner to 'find their song', which particularly resonates when writing from a land, Australia, full of 'song-lines'? In a similar way, what would it be like to hear what a country 'sounds like'? Much like our gem of a wisdom from the **James Baldwin** reflection in this volume, asking the question of song would be to consider if we are going the 'the way [y]our blood beats', that is, living our own creative truth. Yet, what I will focus on as the gem from Tagore's work is 'discovering the invitation', discussed towards the end.

More about Tagore

In 2011 I was invited to speak at a community work educator conference in Dublin. I can still vividly remember stepping outside of my hotel and crossing the road to stroll in St. Stephen's Green. Somewhat jetlagged and in that fuzzy state where the soul has not yet caught up with the body, in the corner of my eye I caught a glimpse of a beautifully sculptured bust. I was drawn to it and realised it was of Tagore, friend of the great Irish poet Yeats. Yeats wrote the preface to *Gitanjali*, the poem that won Tagore the Nobel Prize in Literature, and here was Ireland paying homage to Tagore – a land that somehow understands how to hold together a terrible history of loss, the defiance of political action, along with soul; maintaining the music, so to speak, along with a good taste for a pint of Guinness. Tagore found the essence of his song in that great poem *Gitanjali,* and I suggest it's the call of each practitioner to find their equivalent.

Indicative of his friendship with Yeats, Tagore was a towering figure, living mainly in Calcutta, but travelling far and wide, engaging with some of the greats. Yet, he was very grounded in his own 'experiments in truth', as Gandhi would put it. His key experiments in community development were through his school called Santiniketan, which started in 1901 as an ashram but was also a place where he was deeply committed to the creation of a new kind of world university that could hold both the social and the spiritual (Dutta & Robinson, 1995: 135). This school for students was complemented with the setting up of his Institute for Rural Reconstruction, later named Shriniketan or 'Abode of Welfare', focused on agronomy and social experimentation. Shriniketan was started by Tagore along with economist and agronomist Leonard Knight Elmhirst, who also later founded Dartington Hall, in Devon, the UK (along with his wife). Combining the university and school, his pedagogical inclinations were towards the aesthetic, with students learning dance, art, poetry, languages, and literature, as well as agricultural labour and social literacy. Again, linked to his view of life, Tagore advocated that, 'education is a living, not a mechanical process, a truth as freely admitted as it is persistently ignored' (Dutta & Robinson, 1995: 323).

In dialogue with Gandhi – the soul and the social

Turning to the idea of bringing the social and soul together, importantly there is a historical context that needs understanding. This context is a somewhat antagonistic dialogue between Gandhi and Tagore, which is indicative of some misgivings about Gandhi's idea of 'soul-force' (in the midst of a beautiful enduring friendship, with Gandhi viewing Santiniketan as his second home).[1] For Tagore, Gandhi's interpretations of 'life's training was different' to his own, with Gandhi's focus being 'the eradication of life's joy', and his own being 'the purification of life's joy' (Hill, 2014: 144). For Tagore, there should be no aesthetic antagonism to social life itself – in fact, the hope was harmony. He explains in his typically beautiful words:

> [Life] was like our musical instrument *tambura* whose duty is to supply the fundamental notes to the music to save it from going astray into discordance. It believed in *anadam,* the music of the soul, and its own simplicity was not to kill it but to guide it (Hill, 2014: 144).

Tagore's disagreement with Gandhi is that Gandhi's struggle could easily become *primarily* a struggle 'against something' rather than 'for something'. In contrast, Tagore is arguing *for life*, for a deeper vision of how to live, and sees nonviolent action as it was being deployed by Gandhi as essentially anti-life (in the form of asceticism). As I move into my 50s I become more and more conscious that I can only sustain what I am *for, what I love*. Cognizant that this 'for love' represents a somewhat privileged position in the world, Tagore's love of the bringing together of soul and social has captivated me for decades. If Tagore could 'hold' this position in the midst of the violence and suffering of colonization, then all is possible.

Somewhat like Allen Ginsberg's poetic cry against Moloch in the poem 'Howl', Tagore also saw that 'today the human soul is lying captive in the dungeon of the Great Machine' (Hill, 2014: 163), and he wanted people to rediscover a life-giving vision of love, art, philosophy, conviviality, play, joy, dance, and music. Even in Tagore's lifetime, people were questioning whether it was possible at the same time to be socially radical and to talk of soul. Later in his life Tagore noted that, 'I have not convinced a single sceptic that he has a soul, or that moral beauty has greater value than material power' (Hill, 2014: 166). In a sense, while Gandhi drifted towards social action and asceticism, Tagore was able to hold a view of the world that was both socially revolutionary and also more poetic, more philosophical, more sensual and embodied, characterized by 'the clean and radiant fires of individual expression' (Hill, 2014: 219). Tagore wanted us to cultivate a love *for* something!

Discovering the invitation

As would be clear by now, Tagore's orientation was towards *honouring life* rather than purifying it. But, intriguingly, what's crucial to understand about the opus of Tagore's poetic work is the insistence on 'celebrating of the occurrence of life and consciousness ... and the deliberate celebration of contingency' (Alam & Chakravarty, 2011: xxvi). In the same way, the same commentators suggest that, 'much of Tagore's work, then, is preoccupied with – indeed mesmerized by – coincidence and possibility' (ibid). It reminds me of that old saying, 'life happens when we're making plans.' To be attuned to life in this Tagorean way is to be open to the surprise, and my focus here is the surprise of invitation. Are we attuned to life's invitation? Are we open to the invitation into relationship or practice in such a way that we work *with* what is unfolding, rather than working in a way of wilful planning or preoccupation? To be attuned to life, to soul then, is to be open to the invitation into people's worlds, which I suggest is the beginning of generative community development. I have few rules in my community development practice, but one of them is to *only work when and where I am invited*. I never push, pull, probe. I wait. I am attentive. I nurture relationships; I dream and hope, but I see what unfolds. This is a poetic practice. This is the gem of Tagore's wisdom.

Endnotes

1. For Gandhi, soul-force, sometimes translated as 'truth-force', was at the core of his programme and ethic of nonviolent civil disobedience.

References

Alam, F. & Chakravarty, R. (2011) *The Essential Tagore,* Harvard University Press Cambridge, MA & London, UK.

Dutta, K. & Robinson, A. (1995) *Rabindranath Tagore: The Myriad-Minded Man,* St Martin's Press, New York.

Gupta, U. D. (2006) *Rabindranath Tagore: My Life in My Words,* Penguin, Viking Press, New Delhi & New York.

Hill, B. (2014) *Peacemongers,* The University of Queensland Press, Queensland, Australia.

Kelly, A. & Westoby, P. (2018) *Participatory Development Practice: Using Contemporary and Traditional Frameworks,* Practical Action Press, Rugby, UK.

CHAPTER 39

Thich Nhat Hanh: *Being, not doing*

By Peter Westoby

Thich Nhat Hanh 1926—

Duc

I have journeyed with Thich Nhat Hanh's work for many years. His life has combined peace work and protest, along with bringing the practices of mindfulness and meditation into the world. This has occurred particularly through his writing, but also via the inspirational Plum Village community of practice.

It is also hard to know where to start when thinking about his work's relevance to community development. It was tempting to foreground his concept of Interbeing (Hanh, 2010a), a relational way of perceiving and being in the world – one well aligned with some community development philosophies critiquing the atomizing, individualizing, separate/ing approach of globalizing Western philosophy. I could have picked, 'don't be busy', a mantra loved by one of my co-authors Dave Palmer (see the **Bertrand Russell** reflection in this volume on 'idleness'). Of course, waxing lyrical about the power of mindfulness and meditation was tempting too. Yet, I suspect most readers can access plenty of material on such topics. Instead, I have opted for the simple, yet profound idea of 'being, not doing'. In doing so, consider the following words:

> It is not about 'doing' something; it's about 'being' something – being peace, being hope, being solid. Every action will come out of that, because peace, stability, and freedom always seek a way to express themselves in action. That is the spiritual dimension of our reality (Hanh, 2012: 129).

Who is Thich Nhat Hanh?

However, before we reflect further on these words, let us briefly consider Hanh's biography. In a nutshell, Hanh could be described as a Zen master and peace activist. In this, he has avoided the potential

http://dx.doi.org/10.3362/9781788531245.039

binary of either/or, of living a withdrawn hermetic spiritual life, or instead living a busy activist life. He is a strong proponent of integrating the two, living the polarity between both a spiritual and active life.

Having been exiled from Vietnam during the Vietnam/American War,[1] he had to apply for political asylum in the late 1960s to live in France – where he has lived most of his adult life, only returning to Vietnam in the last chapter of his life. Exile has played a huge part is his life, forcing Hanh to come to terms with what is it to be 'at home' (in one's body, heart, and place, when exiled from the place of your ancestors). In his own words, 'the expression "I have arrived, I am home" is the embodiment of my practice' (2016: 13), or to be more pointed, 'It expresses my understanding of the teaching of the Buddha and is the essence of my practice' (ibid: 13–14). His emphasis on 'being' requires this constantly 'coming home' to our bodies, ourselves, aware that the turmoil in the world must first be understood within ourselves. To not be at home within our bodies wherever we are in the world is to potentially bring violence to the world – for to not be at home in our bodies is to be unsettled, and to be in a violent relationship with ourselves.

France has become his physical home, where he set up in the late 1970s, with others, the Plum Village Mindfulness Practice Centre. This has continued to blossom and many aspiring and experienced practitioners alike make pilgrimages to the Centre to renew their meditation practice.

Being and 'right action'

Returning to the words quoted above, Hanh, like most Buddhist practitioners, tries to avoid binaries – the either/or of, for example, being and doing. Yet, in the binaries that do exist for most people, one tends to be dominant in the perceived and therefore practised hierarchy – that is, one is more important than the other. As such, most community development workers lean towards the tendency of doing or action in the world. Eschewing this hierarchy of doing over being, Hanh insists that 'being' should be primary, but actually a more careful reading does expose the critique of dualistic thinking and his argument is that within a non-duality worldview, 'right action' would flow organically or naturally from this 'being'. Meditating on this, I am reminded of the popular discourse of 'I'm busy'. More or less all community development workers I talk to, and when asked, 'How are you?', answer with some version of, 'I'm too busy'. Hanh's words strike to the heart of this discursive habit. His wisdom invites questions such as, 'In being so busy are you actually creating community?' (Or are you undoing community with your busy activity), or 'Are you enabling development, an emergent process from inside-out of a person, group, or community?' Or in your busy activity, are you intervening into a person, group or community's life, undoing what's organically growing – therefore actually blocking authentic development?

Quality of the practitioner

At the heart of foregrounding the wisdom of 'being, not doing', is actually a call to non-duality whereby action and doing flows from being. To be at peace is to bring peace to the world. To be living in convivial community is to bring community to the world. It is to actually foreground that our real practice challenge is not so much learning a bunch of community development skills, techniques, or even practices, but is cultivating ourselves as a human being. Perhaps, *it is the quality of the practitioner which will determine the quality of the practice.*

What is also powerful about Thich Nhat Hanh's work is that – like much of the Buddhist philosophical and spiritual traditions – it provides pathways to cultivate the actual 'practice' – *the how.* For example, it is one thing to talk about the importance of love in cultivating community. Delightfully, Hanh's work provides actual signposts of how to cultivate love-in-practice (see for example, *True Love: A Practice for Awakening the Heart* (2006)). So, with the wisdom 'being, not doing', Hanh is not just offering a mantra, but a set of practices to cultivate the qualities of being that community development workers aspire to.

Being in the present moment

In turn, most of these practices – enabling true love, and many other capacities – come from 'discovering the magic of the present moment', a title of one of Hanh's best works, (2010b). To focus on being is to focus on the here and now, not to be caught in activities of the mind, feelings, perceptions, consciousness, that take us forever into either the past or future. The present is what is here, and to be attentive to the present – within his framework, enabled through the disciplines of mindfulness and concentration, cultivated through meditation (sitting, walking, but actually available in everyday life)

– is to be fully attentive to a state of being. How am I right now? Am I listening to the person sharing their story with me, or is my mind wandering? Am I really with this group I am facilitating, or wishing I was elsewhere? Are the feelings provoked by the annoying white male who keeps interrupting now linked to other stories in my life rather than the phenomenon occurring right now? Am I listening to my body, for its intelligence offers many pathways? (Or is my practice disembodied, caught in wilful action that is detached from what the body is perceiving?)

Endnotes

1. I have grown up knowing it as the Vietnam War, but a visit to Vietnam in 2005 changed all that as I learned of how north Vietnamese refer to it – as the American War.

References

Hanh, T. H. (2006) *True Love: A Practice for Awakening the Heart,* Shambhala, Boston MA & London.

Hanh, T. N. (2010a) *Together We Are One, Honouring our Diversity, Celebrating Our Connection,* Parallax Press, Berkeley, CA.

Hanh, T. N. (2010b) *You Are Here: Discovering the Magic of the Present Moment,* Random House Inc., New York.

Hanh, T. N. (2012) *The Pocket Thich Nhat Hanh,* Shambala Pocket Classics, Shambhala Press, Boston MA.

Hanh, T. N. (2016) *At Home in the World,* Rider Press, London, Sydney, Auckland, Johannesburg.

CHAPTER 40

Greta Thunberg: *Work where there's desire and political motivation*

By Peter Westoby

Anders Hellberg

Greta Thunberg 2003—

Introduction

Walking with thousands of people on the 20 September 2019 Schools Strike for Climate Action was a hope-building moment in many people's lives. It was an inspiration to walk. It was an inspiration to accompany so many young people. It was an inspiration to chant a slogan, dance a jig, sing a song, and briefly 'dare to dream' that some momentum for climate justice action might gain traction.

A few days later, on 23 September, linked to, and building on, that momentum, young Swedish high-school student Greta Thunberg stepped into the UN Climate Action Summit in New York and gave her now famous: 'You are failing us; how dare you' speech.[1] Pleading with the powerful specifically, and adult generations generally, she looked power in the face and made demands.

We all need to be involved in the climate struggle now

Because of her youth, and because she has stepped into the furnace of climate politics, we have included a reflection on her work as a critical thinker for community development. As we said in the Introduction of this book, unlike the other 39 critical thinkers, Greta Thunberg cannot *yet* be said to have a longevity of influence – she might be just a 'flash in the pan'. This would be true of all young people, but we felt that young people should have a voice in this book, even if only marginal. We also said in the Introduction that perhaps, and we say, perhaps, yet with an adult passion of solidarity with her, that much of

http://dx.doi.org/10.3362/9781788531245.040

the thinking of the other 39 critical thinkers means little if the planet becomes uninhabitable. Echoing Rebecca Solnit's argument (2016), Thunberg's plea acknowledges that while many other struggles for justice are important, they are now all subservient to the climate justice necessity. In a sense, all our other struggles – social, structural, identity, and so forth – will mean little if humans become a part of what many are calling a period of 'mass extinction'. Stated in her own words, Thunberg wants adults to:

> … grasp the urgency of the climate and ecological crisis and come together despite their differences – as you would in an emergency – and take the measures required to safeguard the conditions for a dignified life for everybody on earth (Thunberg, 2019a).

All very well – a young person, a plea, a social, political, economic, cultural struggle for climate justice that cannot be avoided – but what wisdoms can community development practitioners learn from her work?

Changing the story

Thunberg has not yet written much, though at the heart of her September 2019 speech was the crucial words: 'We are in the beginning of mass extinction, and all you can talk about is money and fairy tales of eternal economic growth'. Here, like fellow climate activist George Monbiot (2017), Thunberg insists on a new 'story' – because the endless economic growth story of contemporary hyper-capitalism is wrecking the ecological base of life. Part of the challenge of community development practice is tuning into new stories, reaching for second-order social change – not just surviving the current 'system', but changing it. To name the fantasy of eternal economic growth, one of the core fairy tales of the current story-system, is crucial in the process of reaching for a new story.

Aligning experiments with desire and political motivation

Yet, stories do not change without addressing power. In reaching for a new story, Thunberg has become a moral spokesperson for the climate justice social movement. Such movements recognize that while story generates energies, power is never given away by the powerful. In a sense power needs to be taken, or at least the powerful need to be forced to negotiate through a counter-veiling force. A climate movement now led by young people has the potential to provide this counter-veiling force. The sentiment, 'to fight for justice, one needs to escalate conflict' is apt. Some of our critical thinkers had a similar analysis. For example, **Rosa Luxemburg**, who argues:

> … the modern [worker's] struggle is a part of history, a part of social progress, and in the middle of history, in the middle of progress, in the middle of the fight, we learn how we must fight (Evans, 2015).

The point is, the people for climate justice and action are 'learning how we must fight'. **Freire** and **Horton** make the important point in their dialogue *We Make the Road by Walking,* that community educators can:

> … start without too much preoccupation concerning methods and techniques and materials because you had the principle ingredient, which was the desire of the people, the political motivation of the people (Horton et al. 1990: 78).

The key wisdom here is the acknowledgment that it's much easier for community development practitioners to initiate community education and mobilization experiments when the issues being explored, and mobilized around, are linked to the 'desire' and 'political motivation' of the people. It is into such energies that community development practitioners can facilitate local learning circles learning about climate change and climate justice; it's into the space of such political motivation that community development practitioners can support local-level campaigns to bring changes to local transport, local 'development', and 'transition initiatives', many of which were highlighted in our discussion on **E.F. Schumacher**.

Who is Greta Thunberg?

At the time of making that 2019 famous speech, Greta Thunberg could be described as a reluctant activist. As the symbolic voice of a global youth movement for climate action and justice she said, 'she'd rather be at school' (hence reluctant) but cannot step back from action. Like **Max-Neef, Bhatt, Shiva** and **Maathai** before her, she was awarded the alternative Nobel Prize, the Right Livelihood, in 2019, consolidating herself a place in activist history.

She first learnt about climate change at the age of eight, when, at school, her class was shown documentaries about climate change. She recounts how she remembers being more affected than the other students:

> My classmates were concerned when they watched the film, but when it stopped, they started thinking about other things. I couldn't do that. Those pictures were stuck in my head (Watts & Thunberg, 2019).

She herself suggests that these pictures being 'stuck in my head' was due to her having Asperger's and selective mutism, something she sees as a gift (Thunberg, 2019b: 30). She chooses to speak when it's important. Whereas many people can compartmentalize knowledge that is uncomfortable, her autism spectrum disorder (not an illness) makes that difficult. By the age of 11 she was suffering from depression due to her knowledge of climate warming, and stopped going to school.

On August 20 2018 Thunberg initiated her first school strike, not going to school for the next 21 days (until the Swedish election), and instead sat down outside the Swedish Parliament. Gradually people joined her, and a momentum and a new chapter in the global climate justice movement began to grow, with an estimated 7 million people participating in the global climate strikes on 20 September 2019.

Moving from dialogue to demands combined with people-power

One crucial lesson from her actions is that there is a time for dialogue – and we have made the case for dialogue in numerous reflections, see for example **Buber** and **Freire** – yet there is also a time to stop dialogue and make forceful demands that are backed up by the counter-veiling force of people mentioned earlier.

Like the South African student activists of #RhodesMustFall that burst onto the scene of 2015 in Cape Town, there is a time when frustration at not being listened to leads to such strident gestures of demanding. We suggest that community development practitioners, recognizing the legitimacy of starting social change processes with dialogue (knowing our desires and demands), must be willing to step into the cauldron of making forceful demands when dialogue is constantly dismissed, and ensuring that 'our' demands are backed by people-power.

The people, leaders, and experts

In some ways Thunberg has said nothing new. Scientists, climate activists, and community leaders have been saying the same for many years. Yet something about her age, her personality, and demeanour has spoken to many of us. Adult allies joined her and her fellow students in their hundreds of thousands at the September 2019 Climate Strikes. Her 2019 UN speech evokes the important work of scientists in her plea for change, foregrounding their expertise. In doing this, she acknowledges the importance of expertise, pleading that 'you must unite behind the science' (Thunberg, 2019a). Much like **Myles Horton's** acknowledgement of needing experts, Thunberg herself is a leader, not an expert. So, to finish, we foreground this dyad of expert and leader, recognizing that a crucial trialectic for community development combines expert, leader, and 'the people'. Bringing these three groups together is crucial for successful social change, avoiding anti-intellectual populisms and elitist-expert control. It's the mix of all three, people-led, leader-guided, yet expert-informed, that makes for a potent process of change. As our survival as a species depends upon it, we say, all power to Greta Thunberg and her post-millennial comrades.

Endnotes

1. <www.youtube.com/watch?v=KAJsdgTPJpU&feature=share&fbclid=IwAR1it3p3zq2dKdCjVghJKsf4jCKJYlYZRmTXrOxtoCcSaL5BAq7Af7kYQW8>

References

Evans, K. (2015) *Red Rosa: A Graphic Biography of Rosa Luxemburg*, Verso Press, New York.

Horton, M. and Freire, P. with Bell, B., Gaventa, J. and Peters, J. (eds) (1990) *We Make the Road by Walking: Conversations on Education and Social Change*, Temple University Press, Philadelphia, PA.

Monbiot, G. (2017) *Out of the Wreckage: A Politics for an Age of Crisis*, Verso Press, London.

Solnit, R. (2016) *Hope in the Dark: Untold Histories, Wild Possibilities*, Haymarket Books, Chicago, IL.

Thunberg, G. (2019a) Speech to UN Climate Action Summit in New York [YouTube video] <www.youtube.com/watch?v=KAJsdgTPJpU&feature=share&fbclid=IwAR1it3p3zq2dKdCjVghJKsf4jCKJYlYZRmTXrOxtoCcSaL5BAq7Af7kYQW8> (posted 23 September 2019) [Accessed 1 October 2019].

Thunberg, G. (2019b) *No One Is Too Small To Make A Difference,* Penguin Books, UK, USA, Australia, Canada, Ireland.

Watts, J. & Thunberg, G. (2019) 'Greta Thunberg, schoolgirl climate change warrior: 'Some people can let things go. I can't'', *The Guardian* [website] <www.theguardian.com/world/2019/mar/11/greta-thunberg-schoolgirl-climate-change-warrior-some-people-can-let-things-go-i-cant> (posted 11 March 2019) [accessed 4 November 2019].

CHAPTER 41
Trinh T. Minh-ha:
Recognizing difference in community

By Dave Palmer

Trinh T. Minh-ha 1952—

The categorization of community

Not long after I had started my first job as a 'streetworker' in the 1980s (a strange and difficult title that many of my friends would scoff at) I remember reading a state-government-commissioned report on the lives and needs of those who were called 'street dependent youth'. What I remember about this work was the variety of descriptors that were attached to the kinds of people I knew and had contact with every day. Variously throughout the report I read about 'street kids', 'at risk youth', 'young people living rough', 'homeless youth', 'street-based recidivists', 'Aboriginal young offenders', and 'unattached youth'. As a novice community worker I was not yet fluent in the language of policy speak and remember being massively perplexed. I also recall reading this report and its abstracted language of difference and finding not a single point of familiarity.

It was many years later that I was introduced to the work of Trinh T. Minh-ha. After many years of working with 'the community' I found in her work considerable wisdom on the limits of our reliance upon identity markers, particularly from those who think they are located at the 'centre', the settled or the 'mainstream'.

Who is Trinh T. Minh-ha?

Trinh T. Minh-ha was born in Hanoi in the early 1950s and lived in South Vietnam throughout the Vietnam War. Before migrating to the United States, she began as student at the National Conservatory of

http://dx.doi.org/10.3362/9781788531245.041

Music and Theatre in Saigon. She has since worked at several presti-
gious US institutions such as Harvard, Smith, Cornell, and Berkley. In
addition, she has been a filmmaker for much of her adult life, often
combining her scholarly, political, autobiographic, and creative talents to produce cinema concerned with culture, nation making, and
the transgressing of borderlines.

Much of Trinh's work is often described as sitting within literary,
film and/or postcolonial theory. At the same time, she is a writer,
filmmaker, artist, critic, teacher, and an activist.

On the imperviousness of categories in the West

Trinh's written and filmic work does not easily sit within conventional
categorization, singular ways of describing or simple theorizing. This
is for at least two reasons. The first is that she moves between forms
and genres. Some of her work is more comfortably described as film,
some criticism, and some poetic. The second is she makes it her business to challenge much of our taken-for-granted ideas about identity,
categorizing, and border-making.

In Trinh's view, what gets in the way of respectful human relationships is the long-standing habit of creating categories to describe
communities through their opposition to 'us'. In other words, the
practice of coming to definitive ideas about others using what we
take for granted about ourselves is unhelpful, often even ridiculous.
Although uneasy with the notion of a fixed and unified West she
makes the argument that this practice has become particularly potent
for those who position themselves against categories such as the
Third World, the Orient, Asia, and more recently Islam.

Trinh puts this powerfully when she says:

> The imperviousness in the West of the many branches of
> knowledge to everything that does not fall inside their prede-
> termined scope has been repeatedly challenged by its thinkers
> throughout the years. They extol the concept of decolonization
> and continuously invite into their fold 'the challenge of the
> Third World.' Yet, they do not seem to realize the difference
> when they find themselves face to face with it – a difference
> which does not announce itself, which they do not quite antic-
> ipate and cannot fit into any single varying compartment of
> their catalogued world; a difference they keep on measuring
> with inadequate sticks designed for their own morbid purpose
> (Trinh T. Minh-ha 1991: 16).

Trinh wisely points out that all of us live in a world where our interactions are transcultural. Increasingly we move across national, language, economic, and cultural borders, concurrently possessing multiple identities, life experiences, and transitions, and negotiating an array of technologies, relationships, and knowledge systems. More recently she says there has been an explosion of influences on the 'making and unmaking' of our identities and ways of knowing ourselves and others through the influence of technology and cyberspace (Grzinic, 1998). Consequently, it is much more valuable to think about cultural heritage, identity, and social categorization as things that are constantly transgressing borderlines rather than fixed or settled. Somewhat in common with **Homi Bhabha**, Trinh sees this as both troubling and productive. What she calls the 'multi-hyphenated subject' moves between borders, a liminal being that has a shifting existence and disrupts the ideas, identities, interests, and certainties of those who claim to be located in the centres of influence.

In this way Trinh offers us an insight into how useful it is to shake up many of the conventions and practices we rely on to govern. For example, she points to the part played by much social research, the professionalizing of community work and codifying of practice in constituting as 'Other' groups such as 'Third World' communities, 'Indigenous' communities, and 'disadvantaged' communities. She points out that this practice of producing what Foucault (1979) calls 'expert knowledge' exists to prop up and legitimize an unhelpful way of thinking about communities. This means that ideas about 'the community' often act as a kind of mirror against what Westerners think about themselves. Here she draws on an understanding similar to that proposed by Edward Said in his book *Orientalism*, arguing that the lives of those constituted as Other usually bear little resemblance to those being talked about. Rather they are 'more useful as a sign of the European-Atlantic than an accurate reflection of people described' (Said, 1978). We might say discourses on those we call 'the community' are far more likely to tell us much more about those who are planning on working with 'the community'.

Woman, Native, Other: So how else can we think about people?

In contrast to the conventions of speaking about the Other, Trinh posits that people themselves, particularly if we see them as inhabiting a multitude of 'interstitial spaces', should be encouraged to talk, to be able to draw upon their own new modes of thinking without being expected to recirculate the ideas used to describe themselves.

Here again there are hints of Said (1978) who observes that one of the features of what he calls Orientalist discourse is the almost total absence of the Orient in discussions about themselves.

In her book *Woman, Native, Other* Trinh focuses particularly on the value of oral traditions in the formation of the knowledge of 'women of colour'. Like many communities that do not use technical, academic, and anglicized written work she makes the point that many 'women of colour' articulate, theorize, and frame their world using oral forms that are rich, layered, and deeply sophisticated. Indeed, Trinh cautions against trusting too heavily in what she calls 'well-written' text, proposing instead that we begin to 'unlearn' the language and genres of knowledge. Importantly this demands that we shift from the 'written-woman' to the 'writing-woman'. It also demands that we move towards other genres and ways of coming to know, such as film, poetry, visual art, and music. She does this elegantly herself by combining stories, critiques, and photographic images of women of colour in her films.

Trinh's work and community development

Like many of the authors featured in this book Trinh does not speak a great deal directly about community development, although it is worth noting that she does specifically mention 'community organizers' when she cites Ivan Illich:

> Whereas its by-now-familiar purpose is to spread the Master's values, comforting him in his godlike charity-giver role, protecting his lifestyle, and naturalizing it as the only, the best way. The United States idealist turns up in every theatre of war; the teacher, the volunteer, the missioner, the community organizer, the economic developer. Such men define their role as service ... They especially are the ones for whom 'ingratitude' is the bitter reward. 'Don't they see We are only trying to help?' (Trinh T. Minh-ha, 1991: 22).

However, in her analysis of the West's project of constituting the Other, Trinh argues that community workers are routinely asked to speak *for* rather than *with* those described as the 'community'. She points out that many activities associated with research and knowledge acquisition by community workers (i.e. community mapping exercises, community needs assessment, identifying of various groupings with a community, boundary making, and naming of groups) are so often assumed to be benign. However, these methods are themselves tied up with what she calls the Master's territories, representations, and knowledges. This is particularly so when embarking on work with communities constituted as Third World, Aborigines, Africans, and Asians, where old totalizing and worn-out boundary making gets used as the starting point. In sinister and subtle ways this manifests itself in formal organization of professional bodies, codes of ethics, research institutes that create knowledge about 'the community' (usually in their absence). This 'research data' generally bears little relationship to the way in which these 'communities' know and name themselves. Importantly, says Trinh, this reinforces binary and polarizing distinctions between the illegitimate 'them' and the legitimate 'us'. Finally, this serves as a powerful tool in the governing, excluding, containing, and speaking on behalf of these 'communities'.

Importantly Trinh offers us some insights into how we can act otherwise. In *When the Moon Waxes Red: Representation, Gender and Cultural Politics* she writes poetically and allegorically about how we might seek creative and imaginative ways of coming to know the communities with which we walk and work. She calls this a 'passion named wonder'.

> Wonder never seizes, never possesses the other as an object. It is the ability to see, hear, and touch, to go toward things as though always for the first time. The encounter is one that surprises in its unexpected, if not entirely unknown character. It does not provoke conflict, rejection, or acceptance, for it constitutes an empty, 'no baggage' moment in which passion traverses the non-knowing (not ignorant) subject. (Trinh T. Minh-ha 1991: 23).

References

Foucault, M. (1979) *The History of Sexuality, Vol 1: An Introduction*, Allen Lane Penguin Press, London.

Grzinic, Marina (1998) 'Inappropriate/dartificiality' Interview with Trinh T. Minh-Ha on Trinh T. Minh-Ha's website: <http://trinhminh-ha.squarespace.com/inappropriated-articificiality/> (posted 2 June 1998) [Accessed 4 November 2019].

Said, E. (1978) *Orientalism*, Penguin Press, Harmondsworth, UK.

Trinh T. Minh-ha (1982) *Reassemblage* (40 mins). Film.

Trinh T. Minh-ha (1989) *Woman, Native, Other: Writing Postcoloniality and Feminism,* Indiana University Press, IN.

Trinh T. Minh-ha (1991) *When the Moon Waxes Red: Representation, Gender and Cultural Politics*, Routledge, New York.

Trinh T. Minh-ha (2011) *Elsewhere, Within Here: Immigration, Refugeeism and the Boundary Event*, Routledge, New York.

CHAPTER 42
Conclusion

The conclusion uses the genre of dialogue, an approach consistent with how the three of us prefer to engage with the world, with one another, and with community development practice. Inspired by the examples of dialogical exchanges that we dearly love, particularly of **Freire** and **Horton** (Horton et al. 1990) and **hooks** (her many dialogue books with the likes of **Hillman** and Stuart Hall), we have experimented in the genre. This dialogue, always shaped in the singularity of a time and space, took place in July 2019 at the Queensland State Library in a genuine conversation shaped around a few questions that we pre-curated.

Peter: So, we've written an Introduction and forty reflections from critical thinkers. Each one has a 'gem of a wisdom', several other key ideas, and a bit of a biography. What do you think this book really can offer emerging, or any, community development practitioners? Are they meant to just read the book and take away all these new themes and ideas?

Dave: Well, during the writing process I was reminded of what it was like being a new practitioner. I came into youth and community work having only passed year 10 high school and with an apprenticeship under my belt. I was working largely with young Aboriginal people, and, as a consequence had a hundred different questions every day. I really didn't have a place to put those questions. I didn't have great literacy, didn't have a lot of time, and so I would have loved something that introduced me to an array of people who had done similar work, and were able to really clearly distil a gem or a key short little lesson, or message, or wisdom for me. And the value of having forty of those, just the emotional, psychological message that there are lots of people who have come before you, would have been great. It would have been wonderful to know that there are lots of different lessons here, lots of different ways of coming to the work – that would have been really a powerful message for me. And it wasn't until I went to university and years later that I

http://dx.doi.org/10.3362/9781788531245.042

started to get a little hint of how important the ideas are of those who have 'travelled the road of practice'. So, I think, in a way, I'm speaking to an 18-year-old Dave, saying, here I am 37 years down the track. Here's what some of my colleagues and I might want to give you as a gift. So that, after you've received some of those little gems, you can go off and have a deeper look at them.

Tina: Yes, Dave, and I would say almost the opposite, but with the same message. That when I was starting out, my context was an intentional community and it was pretty much a dominant philosophy that was being given to us, and almost, a very narrow *one way* only, way of working and practising. And similar to you, Dave, when I started studying as a mature-age student and was exposed to all those ideas, I started to think there are other ways of practising. So, I would say this book will help people perhaps think a little bit more critically and introduce more ideas to their practice – expanding people's practice as we say in the Introduction. And start to think about 'what would my practice mean in the light of all these new ideas?' 'What could I start to change in my practice?' This is how I hope the book may be used.

Dave: Peter?

Peter: Yeah, I think I'd say three things. One, when I was a young practitioner, I remember spending time with a mentor for many years – Dave Andrews – and just doing the work, learning on the job. And learning what we would now think of as tacit knowledge. And I remember one day saying to Dave, 'I'm seeing a lot of activity and I'm not quite sure what's guiding us'. And he said, 'There is a method in this madness', and he introduced me to frameworks. He said, 'Actually that is a framework' [as he shared his]. And what I love about our book, is that it would be able to help people name or give words to what they are already doing. Or, as we say in the Introduction, challenge, or disrupt, some assumptions about what they're doing. So, you know, for all those workers that read this, that have got good intuitive capabilities, they're learning on the job. It's important to bring ideas to reflect on, expand, and disrupt.

The second thing I really like about this book is similar to what Tina has said. It's in the principle of diversity, which is really important. And this book, the way we've chosen the forty critical thinkers, is representative of a huge diversity of traditions and ideas. So, I'm hoping that it offers practitioners rich, new archives of thinking that have just not yet been encountered, you know, work from elsewhere.

And the third thing I want to say to practitioners is in the hierarchy of … well, there is a binary in our practice of theory and practice. And I think many community workers think that practice is more important than theory. And in this book, we're saying, no. Ideas, which is theory, are as important as practice. And if you want to be a reflective practitioner, you do your daily work. And this book could be a lovely thing to occasionally pick up and read, and say, 'Oh, there's a new theory. Wow, what does that mean for my practice?' And so, the book could contribute, in a very user-friendly way, to reflective practice. So that's kind of what I'd like to see.

Dave: In the Introduction we talk about how the forty critical thinkers can help individuals build their framework, build their language. That's one of our three goals of the book. But what are the strengths, and what are the limits, of thinking about a framework? Particularly building a framework as we're entering the work, entering the practice.

Peter: So my understanding is that when you're a new practitioner you will start probably working intuitively, being guided 'on the job' by a mentor or senior practitioner, and perhaps they'll introduce their framework – the ideas that guide their work – and then eventually you might start reading and using someone else's framework. You know, read something, a book, and go, 'that's helpful'. You know, Tony Kelly's and Sandra Sewell's, *With, Head, Heart and Hand*, or *Participatory Development Practice* (Kelly & Westoby, 2018). But what this book will do is open that up, you know, give people access to more rich ideas. So, I think that's the strength. If a framework is a conceptual tool that helps people structure their thinking about what they do, I guess the limit of it is that it's conceptual, and that we're learning a lot about practice being embodied and relational. And so, even though a book can hardly escape being a conceptual device, to help people build their framework, we also understand the limits of that. Actually our community development practice is going to be socially constructed in relationships with people we're working with. It's going to be embodied in terms of the very personal – who we are, how we carry ourselves in the world, the things we love, the passions we bring to life. So, it's the limits of conceptual, I think.

Tina: I think, why I like the idea of frameworks is because once you kind of get that you have a framework, and you've done that work even to create one, say a beginning one, then it also helps to understand other people have different frameworks. So that idea of, you know, I walk into a meeting and have a conversation – and we might all even have the same job title or the same training even. Yet, there's almost conflict, or that, because of an individual's value base, values, and theoretical frameworks and so on where people are coming from, there is a clash. So, it's easier to sometimes think of it as a clash of frameworks, rather than, 'I don't like that person', or whatever. You know what I mean?

Peter: Yep. Yes, yes, I do.

Dave: Hmm, yep. I remember coming into youth and community practice without the language that other people were using. When I started, my way of thinking about what I was doing was kind of driven lots by, pretty fundamentalist Christian frames. However, I had little idea that this was the case. All I knew was that I couldn't understand what other practitioners were talking about. As a youth worker, I'd go to conferences and think, 'I've got no idea what they mean, what they're doing'. I think I know what I'm doing, but I'm not sure that these people are doing the same thing, because I don't understand the words they are using. Part of me just thought I had to learn and adopt those words to be good at what I did. Of course this was a little bit naive and a little bit ridiculous.

However, this was an important observation because eventually it helped me realize the point you just have just made, that people around me had different ways of thinking and doing 'practice'. And, subsequently, it helped me invest time in trying to extend my repertoire, both my language and my practice repertoire. And as you said, it really can be a great liberation to build your language and your ideas.

I'd also say that learning about other people's wisdom about practice helps you deepen your practice and helps you move beyond clichés. Recently I did some work with local government community development workers throughout regional Western Australia. I remember early on in the work being in one country town. We were doing a couple of days training in community development and people came from a range of local councils. In the first session one guy, who was a Director of Community Development in his local government authority, jokingly said, 'Two days of a community development, workshop? How many different ways can you learn to sing "Kumbaya"?' This prompted a discussion where people subsequently talked about how their work is often seen as 'fluffy', 'soft', and 'simple' work. They shared that many saw community work as something that sounds 'nice' but not something with a great deal of substance, not serious, and not central to the 'main game'. Many shared their frustrations at not being able to counter this perception and not being able to articulate what they did. What became important was to extend people's repertoire by noticing what it was they did and putting a language to it. In a way I think this began the process of people framing what they were doing so they could describe it to others.

Peter: Yep, and it's crucial. Now how can we say to anyone, 'we have something to offer', if we can't describe what we do, with language?

Dave: Yep, yep. Although, I am still a little reluctant with the language of 'frameworks'. I know, Peter and Tina, you don't approach it this way but many talk about 'frameworks' as if they are things that we have to have or do before going to practice or doing the work. Yet the idea that there is a linear and ordered way of going about things that involves being clear and authoritative before starting something is a very a Western and modern habit. Particularly if you're working in places like university, government authorities, or organizations that have been struck by the outcomes-driven disease – that it's our job, to be clear, to present things with authority, and to know with great certainty what we are doing before we embark on our work.

Of course, a number of those we examine in this collection imply that the art of community development has us holding our plans lightly. People like **Freire** are very critical of this in Western education and development. **Keats** with his idea about negative capability encourages us to build the skill of being comfortable in chaos. **Bhabha** reminds us that ambivalence is healthy, indeed it produces new things.

My own experience of being a community worker is that I would be pretending and mighty dishonest if I claimed that I had even the most basic of frameworks nicely set out before I went about my work. Perhaps even one of the things that sets community development apart from other ways of working is that we learn much more about frameworks in retrospect, after we have acted, built relationships with a community, and together talked through and reflected on what we did.

So I think I'd be more comfortable in seeing 'frameworks' as always more provisional, exceedingly complex, and humbly thought about. Many of the people we visit in this collection talk about the importance of either suspending, or putting in your back pocket, your frame, when you move into a new community. You need to listen to what the people said. What was his name, Halloway? The, the, who, Les?

Peter: Les Halliwell.

Dave: Halliwell said, 'Listen to the people …' For some reason this reminds me of John **Keats**, and his idea of negative capability. Both involve a practice of being able to walk into the room, knowing that you will be confronted by what looks like chaos, and being comfortable enough in that chaos, to be able to listen, to be able to contemplate, to be able to accept that there are lots of things that cannot be included in your framework. There are lots of things that you can't know. You're often going to feel like a fish out of water. And so, therefore, our frames, or my frames, are constantly spinning, and you're using one to test out the other, and finding, and sometimes finding, that my one was terribly inadequate. It's what we talk about in the Introduction as disruption or expanding.

And what I like about a dialogue as a way of writing, is that it opens things up, is a little bit more honest about how our worlds, our ideas, and our practice is often cyclical. The typical writing voice is usually linear, presented as if our ideas are clear, tidy, and said with great authority. Of course this is not how things are. Our communities, our relationships, indeed our minds, are way more complex, transient, and alive than this. And I think some of the wonderful gems from the writers we've chosen kind of touch on that.

Tina: You've said something and now I remember what I wanted to add. And it's that business of the 'aspirational' versus the 'actual'. That in a framework, sometimes – because the idea of creating a framework is to look at what you actually *do,* not what you *want to do*. But often, I think we go to the aspirational, at what we wish we were doing.

Peter: And we're offering a book with wisdom that invites people to move into new aspirations, again, that expanding and deepening we talk about as one of our goals in the Introduction.

Tina: New aspiration, yes. But I mean I think that's good, in the sense that having an aspiration can also then be a tool to check back to see what the actual is, and how far we might have strayed. You know, I was just saying to my students a couple of weeks ago: 'You know, co-operation is one of the principles in my framework, but, bloody hell, sometimes I'd rather just do it myself than co-operate with others! It's so much easier to just do it yourself. Co-operation is hard work'. You know?

Peter: Yep.

Tina: So, that's the kind of thing that I'm talking about. Like, the actual versus the romantic notion of a value or a principle. Hmm.

Dave: Peter, Tina was looking at you more than she was looking at me, when she said co-operation is hard work.

Tina: Ha, ha, ha.

Peter: I do think, though, when I look at this book, and the work we've done, and researching and writing about a mix of critical thinkers, that, each of us is familiar with some, and yet each of us has had to stretch into new territory as well. All of them are challenging; they all in some way disrupt the hegemony, the common-sense world that we now live in. Almost, every single one of these wisdoms says, 'Community development offers a different way of being'. For example, instead of the common-sense world of professional human service or the welfare world, it says de-professionalize. Or be more human – be with the people as friends, not as a professional. You know, don't listen to the powerful, and do revolutionary listening at the margins. So, I do think this book is a profoundly challenging book. If people want to take the wisdoms seriously. We have picked forty people who have given their lives to pretty serious shit.

Tina: Hmmm, and some have *literally* given their lives.

Dave: I like that each writer has a gem that is easy to remember, a catchy phrase that we can pick up and apply. We had students visit a wonderful organization called – it used to be called Men of the Trees – and now it's called Trillion Trees. My friend Chris Ferreira who works there made this interesting comment, when he was talking to a group of young students, he said, 'At the moment, it's really difficult for young people to find a place in the world, to find a place in work, because we're taught to all be ziggers'.

Tina: What's that?

Dave: 'A zigger', he said. In a world where you all need to zig and zag. Zagging – or going the other way – can actually give you an edge. There's spaces, there's not so many spaces for corporate bankers, but there is lots of spaces for people who are working in community development. Anyway, that little, his little gem worked, I think, because it was catchy, illustrative, and relevant to his audience.

Peter to Tina: What has it been like researching and writing about the critical thinkers?

Tina: Well, for me, it's been an opportunity to read, do some reading, and, yes because you would think that in my job, as an academic, that I would be given the time to read, which I am not. So, having a book, with those deadlines, has really been helpful to really put time aside to get stuck in.

Peter: And reading is so important!

Tina: Yes.

Peter: I mean, I just want to say that. Reading and reflection on practice. Theory dancing with practice. Praxis.

Tina: The hard thing is, what to write about. But there's that old wisdom of 'trust the process' and if you read enough, the idea comes forward, about what to write. But I was just going to finish by saying that, distilling the gem of a wisdom – that's been tricky. Because I guess, there's been many that could have been chosen. So, what I hope is that people will read the little snapshot of the critical thinker, and take on board what we think might be the gem of the wisdom. But then, that they'll be encouraged to go then and read the actual authors, and find their own wisdoms. Yeah.

Tina: How about you Dave?

Dave: Well, like you, reading other people's work in preparation for the writing of the book, has given me the chance to be a student again. Again and again. So, it's been like going to university and doing my undergraduate degree. Being introduced to people that I hadn't met before, intellectually. I've enjoyed, particularly those writers that I'm not as familiar with, because that's just been a, you know, just been a treat. And reading your work – reading other people who are coherent – has been good.

The final thing that I want to say about what's lovely about researching, is that as three co-authors we are what **Simmel** might observe as a triad, the beginning of a community. There's no way that I could embark on such a writing project on my own. My experience and frameworks are too limited. To have two other colleagues means that the quality and the quantity of the interesting things that are in front of me have just magnified. And in a way, kind of in a way, we've been working as a community. And that's where I find the really interesting moments.

Tina: Yes: And Peter?

Peter: Well, yeah, I mean on one hand I'd say half the 16 I've written are familiar authors. But familiarity does not breed contempt for me. I have spent my whole life working with **Buber**, or **Freire**, or **Tagore**, and it just gets richer and richer the more you go, the deeper you go. So, I've loved that, you know, another chance to go back, to the familiar. Because, in getting their ideas, doesn't mean we get the practice. And this is that fallacy of: theory first, practice second, and practice follows theory. As we say in the Introduction, this book offers a way of building 'practice wisdom', something learned 'on the job', and through reflection and reading. I'm living with these ideas, all my whole life, and, you know Martin Buber's idea of a dialogue, of dialogue, that's life changing. I'm in the job, trying dialogue, getting it, failing, and then I go back to Buber and read and reflect, and challenge myself. The theory interacts with my practice, and vice versa, and there's a dance that becomes my praxis. And so to revisit it is challenging, and now I've been introduced to, you know, the other eight of mine, that are unfamiliar, and the other 24 you two are introducing. And it's just a beautiful tapestry, a mosaic of new ideas. And I wish I had another 50 years of doing it too. Journeying with their practice, that is, because we know practice is a life journey of embodying practice wisdom. And, as we say in the Introduction, to research these people is again to feel that solidity, to feel that we stand on the firm foundations of tradition, and that deep wisdom is not just coming out of Twitter world, the Twittersphere. Like, this is solid.

References

Horton, M. and Freire, P. with Bell, B., Gaventa, J. and Peters, J. (eds.) (1990) *We Make the Road by Walking: Conversations on Education and Social Change*, Temple University Press, Philadelphia, PA.

Kelly, A. and Sewell, S. (1994) *With Head, Heart and Hand: Dimensions of Community Building*, 3rd edn., Boolarong Press, Brisbane, Australia.

Kelly, A. and Westoby, P. (2018) *Participatory Development Practice: Using Traditional and Contemporary Frameworks*, Practical Action Press, Rugby, UK.

Coda – map of practice

As a final movement, we offer a map of practice elicited from this book. As a coda, this map, portrayed as an image, is an addition to the basic structure of the book which consists of the 40 reflections. As such, like any coda, it is our concluding remark.

Drawing on the likes of radical cartography we like to imagine the map as a radical map of community development wisdom. As such it is a political map of practice. It is possible for you to photocopy the map and gems, blow it up to A3 and put it in your study or work desk area as a reminder of helpful things as you go about your working life.

In curating the image, each of us drew with simple lines a map of our place – where we reside, where our community is, where our connections are. In a sense, as per Mary **Graham's** reflection, we made more conscious the three places that have become the template for who each of us are. Peter has mapped the Brisbane river, Maiwar, from near the centre winding through West End, St. Lucia to Yeronga. Enfolded within that is Tina's map of the Glass House Mountains of the Sunshine Coast region, which include Mt Beerwah, Mt Tibrogargan, Mt Coonowrin, and Mt Ngungun. And finally, the third map is that of Dave's Fremantle, the Swan River through to Perth, along with several other key landmarks, such as Rottnest Island.

Then we have clustered the gems of wisdom and located them in parts of the map alluding to gems that 'belong closely together'. Some are more internally related, about the practitioner themselves, a way of being, a gesture in the world. Others are more aligned to what can be imagined as micro-level practices, listening, dialogue, noticing. Others are clearly more overtly political, ranging from the decolonizing, postcolonial gems, to being willing to go to jail. The clustering is somewhat arbitrary but was fun to do.

We acknowledge the artist, Sarah Govus, who then put it all together in a beautiful map.

Peter, Tina and Dave

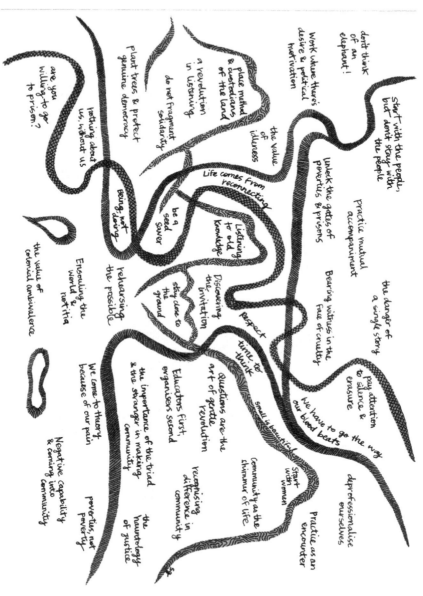

Coda Map of Practice

Photo credits

Chapter 11: Judi Chamberlin, 2000
Photo credit: Judi Chamberlin (2000) upon the publication of the National Council on Disability's federal report 'From Privileges to Rights' Photo by Tom Olin, MindFreedom International, https://mindfreedom.org/ This file is licenced under the Creative Commons Attribution-Share Alike 3.0 Unported Licence. https://creativecommons.org/licenses/by-sa/3.0/deed.en

Chapter 12: Angela Davis, 2017
Photo credit: Photo by Columbia GSAPP, this file is licensed under the Creative Commons Attribution 2.5 Generic Licence, https://creativecommons.org/licenses/by/2.5/deed.en

Chapter 13: Jacques Derrida, 2013
Photo credit: Pencil drawing by Arturo Espinoza. This file is licensed under the Creative Commons Attribution 2.0 Generic license. https://creativecommons.org/licenses/by/2.0/deed.en

Chapter 14: Gustavo Esteva, 2008
Photo credit: Photo by Mark Skipper, this file is licensed under the Creative Commons Attribution 2.0 Generic License. https://creativecommons.org/licenses/by/2.0/deed.en

Chapter 15: Frantz Fanon
Photo credit: Photo by P.J.W. Productions, this file is licenced under the Creative Commons Attribution-Share Alike 3.0 Unported licence. https://creativecommons.org/licenses/by-sa/3.0/deed.en

Chapter 16: Paulo Freire, 1963
Photo credit: Brazilian National Archives, in public domain

Chapter 17: Mary Graham
Photo credit: photo supplied by Mary Graham. Author unknown. Photo in public domain.

Chapter 18: Epeli Hau'ofa, circa 1987
Photo credit: Photo courtesy of Otago Daily Times. Photo supplied by Hocken Collections - Uare Taoka o Hākena, University of Otago

Chapter 19: James Hillman
Photo credit: Cheryle Van Scoy, courtesy of OPUS Archives and Research Center.

Chapter 20: bell hooks, 1988
Photo credit: Photo by Montikamoss, this file is licenced under the Creative Commons Attribution-Share Alike 4.0 International Licence
https://creativecommons.org/licenses/by-sa/4.0/deed.en

Chapter 21: Myles Horton at the Highlander Folk School c. 1936 – 1938
Photo credit: Photo by Annemarie Schwarzenbach. Swiss National Library, SLA-Schwarzenbach-A-5-10/115 Public Domain

Chapter 22: John Keats, 1854
Photo credit: Illustration by George Scharf, in "The Poetical Works of John Keats. With a memoir by Richard Monckton Milnes". Source British Public Library. Public domain.

Chapter 23: George Lakoff, 2012
Photo credit: Photo by Mikethelinguist, this file is licensed under the Creative Commons Attribution-Share Alike 4.0 International license. https://creativecommons.org/licenses/by-sa/4.0/deed.en

Chapter 24: Rosa Luxemburg, 1910, Berlin.
Photo credit: Photo in public domain.

Chapter 25: Wangari Maathai, 2006
Photo credit: Photo by Antônio Cruz, Agência Brasil, this file is licenced under the Creative Commons Attribution 3.0 Brazil License
https://creativecommons.org/licenses/by/3.0/br/deed.en

Chapter 26: Joanna Macy, 2012
Photo credit: Adam Shemper, photo reproduced with permission of Adam Shemper.

Chapter 27: Manfred Max-Neef, 2007
Photo credit: Photo by Olga Berrios, this file is licenced under the Creative Commons Attribution 2.0 Generic license.
https://creativecommons.org/licenses/by/2.0/deed.en

Chapter 28: Chandra Talpade Mohanty, 2011.
Photo credit: Photo provided by Chandra Talpade Mohanty. Photo author unknown. This file is made available under the

Creative Commons CC0 1.0 Universal Public Domain Dedication. https://creativecommons.org/publicdomain/zero/1.0/deed.en

Chapter 29: Fran (Frances) Peavey
Photo credit: Photo author unknown. Public domain. Source: Great Thoughts Treasury [website] http://www.greatthoughtstreasury.com/index.php/author/fran-peavey [Accessed 24 September 2019].

Chapter 30: Arundhati Roy, 2010
Photo credit: Jean Baptiste Paris, this file is licensed under the Creative Commons Attribution-Share Alike 2.0 Generic license. https://creative commons.org/licenses/by-sa/2.0/deed.en

Chapter 31: Deborah Bird Rose
Photo credit: Photo courtesy of Chantal Jackson

Chapter 32: Bertrand Russell, 1957
Photo credit: Author unknown, Dutch National Archives, Public Domain Licensing. https://creativecommons.org/publicdomain/zero/1.0/deed.en

Chapter 33: E.F. Schumacher, 2008
Photo credit: Author unknown. Permission to use from Practical Action.

Chapter 34: Richard Sennett, at the Linz Lectures, 2010
Photo credit: rubra; Ars Electronica from Österreich - flickr: Richard Sennett, CC BY-SA 2.0. This file is licensed under the Creative Commons Attribution-Share Alike 2.0 Generic license.

Chapter 35: Vandana Shiva, 2014
Photo credit: Augustus Binu, this file is licensed under the Creative Commons Attribution-Share Alike 3.0 Unported license. https://cre-ativecommons.org/licenses/by-sa/3.0/deed.en

Chapter 36: Georg Simmel, circa 1901
Photo credit: Julius Cornelius Schaarwächter. Source: http://www.sammlungen.hu-berlin.de/dokumente/10862/, Public Domain

Chapter 37: Linda Tuhiwai Smith, 2019
Photo credit: Photos supplied with permission to use from Linda Tuhiwai Smith

Chapter 38: Rabindranath Tagore, circa 1920
Photo credit: Author unknown. Source: Visva Vharati Archive Public Domain

Chapter 39: Thich Nhat Hanh in Paris, 2006
Photo credit: Author Duc (pixiduc), Thich Nhat Hanh Marche meditative 06 on flickr.com/photos, this file is licensed under the Creative Commons Attribution-Share Alike 2.0 Generic license.

Chapter 40: Greta Thunberg, August 2018
Photo credit: Anders Hellberg, In August 2018, outside the Swedish parliament building, Greta Thunberg started a school strike for the climate. Her sign reads, "Skolstrejk för klimatet," meaning, "school strike for climate". This file is licensed under the Creative Commons Attribution-Share Alike 4.0 International license.

Chapter 41: Trinh T. Minh-ha, self-portrait 2014
Photo credit: Trinh T. Minh-ha, this file is licensed under the Creative Commons Attribution-Share Alike 3.0 Unported license. https://creative commons.org/licenses/by-sa/3.0/deed.en

Coda map of practice: Drawing by Sarah Govus

CPSIA information can be obtained
at www.ICGtesting.com
Printed in the USA
BVHW041518240720
584538BV00020B/566